Fish & Shellfish

by
THE EDITORS OF TIME-LIFE BOOKS

TIME-LIFE BOOKS·AMSTERDAM

TIME-LIFE INTERNATIONAL
EUROPEAN EDITOR: Kit van Tulleken
Design Director: Louis Klein
Director of Photography: Pamela Marke
Chief of Research: Vanessa Kramer
Director of Text: Simon Rigge (acting)
Chief of Design: Graham Davis
Chief Sub-Editor: Ilse Gray

THE GOOD COOK
Series Editor: Windsor Chorlton
Series Designer: Douglas Whitworth
Series Co-ordinator: Liz Timothy

Editorial Staff for *Fish and Shellfish*
Text Editor: Tony Allan
Anthology Editor: Liz Clasen
Staff Writers: Gillian Boucher, Norman Kolpas,
Anthony Masters
Designer: Rick Bowring
Researcher: Ursula Beary
Sub-Editors: Jay Ferguson, Nicoletta Flessati
Permissions Researcher: Mary-Claire Hailey
Design Assistants: Mary Staples, Elaine Maddex
Editorial Assistant: Molly Sutherland

EDITORIAL PRODUCTION FOR THE SERIES
Production Editor: Ellen Brush
Quality Control: Don Fragale
Traffic Co-ordinators: Pat Boag, Joanne Holland
Picture Co-ordinator: Philip Garner
Art Department: Julia West
Editorial Department: Anetha Besidonne,
Debra Dick, Margaret Hall

THE SEAFARERS
WORLD WAR II
THE GOOD COOK
THE TIME-LIFE ENCYCLOPAEDIA OF GARDENING
HUMAN BEHAVIOUR
THE GREAT CITIES
THE ART OF SEWING
THE OLD WEST
THE WORLD'S WILD PLACES
THE EMERGENCE OF MAN
LIFE LIBRARY OF PHOTOGRAPHY
THIS FABULOUS CENTURY
TIME-LIFE LIBRARY OF ART
FOODS OF THE WORLD
GREAT AGES OF MAN
LIFE SCIENCE LIBRARY
LIFE NATURE LIBRARY
YOUNG READERS LIBRARY
LIFE WORLD LIBRARY
THE TIME-LIFE BOOK OF BOATING
TECHNIQUES OF PHOTOGRAPHY
LIFE AT WAR
LIFE GOES TO THE MOVIES
BEST OF LIFE

Cover: Swathed in a jacket of parboiled lettuce leaves and dotted with butter, a whole sea bass is sprinkled with white wine before being baked. (*page 64*). The leaf wrapping will help to keep the fish moist in the oven's dry heat, while a vegetable stuffing will flavour it from within.

THE CHIEF CONSULTANT:
Richard Olney, an American, has lived and worked since 1951
in France, where he is a highly regarded authority on food and
wine. A regular contributor to the influential journals *Cuisine et
Vins de France* and *La Revue du Vin de France*, he has also
written numerous articles for other gastronomic magazines in
France and the United States, and is the author of *The French
Menu Cookbook* and the award-winning *Simple French
Food*. He has directed cooking courses in France and the
United States and is a member of several distinguished gas-
tronomic societies, including *La Confrérie des Chevaliers du
Tastevin*, *La Commanderie du Bontemps de Médoc et des
Graves* and *Les Amitiés Gastronomiques Internationales*.

THE PHOTOGRAPHER:
Alan Duns was born in 1943 in the north of England and studied at the Ealing School of
Photography. He has undertaken many advertising assignments, but specializes in
food photography. His work has appeared in major British publications.

THE INTERNATIONAL CONSULTANTS:
Great Britain: *Jane Grigson* was born in Gloucester and brought up in the north of
England. She is a graduate of Cambridge University. Her first book on food, *Charcu-
terie and French Pork Cookery*, was published in 1967; since then, she has published a
number of cookery books, including *Good Things, English Food* and *The Mushroom
Feast*. She became cookery correspondent for the colour magazine of the London
Observer in 1968. *Alan Davidson*, special consultant for *Fish and Shellfish*, is the author
of *Fish and Fish Dishes of Laos, Mediterranean Seafood* and *North Atlantic Seafood*.
He is writing *The Oxford Companion to Food*, to be published by the Oxford University
Press. **France:** *Michel Lemonnier* was born in Normandy. He began contributing to the
magazine *Cuisine et Vins de France* in 1960, and also writes for several other important
French food and wine periodicals. The co-founder and vice-president of the society *Les
Amitiés Gastronomiques Internationales,* he is a frequent lecturer on wine and vine-
yards, and a member of most of the vinicultural confraternities in France. **Germany:**
Jochen Kuchenbecker trained as a chef, but worked for 10 years as a food photogra-
pher in many European countries before opening his own restaurant in Hamburg. *Anne
Brakemeier*, who also lives in Hamburg, has published articles on food and cooking
in many German periodicals. She is the co-author of three cookery books.
The Netherlands: *Hugh Jans*, a resident of Amsterdam, has been translating cookery
books and articles for more than 25 years. He has also published two books of his own,
Bistro Koken and *Koken in Casserole*, and his recipes are published in many Dutch
magazines. **The United States:** *Carol Cutler*, a resident of Washington, DC, is the author
of *Haute Cuisine for Your Heart's Delight* and the award-winning *The Six-Minute
Soufflé and Other Culinary Delights*. A contributing editor of both *International Food
and Wine* and *Working Woman* magazines, she frequently lectures about food and
gives demonstrations of cooking techniques. *Shirley Sarvis*, a freelance food writer and
consultant in San Francisco, is the author and co-author of a dozen cookery books.
José Wilson moved to the United States from England in 1951. The food editor of *House
and Garden* magazine for 15 years, she has written many books on food and interior
decoration, including *American Cooking: the Eastern Heartland* in TIME-LIFE Books'
Foods of the World series and, with Arthur Leaman, *The Complete Food Catalog*.

Valuable help was given in the preparation of this volume by the following members of
TIME-LIFE Books: *Michèle le Baube, Maria Vincenza Aloisi, Joséphine du Brusle* (Paris);
Jeanne Buys (Amsterdam); *Hans-Heinrich Wellmann, Gertraud Bellon* (Hamburg);
Bona Schmid, Maria Teresa Marenco (Milan).

CONTENTS

The Harvest of the Waters

Fish and shellfish exist in such astonishing variety that they can be a perpetual source of delight to cook and diner alike. In European waters alone, more than a hundred species are caught for the table—a choice more than ample to satisfy every taste. Some fish and shellfish occupy a distinguished place in the culinary world. A whole poached salmon, for example, is obviously a feast for both the eyes and the palate; the delicate flavour of oysters will, in the words of the French chef Auguste Escoffier, "satisfy the most fastidious of epicures". But for a more modest cost, a relatively plebeian dish of grilled mackerel, cooked before the iridescent colours have faded (*left*), or a bowl of steamed mussels, served in a fragrant broth made with their own juices, are also worthy of a cook's best skills.

This volume aims to inspire the cook to make full use of the range of seafood that is available. The following pages explain how to select for economy, variety and quality, and also provide the fundamental rules for cooking and timing. An illustrated guide (*pages 8-17*) showing 121 of the principal fish and shellfish eaten in Europe is followed first by step-by-step demonstrations of the ways they are prepared for cooking, and then by demonstrations of the techniques for cooking them. The demonstrations will enable you to execute any of the 224 recipes in the Anthology that makes up the second half of the book.

Choosing for economy, variety and freshness

When buying seafood, remember that there is no invariable relationship between price and quality. Since the vast preponderance of fish and shellfish are caught in their natural environment, supplies are more erratic than those of meat or vegetables and therefore more subject to price variation. As a rule, fish that are in season and available in large quantities are inexpensive.

Obvious as this advice may sound, many cooks are surprisingly conservative in their fish-buying habits. They cling to their traditional preferences, ignoring fish of comparable quality, although a shortage of the species they want means that they have to pay high prices. Ironically, seafood that is ignored in one country may be highly prized in another. The Venetians, for example, regard tail of angler-fish as one of the finest marine delicacies; while in North America the same species is virtually unknown, since it is usually thrown back into the sea when caught. Similarly, eel is rarely eaten in the United States, but is highly esteemed in Europe. In the English county of Lancashire, haddock is the preferred fish for the national dish of fish and chips, yet in neighbouring Yorkshire, cod has pride of place.

The moral is clear: while preserving useful traditions, the good cook should supplement them with unfamiliar kinds of seafood. All of the fish and shellfish species illustrated in the Guide make good eating. If you choose a fish or shellfish that you have never cooked before, you can consult the chart on the following pages, which tells you at a glance which cooking methods are most appropriate.

Since seafood is more perishable than meat or poultry, you should take care to ensure that it is absolutely fresh when purchased. The ideal, of course, is to keep fish and shellfish alive until the last moment before cooking, but in the case of fish, this is neither practicable nor necessary. Modern fishing vessels are equipped with efficient refrigerated holds that keep the temperature at 0°C (32°F)—low enough to inhibit the action of harmful bacteria, but not so low as to significantly affect the flavour or texture of the fish. Once a catch has been landed, it is kept chilled—usually by being packed in ice—during its journey to market and while it is on display at the fishmonger's. It is natural to suppose that the greater the time that elapses between the capture of a fish and its appearance on the fishmonger's slab, the less fresh it will be. In fact, a fish caught a thousand miles away and several days ago, but kept properly refrigerated, will be more wholesome than a fish caught yesterday by an angler who has left it unchilled.

Both the appearance and odour of fish provide clues to its condition. When buying whole fish, look for shining skin, pink gills and full, bright eyes with black pupils and transparent corneas. If your fishmonger allows you to touch his wares, press the fish with your fingers: the flesh should be soft but springy. Genuinely fresh fish has a clean, pleasant odour; reject any that have even the suggestion of a "fishy" smell. Exceptions to the rule are sharks, skates and rays, whose flesh contains a chemical called urea, which helps counter the tendency of these fish to lose body fluids to the sea by the process of osmosis. When sharks, skates and rays die, the urea breaks down and produces ammonia. The smell of ammonia should not worry the cook; it indicates that the urea is disappearing. But the process may take a day or two, so do not cook sharks, skates and rays immediately after they have been caught. (Any lingering ammoniac smell will be driven off by the heat of cooking.)

When buying pieces of fish, look for transluscent, rather than milky, flesh. Fillets that are dried up around their edges and show traces of discoloration will be stale.

If you are fortunate enough to catch your own fish, remove its viscera immediately; the digestive organs contain powerful enzymes that will attack the body wall. The only fish that can be kept intact for any length of time are those, such as salmon and sea trout, that return to fresh water to breed and stop feeding when they leave the sea. During the breeding period, the digestive organs of these fish atrophy.

Shellfish deteriorate more rapidly than fish; they are therefore usually sold alive or—in the case of lobsters, crabs and other crustaceans—pre-cooked. The methods for ascertaining whether shellfish are alive and in good condition differ according to the species; they are described on pages 26-31. As a general rule, however, fresh shellfish can be recognized by their lack of smell.

Seafood will keep fresh for no more than a day if stored in a refrigerator, loosely wrapped in plastic film or aluminium foil to prevent their smell from penetrating other foods. Neither fish nor shellfish respond well to deep-freezing: when chilled to below −7°C (19°F)—the temperature required to stop bacterial action—their flesh looses its springiness and cooking makes it dry, tough and tasteless. But fish do lend themselves to drying, salting, smoking and combinations of these curing techniques. Cured fish are not given a special place in this book, since most kinds can either be cooked in the same ways as fresh fish or can be eaten without cooking. A notable exception, however, is salt cod, which requires special preparation before it is cooked (*page 90*) and lends itself to a wide variety of dishes that are designed to make the most of its unique, briny flavour.

Special cooking needs

Fresh fish and shellfish are cooked by the same methods used for meat—frying, grilling, stewing and braising, for example. In one important respect, though, the methods differ. Whereas many cuts of meat are tough and require long cooking to become tender, all fish are naturally tender and require relatively brief cooking. The amount of fibrous connective tissue in fish is much less than in meat, and it breaks down more rapidly when exposed to heat. When it is possible without harming the presentation, fish can be checked for doneness by cutting into the flesh with the point of a knife at its thickest part, just behind the gills. When the flesh no longer clings to the bone the fish is cooked. At the same time, the

flesh will have changed from transluscent to opaque. If fish are not removed from the heat at this point, their flesh will shrink, toughen and flake apart.

Obviously, the time required to cook a fish will depend on its size and the degree of heat to which it is subjected. Various methods of gauging cooking time has been proposed; one of them, devised by the Canadian Department of Fisheries, calls for the fish to be measured at its thickest point and then cooked for 10 minutes for each 2.5 cm (1 inch)—irrespective of the cooking method used. The formula is a useful guide, but do not rely upon it exclusively; use the evidence of your eyes to see if the fish is done.

Suitable Cooking Methods at a Glance

The chart below suggests the cooking methods that are most appropriate for each of the fish and shellfish included in the Guide on the following pages. For ease of reference and for purposes of comparison, the entries are arranged in the same groupings used in the Guide and the Anthology of recipes.

	Freshwater Fish																	Herring Family						Cod Family								Flat Fish												Mackerel, Bonito, Tuna, Swordfish						Sharks, Skates, Rays						
	PIKE	PERCH	PIKE-PERCH	POWAN	SEA TROUT	BROWN TROUT	GRAYLING	ATLANTIC SALMON	RAINBOW TROUT	GUDGEON	BARBEL	CARP	BREAM	STURGEON	BURBOT	EEL	ELVERS	SMELT	SHAD	PILCHARD/SARDINE	SPRAT	ANCHOVY	HERRING	COD	HADDOCK	BLUE WHITING	WHITING	LING	COLEY	HAKE	POLLACK	DAB	LONG ROUGH DAB	FRENCH SOLE	WITCH	PLAICE	LEMON SOLE	HALIBUT	SOLE	FLOUNDER	TURBOT	MEGRIM	BRILL	FRIGATE MACKEREL	MACKEREL	SKIPJACK	BLUEFIN TUNA	BONITO	SWORDFISH	PORBEAGLE SHARK	DOGFISH	SMOOTH HOUND	SPUR DOG	ANGEL SHARK	BLUE (OR GREY) SKATE	THORNBACK RAY
Poaching and Steaming	●	●	●	●	●	●	●	●	●	●		●	●		●	●								●	●	●	●	●	●	●	●	●	●	●	●	●	●	●	●	●	●	●	●		●					●	●	●	●	●	●	●
Stewing and Braising	●	●	●	●	●	●	●	●	●			●	●	●	●	●	●		●		●	●	●	●	●	●	●	●	●	●	●							●						●		●	●	●	●	●	●	●	●	●	●	●
Baking	●	●	●	●	●	●	●	●	●			●	●	●	●	●		●	●	●	●	●	●	●	●	●	●	●	●	●	●	●	●	●	●	●	●	●	●	●	●	●	●	●	●	●	●	●	●	●	●	●	●	●	●	●
Frying	●	●	●	●	●	●	●	●	●	●	●	●	●	●	●	●	●	●	●	●	●	●	●	●	●	●	●	●	●	●	●	●	●	●	●	●	●	●	●	●	●	●	●	●	●	●	●	●	●	●	●	●	●	●	●	●
Grilling	●	●	●	●	●	●	●	●	●				●			●		●	●	●	●	●	●	●	●	●	●	●	●	●	●	●	●	●	●	●	●	●	●	●	●	●	●	●	●	●	●	●	●	●	●	●	●	●	●	●

Shellfish, of course, have their own cooking requirements, and these are explained on the appropriate pages.

Serving wine with seafood

Most fish and shellfish dishes will be enhanced by a white wine served well chilled. There are exceptions, of course. A rosé or a cool, young, relatively light-bodied red wine is an excellent accompaniment to salmon, tuna, sturgeon, mackerel, sardines and other richly flavoured fish; and a robust red wine, in the fruit of its youth, can be an exhilarating accompaniment to a lobster *à l'américaine,* a *bouillabaisse* or other fish stew that is flavoured with tomatoes, garlic and the assertive ingredients of Mediterranean cookery. But generally, red wines are so robustly flavoured that they would overwhelm the taste of seafood.

The light acidity of a dry white wine provides a pleasant contrast to the slight sweetness of most fish and it is the best foil to the rich cream or egg-bound sauces that marry so well with simply poached white fish. Dry white wines suitable for everyday use include Muscadet, Pouilly-Fuissé, Pouilly-Fumé, the Hermitage whites from the Rhône and—from Italy—Soave and Frascati. Champagne—including the still variety, called *coteaux champenois*—is associated with shellfish, especially with oysters and lobster, but the association owes less to the impressions of the palate than to notions of luxury and celebration. Champagne, however, is an acceptable accompaniment to cold poached lobster; and the dryest of white wines—Muscadet and Sancerre, for example—are the best accompaniment to oysters.

The wonderfully rounded flavour of one of the finer Burgundies—especially the first growths from the communes of Aloxe-Corton, Meursault and Puligny-Montrachet—is the perfect complement to a dish of sole, turbot or other fish of superior quality. Grand Cru Chablis, from northern Burgundy, has a delicate greenish colour and a lingering flinty taste that justifies its reputation as a classic accompaniment to seafood. Fine wines from outside France include the dry, delicate but beautifully fragrant Moselles from Germany.

Although dry wines have a natural affinity with seafood, some people prefer a wine with more than a hint of sweetness—a Vouvray from France, a Riesling or Gewürztraminer from Alsace, or a Spätlese or Auslese from Germany's Saar region, for example. The sweetest white wines, such as Sauternes, may be the ideal choice for a rich seafood dish—Lobster Newburg, for example. Nowadays, they are usually reserved for the dessert, but this practice was not always followed. At the turn of the century, a chef who prepared a fish dish for King Edward VII of Great Britain was seen to be delighted by His Majesty's reception of the meal. "But the King didn't say anything about your dish," the chef's colleagues pointed out. "Didn't you hear?" the chef asked, "His Majesty said that his Château d'Yquem [the first great growth of Sauternes] had never tasted so delicious. Wasn't that a tribute to my dish?". The story may be apocryphal, but it serves to show that in choosing a wine, as in cooking itself, your own palate is the surest guide.

	A Mixed Catch																										Crustaceans														Squid, Cuttlefish Octopus						Shellfish															
	RED SEA BREAM	PANDORA	GILT-HEAD BREAM	SAR COMMUN	DENTEX	BOGUE	SEA BASS	GROUPER	CONGER EEL	ANGLER-FISH	WOLF-FISH	GREY GURNARD	RED GURNARD	REDFISH	OMBRINE	BLUEFISH	SCAD	JOHN DORY	GREY MULLET	BALLAN WRASSE	WEEVER	GARFISH	RED MULLET	DOLPHIN FISH	LUMPFISH	SPINY LOBSTER	DUBLIN BAY PRAWN	EUROPEAN LOBSTER	FLAT LOBSTER	FRESHWATER CRAYFISH	DEEP SEA PRAWN	PRAWN	SHRIMP	EDIBLE CRAB	SHORE CRAB	SWIMMING CRAB	SPIDER CRAB	MANTIS SHRIMP	CUTTLEFISH	LITTLE CUTTLEFISH	FLYING SQUID	SQUID	OCTOPUS	PORTUGUESE OYSTER	EUROPEAN OYSTER	ORIENTAL OYSTER	MEDITERRANEAN SCALLOP	SCALLOP	QUEEN SCALLOP	WARTY VENUS	TELLIN	SOFT-SHELLED CLAM	CARPET-SHELL	CLOVISSE	SMOOTH VENUS	STRIPED VENUS	COCKLE	WINKLE	ORMER	WHELK	RAZOR-SHELL	MUSSEL
	•	•	•	•	•	•	•	•	•	•	•				•	•	•	•	•	•			•	•	•	•	•	•	•	•	•	•	•	•	•	•	•	•		•	•	•	•	•	•	•	•	•	•	•	•	•	•	•	•	•	•	•	•	•	•	•	•
	•		•				•					•	•	•				•	•	•	•	•	•	•		•	•	•				•							•	•												•						•		•		•
	•	•	•	•	•	•	•	•	•	•	•				•		•	•	•	•	•	•		•	•	•	•	•	•	•	•	•	•	•	•	•	•	•					•	•	•	•	•	•	•	•		•				•		•	•	•		•
	•	•	•	•	•	•	•	•	•	•	•				•		•	•	•	•	•	•					•				•	•	•	•	•	•	•							•	•	•	•	•	•	•		•				•		•	•	•		•
	•	•	•	•	•	•	•	•	•	•	•				•	•	•	•	•	•	•	•		•	•	•	•	•	•	•	•	•	•	•	•	•	•	•					•	•	•	•	•	•	•	•		•				•		•	•	•		•

7

A Guide to Fish and Shellfish

Of the hundreds of fish and shellfish species sold in Europe as a whole, most shoppers have access to several dozen but can identify only a fraction of the available range. Even if you are familiar with all the species that are customarily sold in your locality, the changing patterns of commercial fishing and marketing mean that you are likely to encounter new types of seafood from time to time.

The Guide on the following pages shows 121 of the important food fish and shellfish caught in Mediterranean and North-East Atlantic waters. By familiarizing yourself with the appearance of the seafood, you will be able to identify fish that are displayed without a label—and perhaps detect misleadingly labelled wares. Many fishmongers endow commonplace fish with euphemistic names: dogfish, for example, is traditionally sold as "rock salmon", although its appearance and flavour have nothing in common with those of true salmon. Also, for the cook who moves home from one part of the country to another, visual clues may at first be the only means of identifying a fish since the names of many species differ from region to region.

Used in conjunction with either the cooking chart on pages 6 and 7 or the Anthology of recipes on pages 94-175, the Guide will help you to choose a substitute if the fish that you ask for is not available or is too expensive. Most of the recipes in the Anthology list one or more suitable substitutes for the fish specified; recipes that do not call for a particular fish include a list of options. All the fish given as options are included in the Guide, and the methods of cooking them are listed in the cooking chart. Finally, the Guide should encourage you to buy some of the delicious, but strange-looking, species that you may come across.

Size is an important consideration when choosing fish; for this reason, all the fish and shellfish in the Guide are drawn to scale—necessarily a sliding scale, since the range of sizes is great (box, below). For ease of reference and for comparison, the entries are divided into nine groups: freshwater fish; the herring and cod families; flat fish; mackerel, bonito, tuna and swordfish; sharks, skates and rays; a mixed catch (other sea fish); crustaceans; squid, cuttlefish and octopus; shellfish.

All but two groups are arranged in accordance with the scientific system of classification. Not surprisingly, fish belonging to the same family, or to closely related families, tend to have culinary features in common and can be prepared in the same ways. All the cod family, for example, have lean, white flesh; and the recipes for species in this group are interchangeable. The general cooking characteristics of each group—together with salient information about individual species—are given in the text that accompanies the illustrations.

The two groups that do not conform to this system are the freshwater fish (opposite) and the species arranged under the heading "A Mixed Catch" (page 14). Both groupings list species from many different families and with varying flavours, textures and cooking requirements. The so-called freshwater fish include some species, such as bream and carp, that are found only in fresh water, and others, such as salmon and eel, that spend part of their lives in the sea but are caught in rivers and lakes. In the sea fish grouping, Mediterranean species are well represented. Unlike the colder waters of the North Atlantic, which contain relatively few species, mostly occurring in huge numbers, the Mediterranean contains numerous species, most of which occur in relatively small numbers. Local cuisines reflect this difference, since they feature many dishes of mixed fish and shellfish—including the sea fish stews for which the Mediterranean region is famous.

A Key to the Fish Drawings

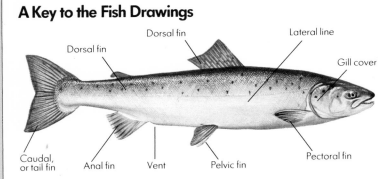

Dorsal fin

Dorsal fin

Lateral line

Gill cover

Caudal, or tail fin

Anal fin

Vent

Pelvic fin

Pectoral fin

The fish illustrated in the Guide range in size from the porbeagle shark, which may attain a length of 4 metres (13 feet), to the sardine. In order to show species of greatly differing sizes on the same page, gradations in the fish's length are represented on a diminishing scale (below). Thus the Atlantic salmon (left) appears only twice as large as the brown trout on the opposite page, but is actually four times as long. The drawing of the salmon also gives the terms for the main external features of fish: the terms are those used throughout the book. Each fish is identified by its common and scientific names.

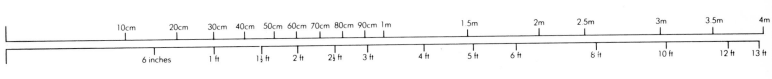

10cm 20cm 30cm 40cm 50cm 60cm 70cm 80cm 90cm 1m   1.5m   2m 2.5m   3m 3.5m 4m

6 inches   1 ft   1½ ft   2 ft   2½ ft   3 ft   4 ft   5 ft 6 ft   8 ft   10 ft   12 ft 13 ft

Freshwater Fish

Among fish caught in fresh water, members of the salmon and trout family are universally esteemed, but there are many less familiar species that make fine eating—notably grayling, powan, perch, pike-perch and eel.

Both grayling, which has a scent of thyme when freshly caught, and powan are related to trout. Perch has an especially good flavour but is very bony; its relative, the pike-perch, has flesh that has been likened to that of sole. Eel has dense, fatty flesh that is enhanced by highly flavoured sauces; its young, called elvers, are delicious sautéed, deep fried, or stewed with garlic. Sturgeon can be braised like tuna (*page 60*).

The other fish shown include gudgeon, which is good pan fried or deep fried; carp, admired for its firm, sweet flesh; barbel and bream, two less distinguished cousins of carp that need well-seasoned sauces; pike, a bland fish that is a good choice for mousselines (*page 84*); and burbot, a relative of cod.

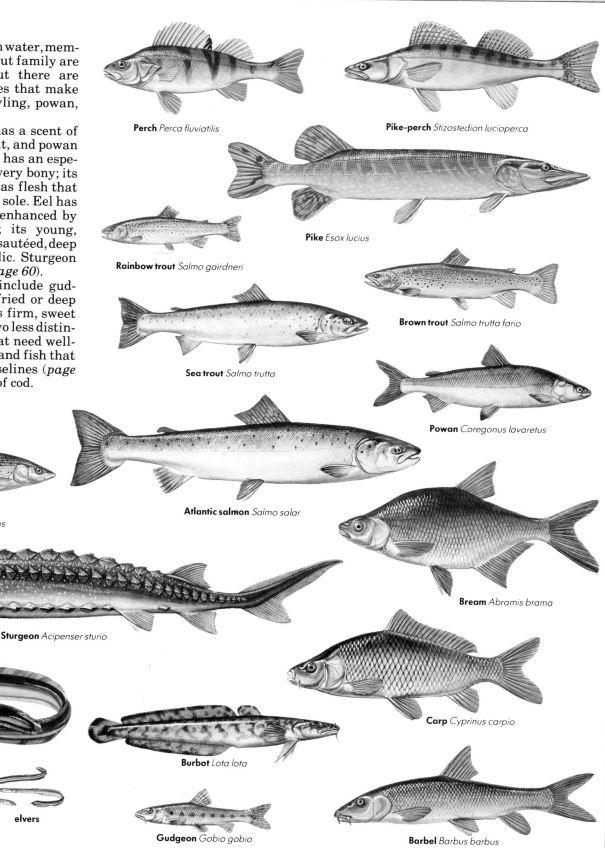

Perch *Perca fluviatilis*

Pike-perch *Stizostedion lucioperca*

Pike *Esox lucius*

Rainbow trout *Salmo gairdneri*

Brown trout *Salmo trutta fario*

Sea trout *Salmo trutta*

Powan *Coregonus lavaretus*

Atlantic salmon *Salmo salar*

Grayling *Thymallus thymallus*

Bream *Abramis brama*

Sturgeon *Acipenser sturio*

Carp *Cyprinus carpio*

immature eel

mature eel

elvers

Burbot *Lota lota*

Eel *Anguilla anguilla*

Gudgeon *Gobio gobio*

Barbel *Barbus barbus*

The Herring and Cod Families

Richly flavoured, with somewhat fatty flesh, fish of the herring family—herring itself, sprat, anchovy, shad, pilchard and its immature form, sardine—are best grilled or fried. The smelt is a delicately flavoured relative that is delicious grilled, fried, poached in a wine court-bouillon or braised.

Herrings, sprats and anchovies are sold in a variety of cured forms. Salted anchovies make a valuable flavouring agent in many sauces and stuffings.

The members of the cod family are lean, white fish. The North Atlantic cod, its Baltic cousin and haddock have firm, sweet flesh. Whiting has an especially delicate flavour and fine texture. Hake resembles cod, but has closer-grained flesh. The other members of the cod family—pollack, coley, blue whiting and ling—tend towards blandness, but they are inexpensive choices for any recipe that simply calls for white fish.

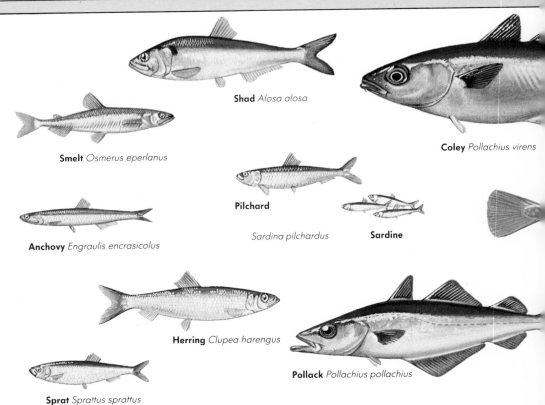

Shad *Alosa alosa*

Smelt *Osmerus eperlanus*

Coley *Pollachius virens*

Pilchard

Sardina pilchardus

Sardine

Anchovy *Engraulis encrasicolus*

Herring *Clupea harengus*

Pollack *Pollachius pollachius*

Sprat *Sprattus sprattus*

Flat Fish

Two of the most exquisitely flavoured sea fish—sole and turbot—belong to this group. Both have firm, yet tender and succulent flesh. Sole, in particular, has fired the imaginations of chefs, and features in a wide range of dishes.

Like the other smaller flat fish—lemon sole, French sole, plaice, the dabs, witch, flounder, brill and megrim—sole can be cooked whole or filleted. The shallow bodies of all these species make them suitable for grilling and sautéing. Turbot is often so large that it requires a special lozenge-shaped vessel, the *turbotière*, for poaching it whole; however, it is generally cooked as steaks or fillets. The turbot's bones are rich in gelatine, which makes the flesh succulent and gives body to sauces made from a liquid in which the bones have been poached.

The largest flat fish is the halibut, which is always sold as fillets or steaks. It has a pleasing flavour, but a tendency to dryness: take special care to keep it moistened during cooking.

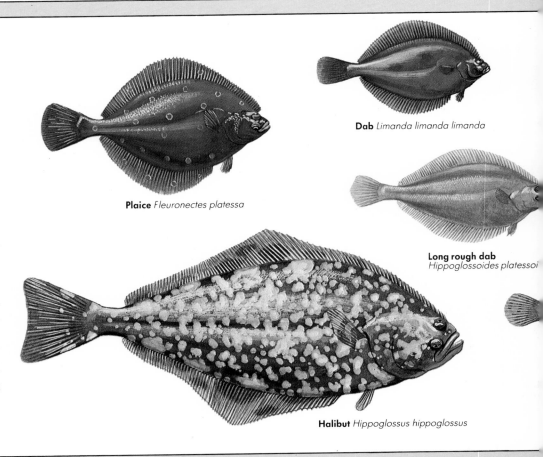

Dab *Limanda limanda limanda*

Plaice *Fleuronectes platessa*

Long rough dab
Hippoglossoides platessoi

Halibut *Hippoglossus hippoglossus*

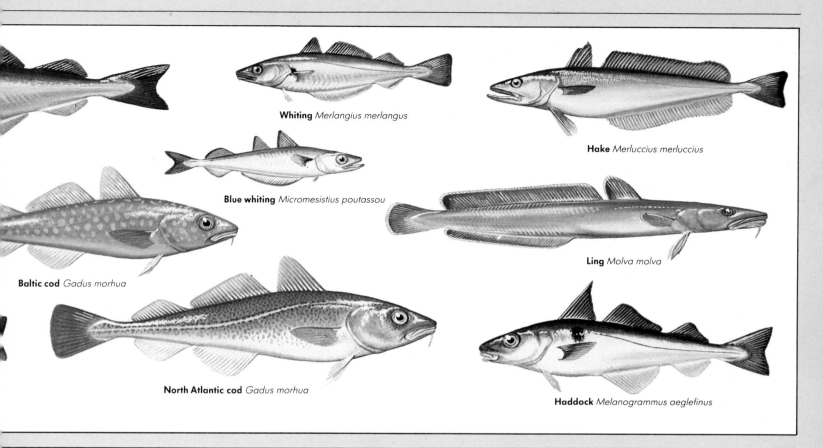

Whiting *Merlangius merlangus*

Hake *Merluccius merluccius*

Blue whiting *Micromesistius poutassou*

Ling *Molva molva*

Baltic cod *Gadus morhua*

North Atlantic cod *Gadus morhua*

Haddock *Melanogrammus aeglefinus*

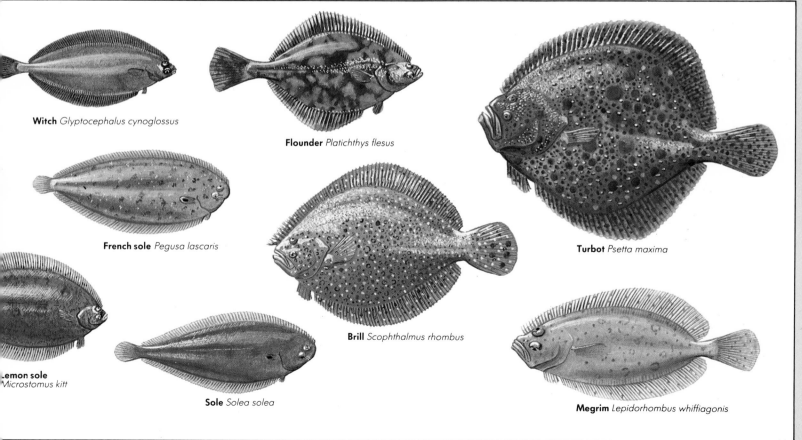

Witch *Glyptocephalus cynoglossus*

Flounder *Platichthys flesus*

Turbot *Psetta maxima*

French sole *Pegusa lascaris*

Lemon sole *Microstomus kitt*

Sole *Solea solea*

Brill *Scophthalmus rhombus*

Megrim *Lepidorhombus whiffiagonis*

Mackerel, Bonito, Tuna and Swordfish

Powerful swimmers with compact, muscular flesh, these surface fish can be divided for practical cooking purposes into two groups—mackerel and the rest.

Mackerel is distinguished by its comparatively soft texture and by its oiliness. During summer and autumn, its fat content may rise to 20 per cent—a very high proportion for fish. Traditional ways of countering mackerel's fattiness include poaching it in white wine and serving it with sharp sauces based on gooseberries, sorrel or mustard.

Swordfish, bonito, tuna, skipjack and the misleadingly named frigate mackerel (actually a member of the tuna family) have firm, close-grained flesh. These fish lend themselves to grilling (*page 80*) and lengthy oven braising with vegetables (*page 60*).

The colours of their flesh range from the near-white of the swordfish to the deep red of the bonito and frigate mackerel; lighter-coloured flesh indicates a more delicate flavour. The larger fish are usually sold as steaks.

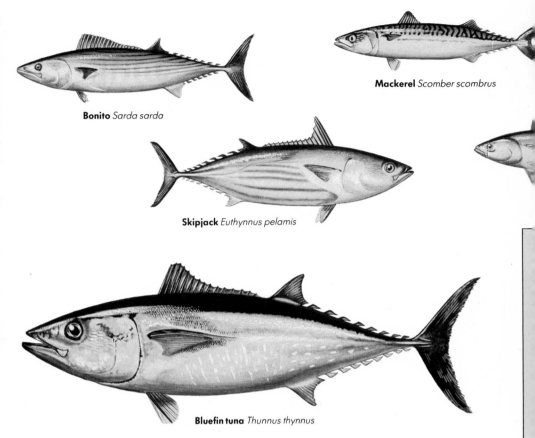

Bonito *Sarda sarda*

Mackerel *Scomber scombrus*

Skipjack *Euthynnus pelamis*

Bluefin tuna *Thunnus thynnus*

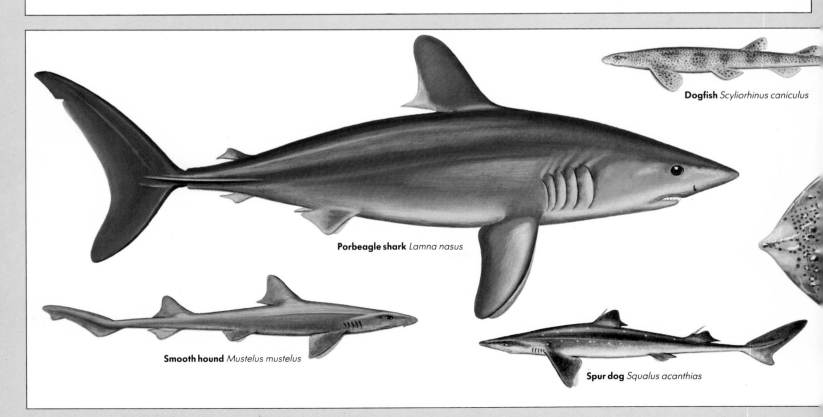

Dogfish *Scyliorhinus caniculus*

Porbeagle shark *Lamna nasus*

Smooth hound *Mustelus mustelus*

Spur dog *Squalus acanthias*

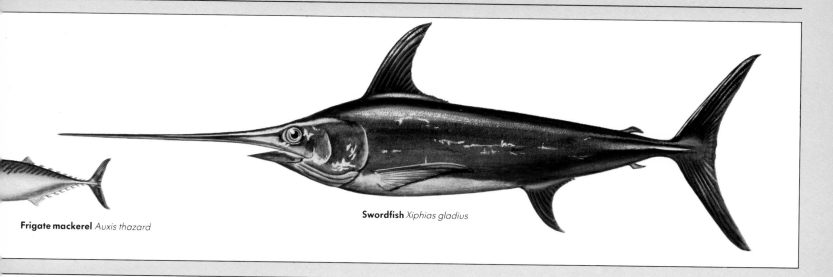

Frigate mackerel *Auxis thazard*

Swordfish *Xiphias gladius*

Angel shark *Squatina squatina*

Blue (or grey) skate *Raja batis*

Thornback ray *Raja clavata*

Sea lamprey *Petromyzon marinus*

Sharks, Skates and Rays

One characteristic of these fish that should endear them to the diner is their lack of true bones. Their skeletons are composed of a cartilaginous material that separates easily from the flesh after cooking. The skeletons yield gelatine during cooking: a fumet (*page 35*) made from a shark or skate carcass will have enough body to set after cooling.

As explained on page 5, these fish have an ammoniac smell when freshly caught which disappears on cooking.

Of the sharks and dogfish, the porbeagle enjoys the most favourable culinary reputation. It has several features in common with veal: close-textured pink flesh with a delicate flavour and a tendency to dryness, which can be countered by larding the flesh with strips of pork fat. Porbeagle is good for grilling or braising. Angel shark, spur dog, smooth hound and dogfish have less refined flavours, but they lend themselves well to highly seasoned dishes. Their flesh can be cut into cubes and steeped in an aromatic marinade to make excellent brochettes (*page 81*).

Only the "wings" of blue skate and thornback ray are used in cooking. Delicately flavoured but delicious when fried or poached, they are traditionally sauced with butter heated until nut-brown, and then sharpened with a dash of vinegar and a sprinkling of capers.

The sea lamprey can be prepared and cooked like an eel (*page 50*); *afficionados* of this unusual fish consider its flavour superior to that of the eel.

A Mixed Catch

Unlike the cold waters of the Atlantic, the Mediterranean contains many different species, most of which occur in relatively small numbers. Shown here are some of the most important Mediterranean species, with preference given to those that range around the Iberian peninsula into the Bay of Biscay and as far north as the English Channel. In addition, some of the less familiar North Atlantic species are exhibited. All of these fish make good eating.

Among the finest flavoured is red mullet, whose liver is a delicacy; grouper, with its firm and relatively bone-free flesh; the sea bass, a relation of the grouper; John Dory, which can be cooked like flat fish; and the family of sea breams—notably, sea bream itself, red sea bream, pandora, gilt-head bream and dentex—all with firm, lean flesh.

The wrasse, gurnards, weever and grey mullet are often included in the fish stews for which the Mediterranean region is famous. Grey mullet—no relation of red mullet—has rather soft flesh, and is prized chiefly for its roe.

An unappetizing appearance has prevented some of the species shown here from winning the favour they deserve. The angler-fish, for example, has a hideous head; but the flesh from its tail is firm and sweet. The wolf-fish has an array of fearsome teeth that enables it to feed on mussels and whelks—a diet that gives its firm flesh a delicious flavour. The garfish's green bones do not affect its delicate flavour, but do keep down its price. Conger eel is another inexpensive fish, with firm flesh that makes it valuable in fish stews.

Of the remaining species illustrated, small bluefish and the robustly flavoured dolphin fish are especially worth seeking out. Sar commun and bogue can be substituted for the sea breams. Ombrine can be treated like sea bass. Scad is similar, but inferior, to mackerel. Redfish is undistinguished, but economical.

Lumpfish are sought for their eggs, which make an inexpensive substitute for sturgeon caviar. The flesh of the male is edible; but that of the female during the breeding season has aptly been described as "glue-pudding".

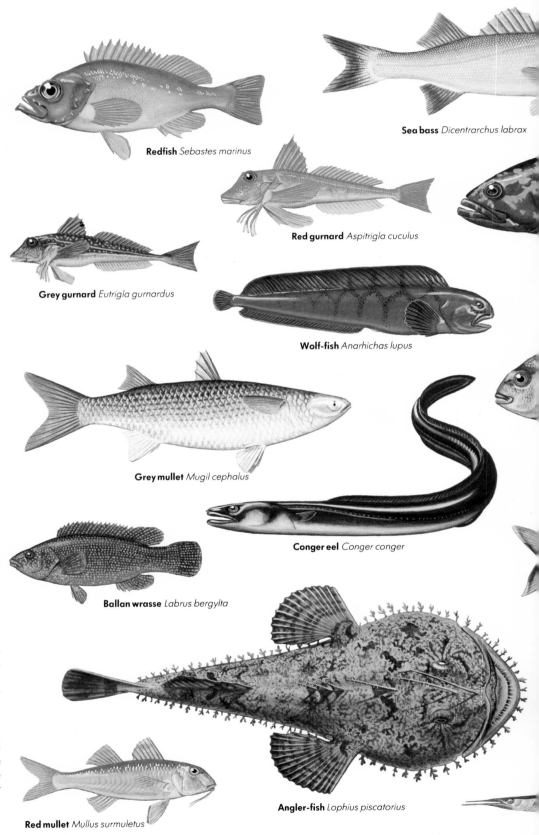

Redfish *Sebastes marinus*

Sea bass *Dicentrarchus labrax*

Red gurnard *Aspitrigla cuculus*

Grey gurnard *Eutrigla gurnardus*

Wolf-fish *Anarhichas lupus*

Grey mullet *Mugil cephalus*

Conger eel *Conger conger*

Ballan wrasse *Labrus bergylta*

Angler-fish *Lophius piscatorius*

Red mullet *Mullus surmuletus*

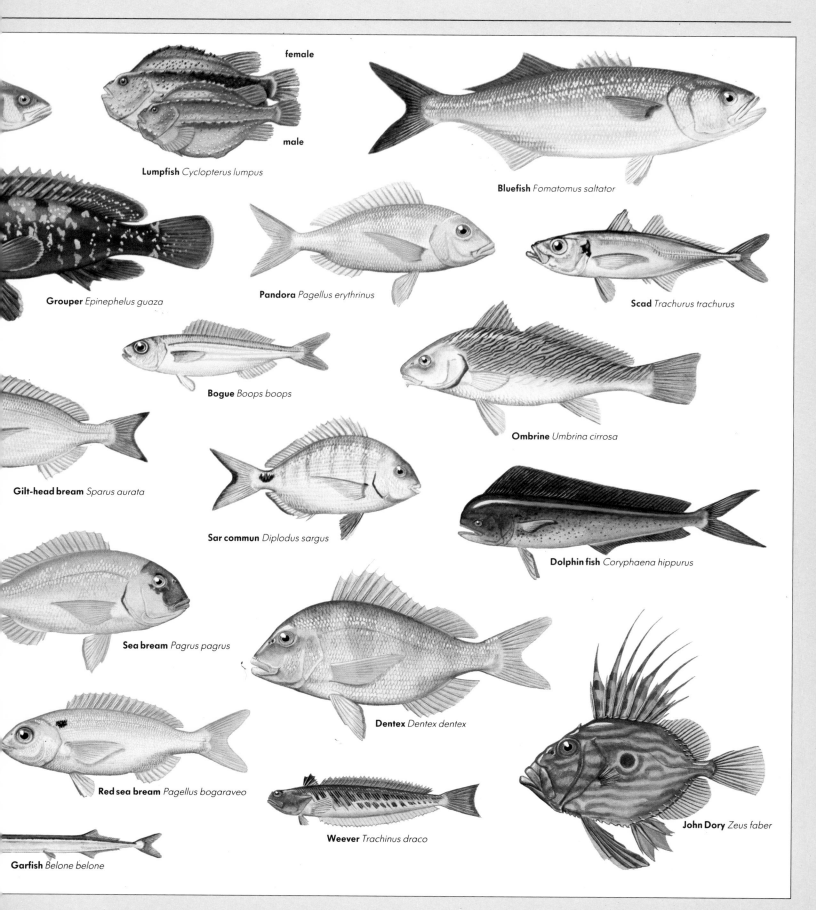

Lumpfish *Cyclopterus lumpus*
female
male

Bluefish *Fomatomus saltator*

Grouper *Epinephelus guaza*

Pandora *Pagellus erythrinus*

Scad *Trachurus trachurus*

Bogue *Boops boops*

Ombrine *Umbrina cirrosa*

Gilt-head bream *Sparus aurata*

Sar commun *Diplodus sargus*

Dolphin fish *Coryphaena hippurus*

Sea bream *Pagrus pagrus*

Dentex *Dentex dentex*

Red sea bream *Pagellus bogaraveo*

John Dory *Zeus faber*

Weever *Trachinus draco*

Garfish *Belone belone*

Crustaceans

All of the crustaceans have firm, sweet flesh and hard, jointed shells that are shed periodically as the creatures grow. The European lobster is generally regarded as the finest flavoured; but the spiny lobster and the flat lobster are of comparable quality and lend themselves to the same dishes. All three species are prepared for cooking in basically the same way (*pages 26 and 54*).

Shrimps, prawns and deep-sea prawns are often poached and used as garnishes; but like the larger Dublin Bay prawns and mantis shrimps, they can be prepared as dishes in their own right—coated in batter and deep fried, for example, or skewered with vegetables and grilled. Crayfish are especially esteemed for their delicate flavour. These freshwater crustaceans can be simply poached and served with a sauce, or they can be braised with aromatic vegetables in a sauce thickened and flavoured with the pounded shells.

The edible and spider crabs are usually poached and served in their shells. The small swimming and shore crabs yield little meat and are used mainly for flavouring soups and stews. However, if they are collected after they have shed their old shells and before their new ones have hardened, they can be cooked and eaten whole—claws and all.

Deep-sea prawn *Pandalus borealis*

Spiny lobster *Palinurus elephas*

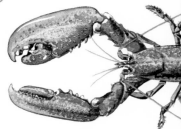

Flat lobster *Scyllarides latus*

Spider crab *Maja squinado*

Shore crab *Carcinus maenas*

Mantis shrimp *Squilla mantis*

Freshwater crayfish *Austropotamobius pallip*

Edible crab *Cancer pagurus*

Swimming crab *Macropipus corrugatus*

European lobster *Homarus gam*

Squid, Cuttlefish and Octopus

Members of the cephalopod family, squid, cuttlefish and octopus are unusually rich in flesh for their weight, since their bag-like bodies and tentacles do not contain true skeletons. Yet until recently, their firm, rather spicy flesh has been widely appreciated only in the Mediterranean region and the Far East.

The squid of European coasts, its relative, the flying squid, and the cuttlefish can be cut up and fried or stewed—or their bodies can be stuffed and braised. Small octopus can be fried, but octopus more than 30 cm (12 inches) long have rubbery flesh that should be beaten and then tenderized by long cooking in a liquid. Little cuttlefish are usually cleaned and fried whole.

Flying squid *Todarodes sagittatus*

Cuttlefish *Sepia officinalis*

Little cuttlefish *Sepiola rondeleti*

Octopus *Octopus vulgaris*

Squid *Loligo vulgaris*

Shellfish

Despite their abundance and the variety of ways in which they can be served, molluscs are neglected by most cooks. Eaten raw, many of them make a delicious hors-d'oeuvre; they can be used in soups or stews; or they can serve as garnishes and stuffings for other seafood dishes. Advice on choosing and opening molluscs appears on page 30.

An exception to the general rule of neglect is the oyster, whose subtle flavour is universally esteemed. To be appreciated fully, European and Portuguese oysters should be eaten raw, with their juices, from the half shell. The Oriental oyster, an exotic addition to European oyster beds, does not have the exquisite flavour of its smaller relatives and is usually baked, or sliced and fried.

Most of the other bivalves—cockles, razor-shells, tellins, clovisses, carpet-shells and the different kinds of Venus shells—can be eaten raw. They also make delicious soups and stews.

Mussels are usually steamed in their own juices, which are served as a broth. Soft-shelled clams can be cooked in the same way, or baked. The firm, white flesh of the scallop, Mediterranean scallop and queen scallop is often poached, then baked in a creamy sauce.

Winkles and whelks, boiled in their shells and served with lemon juice or vinegar, make good appetizers. The white muscle of the ormer is tough; it should first be tenderized by beating and then braised or fried.

European oyster *Ostrea edulis*

Oriental oyster *Crassostrea gigas*

Portuguese oyster *Crassostrea angulata*

Tellin *Donax trunculus*

Warty Venus *Venus verrucosa*

Clovisse *Venerupis aurea*

Smooth Venus *Callista chione*

Carpet-shell *Venerupis decussata*

Soft-shelled clam *Mya arenaria*

Striped Venus *Venus gallina*

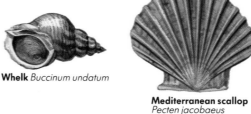

Whelk *Buccinum undatum*

Mediterranean scallop *Pecten jacobaeus*

Queen scallop *Chlamys opercularis*

Razor-shell *Ensis ensis*

Ormer *Haliotis tuberculata*

Winkle *Littorina littorea*

Cockle *Cerastoderma edule*

Mussel *Mytilus edulis*

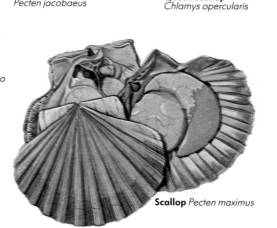

Scallop *Pecten maximus*

ublin Bay prawn *lephrops norvegicus*

hrimp *rangon crangon*

Prawn *Palaemon serratus*

Cleaning and Trimming: the Essential First Steps

However fish are to be cooked—whole, boned, filleted or cut into steaks—they must first be cleaned and trimmed. Most fish netted by deep-water fishermen are eviscerated before being brought ashore; fish caught inshore or in fresh water are usually sold intact. With rare exceptions, the viscera (internal organs) of the latter should be taken out, and the fins and scales removed. These chores will be performed on request by your fishmonger, but you should, nevertheless, learn to do them yourself: how else will you be able to deal with a freshly caught fish presented to you by an angler friend?

Finning (*box, below, left*) is done mainly for aesthetic reasons; fish that are to be served whole look tidier and more attractive if their fins and tails are trimmed, and they are easier to serve and eat. If you are dealing with a spiky-finned species, such as the sea bream shown below, it is wise to trim the fins before going on to other preparations, since the spikes can cause painful punctures if handled carelessly. The dorsal fin and other large fins are firmly attached to the flesh by bones; in the case of fish that are to be boned (*page 22*) the fins and underlying bones should be removed. If you are poaching a whole fish, it is easier to remove the fins by hand after cooking.

With some notable exceptions—which would include the shark and eel families—all fish have scales. In many species the scales are small and form an integral part of the skin; in others—sea bream, carp and grey mullet, for example—the scales are large and bony. Fortunately, they are loosely attached to the skin and can be scraped off with the edge of a knife (*box, below, right*), a serrated blade or a fish scaler.

There are two principal ways to eviscerate a fish—through the belly and through the gills (*box, right*). Eviscerating through the belly is a quick and convenient method if you have to bone or fillet a fish; eviscerating through the gills—which preserves the shape of the fish—is the preferred method for fish that are to be stuffed and cooked whole (*page 64*) or served whole in aspic (*page 40*). To clean flat fish, whose viscera occupy a small area directly below the gills, simply make a small incision below the gills and pull out the viscera.

Once fish have been eviscerated and trimmed, you can go on to fillet or bone them (*pages 20-23*). If you are filleting small flat fish, such as sole, it is convenient to skin them at this stage (*box, opposite page, below*). Flat fish that are to be filleted should be skinned completely; flat fish that are to be cooked whole should be skinned only on their dark, upper side since the white, lower skin helps hold the whole fish intact during cooking. Round fish—and large flat fish, such as turbot—are easier to skin after they have been filleted or cooked.

Removing Fins and Scales

Trimming a spiky-finned fish. Lay the fish—here, a sea bream—on a cutting board. With a pair of heavy scissors, cut away the dorsal fin down to the back. If you are planning to bone the fish, remove the dorsal fin completely. Cut down each side of the fin, ease the knife into the underlying bony structure that connects the fin to the flesh and prise the fin and underlying bones free. Cut off the pectoral, ventral and anal fins (*above*).

Remove scales. Grip the fish by the tail and, using the edge of a knife or a fish scaler, scrape towards the head—against the direction in which the scales lie. Work carefully round the head and the base of the fins. (To prevent scales from being scattered around the kitchen, you can scale the fish in a large basin of water.) When the skin is free of scales, rinse the fish thoroughly.

Methods for Gutting

Eviscerating through the belly. Where a recipe calls for the head to be removed, cut off the head behind the last gill opening: here, a herring is being prepared for boning before it is fried (*page 75*). Using heavy scissors or a sharp knife, cut down the belly as far as the vent (*above*). Pull out the viscera (*above, right*). Run a knife-point down both sides of the backbone to release any pockets of blood. Rinse the fish briefly in cold water.

Eviscerating through the gills. In order to eviscerate a fish for stuffing whole—here, a sea trout—hook a finger through the opening and pull out the viscera in one piece, together with the gill. Reach into the cavity to be sure you have removed all the organs, then rinse out the fish in cold water.

A Rapid Way to Skin Flat Fish

1 Starting the operation. Lay the fish—here, a sole—dark side uppermost on a cutting board. With a sharp knife, cut across the skin where the tail joins the body (*above*). Starting at the cut, use the point of the knife or your fingernails to prise a flap of skin away from the flesh until you can obtain a firm grip on it.

2 Peeling off the skin. Grasp the flap of skin in one hand; with the other hold down the tail, using a cloth to prevent your fingers from slipping. Firmly and decisively, pull the skin towards the head (*above*). On reaching the jaws, turn the fish over and, holding the fish by the head, continue pulling the skin until you reach the tail (*inset, right*).

Separating the Flesh from the Bones

Fillets—full-length sections of fish separated from the bones—are called for in most dishes where fish are to be served in a sauce or deep fried in batter. Fillets are also the raw material for *mousselines, quenelles (pages 84-87)* and fish pâtés. Most fish can be filleted, but best results are obtained with fish that have a well-defined bone structure—such as the sole and whiting shown here.

To separate fillets cleanly from the bones, you need a knife with a long, sharp blade that is flexible enough to ride over the fish's bones. The basic technique is the same whatever fish you are handling, but flat fish and round fish call for slightly different methods of working. Flat fish, which are usually skinned before filleting (*pages 18-19*), yield four fillets—two from the upper side of the body and two from the lower side. Round fish, which are skinned after filleting, yield two fillets—one from each side of the backbone.

Cook fillets as soon as possible after they have been prepared; since they are not protected by skin, they will dry up if exposed directly to the air. For the same reason, do not grill fillets. They should be fried gently in butter, or poached briefly in a rich stock or sauce (*page 42*); or they can be coated with batter and deep fried, or covered with a sauce and baked.

Fillets also lend themselves to decorative presentations. They can be rolled around a stuffing and poached, for example, or used to line a mould filled with a *mousseline* or other stuffing (*page 87*).

Filleting Flat Fish

1 **Freeing the flesh from the backbone.** Lay the skinned fish—here, a sole—on a cutting board with its eyes facing up and its tail towards you. With the tip of a sharp, flexible knife, cut down the centre of the fish along the backbone from the head to the tail. Insert the blade at a shallow angle between the head end of the fillet and the ribs. Steadying the fillet with one hand and cutting with short movements, separate the head end of the fillet from the ribs.

Filleting and Skinning Round Fish

1 **Cutting down the backbone.** Lay the cleaned fish—here, a whiting—on one side, with its tail towards you. Holding the fish steady with one hand, slice along the backbone from head to tail, cutting deep enough to expose the backbone.

2 **Removing the upper fillet.** Separate the fillet from the head by cutting down to the backbone behind the gills. Holding the head end of the fillet, insert the knife between the fillet and ribs. With the blade of the knife parallel to the ribs, cut down the length of the fillet, using short strokes to detach it completely.

2 **Removing the first fillet.** When the head end of the fillet is detached, lift it clear of the ribs with your free hand and continue cutting away the fillet along its length. Let the fish's symmetrical bone structure guide the knife. Cut off at the tail, and trim any fins or ragged edges.

3 **Removing the second fillet.** Cut away the right-hand fillet. If the fish has been caught in the spawning season, it will probably contain a sac of orange roe beneath the right-hand fillet, as shown here. You can save the roe for a fish stock, or it can be served poached or fried as a delicacy in its own right.

4 **A bonus for the stock-pot.** When the upper side of the fish has been filleted, turn the fish over and repeat the process on the under side. You will be left with four fillets and a cleanly picked skeleton (*above*). Save the skeleton for inclusion in a fumet (*page 35*).□

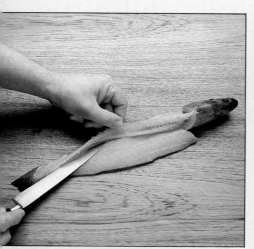

3 **Removing the lower fillet.** Holding the fish by its exposed backbone, use the flat of the knife to separate the lower fillet from the ribs. If you are filleting a fish with a delicate skeleton—a herring, for example—some bones may remain attached to the flesh. Carefully pull them out with your fingers or a tweezer.

4 **Skinning the fillets.** Lay the fillets skin-side down and cut about 1 cm (½ inch) of flesh away from the skin at the tail end. Pressing a finger on the exposed skin, insert the knife at a shallow angle beneath the flesh and, cutting away from you with short strokes, separate fillet and skin. Repeat for the second fillet. Trim the fillets neatly for cooking (*inset*).□

Boning Round Fish Through the Belly

Bones in cooked fish can be a nuisance—but they are easy to remove beforehand. One method is to fillet the fish, but then you will not be able to serve it whole. Another method, which permits you to bone the fish yet preserve its shape, is demonstrated here. You can then cook the whole fish *au gratin* (*page 62*), fill the body cavity with stuffing, or poach it and cover it with sauce. This method should only be used for round fish; when flat fish need boning, the bones should be removed by the method described on page 66.

Most round fish have simple skeletons consisting of a backbone with "ribs" branching off it. Removing the bones simply involves opening the underside of the fish from head to tail and freeing the skeleton from the surrounding flesh. In the case of sea bass—shown here—and other large-boned fish, you can use a knife to help free the "ribs" from the membrane that covers them, and then pick each one out individually.

The skeleton of finer-boned fish, such as herrings, should be prised loose with your fingers alone (*page 75*), since a knife could damage the flesh. Very small fish, such as anchovies, can be boned by slitting the belly with your thumb and peeling away the skeleton (*page 77*).

Alternatively you can—with more finesse than this method requires—bone round fish through the back (*page 66*).

1 Gutting and finning. Check that the fish has been cleanly gutted; if not, first rinse out the gut cavity and wipe away any dried blood. Cut away the dorsal fins, together with the underlying bones that support them (*page 18*). Then slice off the pectoral fins (*above*), cutting forwards, towards the gill apertures.

2 Opening the fish. The fish's belly will already have been opened for gutting. To remove the bones, the opening should be extended along the length of the fish. Using a sharp knife, slit the underside from the vent to the tail.

3 Cutting out the ribs. Hold the fish open to expose the backbone and ribs, which are embedded shallowly in the flesh and covered by membrane. Working down the fish from rib to rib, nick the membrane, and with your fingers—and the aid of a small knife—pull the rib free (*above*). Snap each rib away from the backbone with your fingers (*right*).

4 **Freeing the backbone.** The backbone of the fish is still partly embedded in flesh. To free it, open the fish as wide as possible without tearing the flesh, and run the knife down both sides of the spine. Take care not to press too hard so as not to cut through the skin.

5 **Removing the backbone.** With a pair of kitchen scissors, sever the backbone as close to the head as possible. Grasp the severed end and pull out the bone, working back towards the tail. Snip it free. The backbone can be included in a fumet (*page 35*), if you like.☐

Dressing Cephalopods

Squid, cuttlefish and octopus can be prepared for cooking in no more time than it takes to gut and fillet a fish. Only the tentacles and the fleshy body sac of these species are eaten. The other parts are discarded, starting with the translucent, quill-shaped "pen" of the squid (*right*) and the hard white cuttlebone of the cuttlefish (*box, opposite*). The octopus's body does not have a bony support.

The eyes, skin, viscera and mouth, or "beak", of all these cephalopods are always removed. Among the viscera lies an ink sac, which contains the black fluid the cephalopods secrete when threatened by predators. If they are to be cooked "in their ink"—a practice traditional in Mediterranean and Adriatic cookery—the sac must be removed intact. In specimens that have been frozen, the ink will have coagulated; to restore fluidity, remove the frozen granules from the sac and dissolve them in a little hot water.

The flesh of fresh squid and cuttlefish should be firm to the touch. The tentacles of both species are usually chopped up for cooking, and the body pouch sliced into rings or sections. Very small squid and cuttlefish—up to 2 to 3 cm (1 inch) long—can be fried, but most recipes (*pages 157-160*) call for relatively long simmering to tenderize the flesh. The squid's baglike body also makes an ideal receptacle for stuffing (*demonstration, page 52*).

Octopus flesh should be springy and resilient. Octopus is prepared by cutting away the tentacles in one piece, then inverting the body sac or hood to remove the viscera, and finally taking out the beak. The skin, however, is too firmly attached to be peeled easily; parboil the octopus before stripping off the skin.

Octopus requires a longer time to cook than either squid or cuttlefish, it is generally stewed for anything from 1 to 4 hours, depending on size (*recipes, pages 160-161*). The fishermen of the Mediterranean lands tenderize mature specimens by beating their catch against rocks. You can achieve the same effect by beating the hood or tentacles with a mallet; a very small octopus—less than 10 cm (4 inches) long—does not need beating.

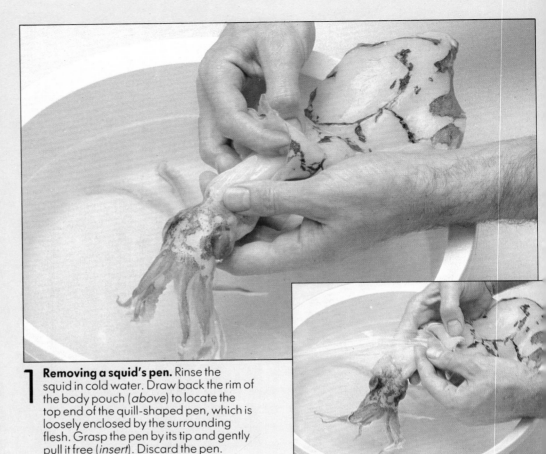

1 **Removing a squid's pen.** Rinse the squid in cold water. Draw back the rim of the body pouch (*above*) to locate the top end of the quill-shaped pen, which is loosely enclosed by the surrounding flesh. Grasp the pen by its tip and gently pull it free (*insert*). Discard the pen.

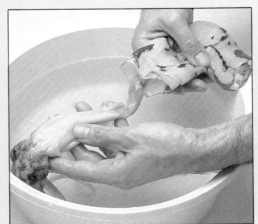

2 **Separating tentacles and body.** Hold the body pouch in one hand; with the other, grasp the head just below the eyes. Pull the two sections gently apart. The viscera, including the ink sac, will come away with the head (*above*). The body pouch will be empty except for a mucous membrane. Pull the membrane away under cold running water.

3 **Skinning the body pouch.** Translucent skin, irregularly patterned with mauve patches, covers the white flesh of the squid's body pouch. Slip a finger under the skin and peel it off the pouch (*above*). Carefully pull off the edible, triangular fins which are on either side of the pouch. Skin the fins.

Opening Cuttlefish without Breaking the Ink Sac

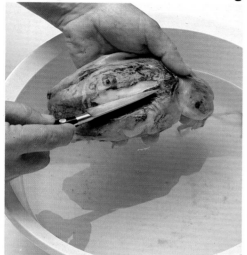

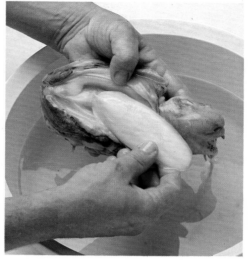

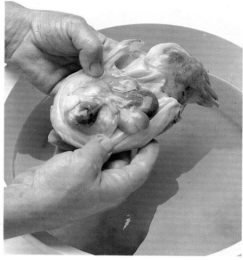

1 Opening the body. Cuttlefish can be prepared in much the same way as squid (*steps 1 to 6 left and below*); but if you intend to cook cuttlefish in its own ink (*page 53*), the body pouch should be cut open to ensure that the ink sac remains intact. Wash the cuttlefish in cold water; then, with a sharp knife, slit the back from head to tail, pressing until the blade strikes the cuttlebone.

2 Removing the cuttlebone. Ease apart the sides of the cut to expose the oval cuttlebone. With your fingers, gently lift the cuttlebone out of the body. You will now be able to see the viscera beneath a thin membrane. Slip a finger beneath the membrane and peel it away from the viscera. Discard the membrane.

3 Extracting the ink sac. The ink sac will be clearly seen among the viscera. With your fingers, carefully detach it. Scoop out and discard the rest of the viscera. Cut the tentacles away from the body and remove the beak in the same way as for squid (*Steps 4 and 5, below*). The cuttlefish is now ready for cooking.

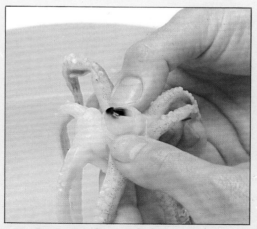

4 Severing the tentacles. Put the squid's head and the viscera on a cutting board and, using a sharp knife, sever the tentacles from the rest of the head, cutting just above the eyes (*above*). The tentacles should come away together, connected to one another by a narrow rim of edible flesh. Discard the head and viscera, saving the ink sac if required.

5 Removing the squid's beak. A bony, beak-like mouth, complete with rasping teeth, lies within the rim of flesh that connects the base of the tentacles. With your fingers, squeeze the beak out of the fleshy rim (*above*) and discard it.

6 The end result. Spread on a plate, ready for cooking (*page 52*), the four edible pieces of squid flesh: the pouch, the tentacles and the two triangular fins. Covered with fine plastic wrap, fresh squid can be stored in a refrigerator for up to two days. ☐

Extracting Every Morsel of a Lobster

To enjoy lobster at its best, buy it live. Choose an active lobster that feels heavy for its size. Sluggish specimens that seem underweight may have been kept for days without food in the fishmonger's holding tank; or they may have moulted recently and not yet grown enough to fill their new shells with firm flesh.

If you intend to serve the flesh plain—the best way to appreciate its wonderful flavour—kill the lobster by immersing it in boiling water or a court-bouillon, which will also cook the flesh (*right*). Then you can conveniently pick out every morsel of meat from the shell, as shown here.

If, however, you plan to use the lobster in a dish that calls for uncooked halves or pieces—such as lobster *à l'américaine*—kill the lobster by cutting it in half, as demonstrated on page 54.

1 Killing and cooking a lobster. Grasp the lobster by the back and drop it into boiling salted water or into a court-bouillon (*page 34*), then hold it under the surface with tongs for two minutes. Turn down the heat, cover the pan and simmer the lobster, allowing 12 minutes for the first 500g (1 lb), 10 minutes for the next 500g, and 5 minutes more for each additional 500g thereafter.

2 Detaching the legs. Using tongs or a wire skimmer, remove the lobster—which will have turned red during cooking—from the pan and lay it on its back. When it is cool enough to handle, snap off the eight legs (*above*) as close to the body as possible. Break each leg apart at the central joint, then, with a skewer, remove the thin slivers of flesh from the hollow centre.

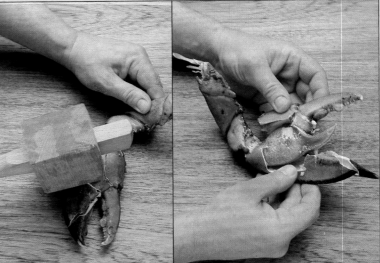

3 Cracking the claws. Snap each claw free near the body. With a mallet, crack the shell (*above, left*). Pull away the shell fragments (*above, right*) and remove the flesh, in one piece if possible. Extract the blade-like cartilage that runs through each claw. Twist free the two small segments attached to the pincers, crack them open and remove the meat inside.

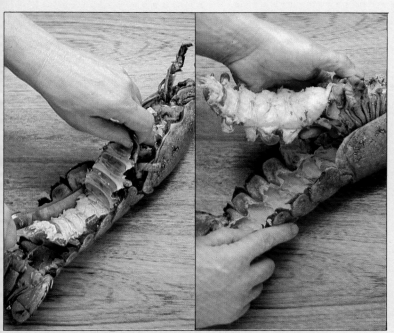

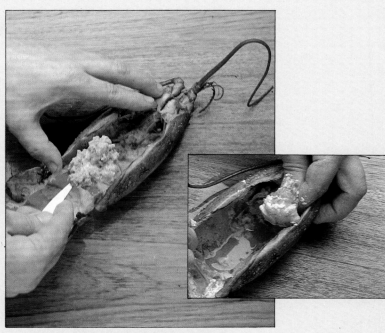

4 **Extracting the meat from the body and tail.** Lay the lobster on its back. With a heavy knife, cut down each side along its entire length. Pull away the bony covering that protects the underside (*above, left*). Starting at the tail, prise the flesh free in a single section (*above, right*). Strip off the brown-grey, feathery gills.

5 **Removing the liver and gravel sac.** The soft grey-green liver, or tomalley, will be left in the shell. Scoop this out with a spoon (*above*) and save it. Female lobsters may also contain a pink roe, or coral, which should be saved. The inedible gravel sac, which serves as a stomach, lies between the eyes. Lift it out with your fingers (*inset*) and discard.

Tail

Liver and coral

Claws

Legs

Body flesh

6 **Chopping the tail meat.** Lay the tail meat on a cutting surface and slice it into several neat serving pieces with a knife (*above*). Cut or break off the section of shell that housed the lobster's body and, using the point of the knife, scrape out any flesh attached to the shell.□

To serve lobster plain, arrange the pieces attractively on a serving plate, using the liver—and coral, if there is any—as a garnish, or to flavour an accompanying sauce (*page 55*). Alternatively, clean the empty tail shell (not shown) and use it as a container in which to serve the lobster. The flesh extracted from the cooked lobster accounts for approximately 30 per cent of its total weight when alive.

Prising Out the Meat of a Hard-Shelled Crab

Crabs are usually sold ready-cooked—a convenient arrangement, since the humane killing of crabs is a job best left to experts. The two surest guides to quality are the crab's weight and the condition of its shell. Reject those crabs that are lightweight; they may have recently shed their shells, in which case their flesh will be soft and porous as it expands to the size of the new ones. Avoid also any cooked crab with holes in its shell; boiling liquid will have penetrated through the holes during cooking, making the flesh watery.

The meat of the male crab is preferable to that of the female; males have a higher proportion of white meat than females and the quality of their flesh is superior. Male crabs can be distinguished from female crabs by the much smaller tail flap on their undersides.

The method of extracting crab meat—demonstrated here on the common or edible crab, the familiar Western European variety—is basically the same for all hard-shelled species. The meat can be served cold in a salad with mayonnaise or some other suitable sauce, or it can be used for a hot dish, such as the gratin demonstrated on page 68.

You may want to keep the empty crab shell. By breaking away the shell along the rim of the underside, you can turn it into an attractive dish in which to serve the dressed crab; or use it as a container for a seafood gratin (*page 68*).

1 **Removing the claws and legs.** Place the crab underside up on a work surface. With your fingers, break the claws from the body by twisting them against the direction in which the pincers face. Then, in the same way, detach the eight legs, snapping them loose at the lowest joint, as close as possible to the shell.

2 **Extracting flesh from the claws.** Crack the shell of each claw with a mallet, taking care not to break up the flesh inside. Peel away the shell (*top*), and extract the flesh, bringing with it the meat concealed in the pincers (*above*). Repeat this for the second segment of the claws and for the eight legs (which can be broken apart with one's fingers).

3 **Opening the crab.** Twist free the bony tail flap on the underside of the crab (*above, left*) and discard it. Insert the tip of a rigid knife between the main shell and the section of the shell to which the legs were attached. Loosen the rim of the underside, then twist the knife to prise it upwards (*above, centre*). Pull the underside free of the shell (*above, right*) and set it aside. With a teaspoon, scoop out the meat from inside the shell and reserve it; but remove and discard the small, baglike, stomach sac and its appendages, which are located just behind the crab's mouth.

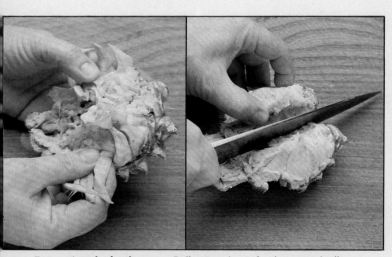

4 **Extracting the body meat.** Pull away the soft, elongated gills along the edges of the underside (*above, left*) and discard them. Using a heavy kitchen knife, split the underside down the middle (*above, right*), then use a skewer to remove the flesh from the many crevices. Turn the underside over, and prise the scraps of white meat out of the leg sockets.□

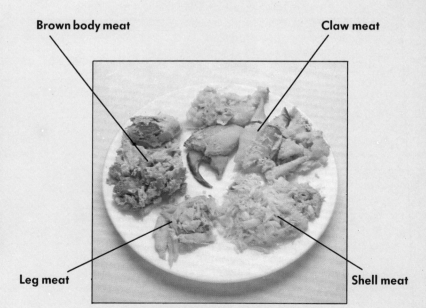

Brown body meat · Claw meat · Leg meat · Shell meat

The brown body meat—most of it liver—and the cream-coloured meat from the shell are usually kept apart from the flaky white meat of the legs and claws. When serving crab cold in the shell, arrange the dark meat in one half of the shell and the white flesh in the other half. The soft brown liver can also be incorporated into an accompanying sauce.

Special Preparations for Molluscs

Because molluscs are cooked only briefly or eaten raw, they must be absolutely fresh. If you gather your own supply, check with local fishermen or the district fishing authority that the area in which the molluscs live is not polluted, since specimens that come from contaminated waters may contain toxic substances.

Most bivalves—mussels, oysters and cockles, for example—are sold live. Their shells are usually closed. Sharply tap any specimens whose shells are open; if they remain open, the shellfish inside are probably dead, and should be discarded.

Univalves such as winkles and whelks are generally sold pre-cooked. Buying from a dealer you trust is the best guarantee of freshness.

Because most of the molluscs inhabit the sandy or muddy regions of the tide line, they tend to ingest sand or other particles when they feed. When you bring a batch home, scrape any growths from their shells under water with a knife or stiff brush, then place them in a pan of clean, salted water. They will stay alive for several hours and expel any sand or grit they contain. Change the water at intervals if it becomes muddied.

There are two principal ways to open bivalves to extract their flesh: prising them open, which sometimes involves cutting the muscles that hold the shells together, or applying heat, which causes the shells to open automatically. Oysters should always be prised open (*box, right*), since heat tends to toughen their flesh. Scallops can either be prised open, or placed in a hot oven for a few minutes; in either case, you then have to separate the edible parts from the inedible (*box, opposite page, above*). Mussels are usually steamed open in a pan as part of their cooking (*page 44*); but a few dishes call for them to be prised open (*page 92*).

Winkles and whelks are almost always steamed or boiled until cooked. Their flesh can then be extracted with a pin or a skewer (*box, above, right*).

Removing a Mussel's Beard

A mussel has a bunch of thin, hair-like strands attached to the hinge of its shell. The strands, known as the beard, serve to anchor the live mussel to rocks. Before cooking, pull the beard off (*above*) or cut it free with scissors.

Pinning Whelks and Winkles

Whelks, shown here, are cooked in boiling water for 10 to 20 minutes; but winkles take only 5 to 10 minutes. Drain off the water. When the shells are cool enough to handle, extract the flesh from each one by pinning it with a small skewer and levering it free (*above*).

A Safe and Efficient Way to Shuck an Oyster

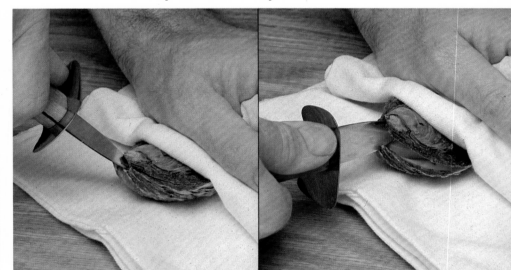

1 **Separating the shells.** Place the oyster, wrapped in a folded napkin, on a firm surface with the flatter shell uppermost and the hinged end towards you. Holding the oyster firmly in place with one hand, take an oyster knife in the other and insert the tip into the small gap in the hinge (*above, left*). Twist the blade to snap the shells apart (*above, right*).

Opening and Cleaning a Scallop

 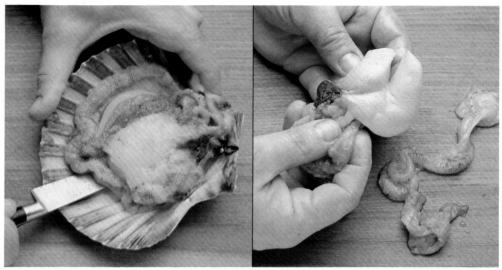

1 Opening the shells. Hold the scallop in a cloth, with the flat shell up. Probe between the shells with a short knife to find a small opening (*above*). Insert the blade and run it across the roof of the shell to sever the internal muscle.

2 Separating the flesh. Pull the shells apart. Slide the blade of the knife under the greyish outer rim of flesh—the skirt—to free the scallop (*above, left*). Remove the flesh from the shell and separate the white muscle and pink coral from the other organs (*above, right*). The muscle and coral are the best parts; the skirt can be used in a stock-pot; the rest should be discarded.

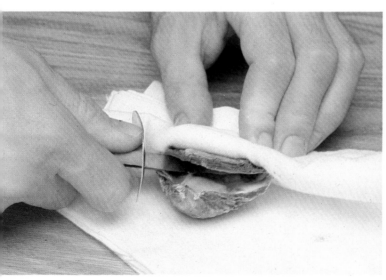 

2 Severing the muscle. Continuing to hold the oyster firmly in the cloth, slide the knife blade along the inside of the upper shell (*above*) to sever the muscle that holds the shells together. Discard the shell, and lift the rounded, lower shell off the napkin, making sure the liquid in it does not spill. Clean out any bits of broken shell with the point of the knife.

3 Cutting the oyster loose. Grip the lower shell firmly with your fingers. Cutting towards yourself, run the blade under the oyster to sever the muscle attaching it to the lower shell (*above*) and so to free it. The oyster can then be swallowed raw directly from the shell, together with its juices, first seasoned to taste with a little lemon juice or freshly ground pepper.

1
Poaching and Steaming
Careful Handling and Controlled Cooking

The simplicity of a properly poached or steamed seafood dish belies the skills that go into it. To serve a fish or shellfish that has been prepared by either method, and that both looks and tastes delicious, the cook must first select a suitable vessel; then choose and prepare a poaching or steaming liquid that will enhance, not mask, the flavour of the fish; control the temperature of the liquid; and—finally—judge, to the moment, when the fish or shellfish is done to perfection.

All these decisions start with the choice of seafood. Firm-fleshed fish such as salmon, trout, sole or turbot are the best candidates for poaching or steaming. Among the shellfish, lobsters, crabs, prawns, mussels and clams give first-rate results. The size and type of seafood then determines the vessel to be used. Whole large fish must be cooked in special poachers that keep them intact (*page 36*). Whole small fish, as well as fish steaks and fillets, can be poached, or—with the addition of a wire rack—steamed, in any straight-sided pan broad enough to hold them flat. Lobsters and crabs require deep pots to accommodate them easily; prawns and bivalves may be poached or steamed in frying pans.

Salted water will do for the poaching or steaming liquid, but most fish and shellfish profit from being cooked in a court-bouillon (*page 34*), often made by simmering vegetables and herbs in water to which wine, lemon, cider or vinegar is then added. If fish trimmings are incorporated, the court-bouillon becomes a fish stock, or fumet, which not only makes a rich liquid for poaching delicate fish—such as whiting—or fillets, but also furnishes the starting material for sauces and aspic coatings.

The poaching process, of course, is never synonymous with boiling; with seafood, however, it is especially important that the temperature of the liquid be adjusted carefully. If fish are agitated in boiling water, their flesh flakes apart, resulting in a dry texture and ruined appearance. The poaching liquid should therefore be kept around 80°C (175°F), at which point the surface will perceptibly shudder, but not bubble. Crustaceans, which have protective shells and denser flesh than fish, can be cooked at a simmer (90°C or 195°F). Fish to be steamed should be cooked over—not in contact with—boiling liquid; bivalves are steamed in a tightly closed pan over a high heat with the addition of a little white wine (*page 44*).

A halibut steak is lowered into a milk and water court-bouillon that is just at the frothing point. The fish's flesh, protected by the intact skin, will emerge with its flavour heightened by the acidity of the lemon slices which have been added to the court-bouillon.

Flavoured Liquids for Cooking and Sauce-Making

Seafood can, of course, be poached or steamed in plain water. But the inherent taste of any fish or shellfish can also be enhanced easily by cooking it in a flavoured liquid. Sea water makes an excellent poaching medium; otherwise use a court-bouillon or a fumet (*recipes, page 174*). A court-bouillon usually combines water with wine or vinegar, but may be based on milk. A fumet, which is a fish stock, is made with water, wine, and fish or fish trimmings. Both may be flavoured with aromatic vegetables and herbs; their composition will vary depending on the type of seafood and how it is to be served, as well as on personal taste and what ingredients are available.

Thyme, bay, onion and carrot are usually present in a wine and vegetable court-bouillon (*below, left*). Parsley, fennel stalks, dill, garlic, leeks or celery are optional additions. You can use red or white wine in any quantity you like. A court-bouillon with a high proportion of wine would be too strong for poaching delicate fish—whiting and turbot, for example; but it would be ideal for cooking strongly flavoured fish such as mackerel, or such shellfish as prawns and mussels.

To draw out the flavours of the vegetables and herbs, simmer them in water for 30 to 40 minutes. Wine inhibits the release of the vegetables' flavours, so it should be added about half-way through the simmering time. If you include peppercorns, add them for the last few minutes, since they will impart a bitter taste to the liquid if cooked too long.

A vinegar court-bouillon (*below, centre*) substitutes wine vinegar for wine, but in a smaller proportion to the water. Its piquancy suits such freshwater fish as carp, trout and pike. Keep in mind that when a freshly caught fish is plunged into a simmering vinegar court-bouillon, the acid will turn its skin a delicate shade of blue. A fish which is treated in this way is said to be cooked *au bleu*.

A milk and lemon court-bouillon (*below, right*) helps keep fish steaks and fillets white. Turbot, brill, cod and smoked haddock are often poached in this mild liquid and emerge with their flavour heightened by the lemon's acidity.

A fumet, literally "flavour", is usually prepared with water and wine, but generally contains less water than a court-bouillon. Indeed, a fumet can simply be a court-bouillon that has already been used for poaching fish and has reduced in the process. The concentrated liquid can be used for poaching any fish or shellfish, but its additional flavour makes it especially good for mild-tasting fillets.

After the poaching, a fumet can be transformed into a sauce (*page 42*) or reserved for a stew or braise (*pages 47-57*). And if it is clarified and strengthened with gelatine, it becomes an aspic jelly that can be used to coat cold poached fish or other dishes (*page 40*).

To store fumet for future use, simply place an intact plastic freezing bag in a small loaf tin or other suitably sized container, pour in the cooled fumet, tie up the bag, label it and freeze. It can be stored for up to three months.

A Trio of Court-Bouillons

A wine and vegetable court-bouillon. Slice an onion, a carrot and a leek, and dice a stick of celery. Add the vegetables, together with parsley, thyme, dill, a bay leaf and salt to about 1 litre (1¾ pints) salted water. Simmer for about 15 minutes, then pour in 30 cl (½ pint) of white wine. Simmer for a further 15 minutes, adding a few peppercorns for the last 10 minutes.

A vinegar court-bouillon. To the same water and vegetable mixture used for the wine court-bouillon, add white or red wine vinegar to taste; as a rough guide, allow 5 tablespoons wine vinegar to 60 cl (1 pint) water. Simmer the court-bouillon for about 30 minutes.

A milk and lemon court-bouillon. Peel the skin and bitter pith from a lemon. Slice the lemon finely and remove the seeds. Add as many lemon slices as you like to a mixture of one part milk to four parts salted water. The court-bouillon requires no preliminary cooking before the fish is placed in it.

Fumet: an Essence Made with Trimmings

1 **Assembling the ingredients.** Prepare a selection of vegetables and herbs as for a court-bouillon (*opposite page*). Rinse some fish carcasses—here, the heads and the bones of sole and whiting— and tear out and discard the gills. Break the skeletons into convenient sizes. Place all the ingredients in a pan, cover with cold water, and salt lightly.

2 **Skimming the liquid.** Bring the liquid to the boil. With a spoon, remove the scum that forms on its surface as its reaches a simmer (*above*). Simmer for 15 minutes, then add white wine in the proportion of up to one part of white wine to one part of water, according to taste. Simmer for a further 15 minutes, but do not overcook, lest the fish bones make the liquid bitter.

3 **Straining the fumet.** Strain the fumet through a colander set over a deep bowl. Pressing the solids speeds the process but also makes the liquid cloudy; do not press the solids if you need the fumet for a clear-textured sauce or aspic. The strained liquid is now ready for use as a poaching medium.

4 **Removing small particles.** If you want to make aspic from the fumet (*page 40*), strain the liquid a second time, through a damp muslin cloth draped inside a fine sieve (*left*). Do not press the liquid. Leave the strained fumet in a refrigerator for several hours to allow the fine solids it contains to form a sediment (*above*). Decant the liquid for making aspic. □

Special Care for a Perfect Presentation

Poached and skinned, a large fish such as the salmon shown here makes a splendid dinner or buffet dish. But it requires a special fish kettle—a long, narrow pan that accommodates the shape and size of the fish, and is fitted with a removable rack that makes it possible to lift the fish into and out of the poaching liquid without damaging the flesh.

Before it is poached, a large fish that has been cleaned through the belly should be trussed to ensure that it retains its shape as it cooks. A fish that has been eviscerated through the gills (*page 19*) does not need trussing. Large fish should always be started in a cold court-bouillon and allowed to warm through gradually—otherwise the surface flesh will be cooked before the inside is done.

A small fish—trout, small sea bass or the whiting shown below—will cook through more quickly, and so can be covered directly with warm poaching liquid. It can also be cooked without a fish kettle: by curling it so that its tail is in its mouth (*box, below*), you can cook it in a sauté pan that would otherwise be too small for it.

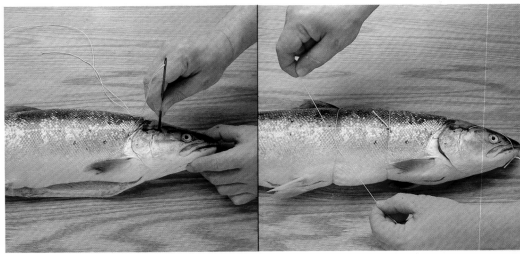

1 Trussing the fish. Gut and clean the fish but do not remove its fins and scales; keeping the skin intact will help hold the fish together. For a neat presentation at table, tie up the fish's mouth: push a trussing needle, threaded with about 30 cm (12 inches) of cotton string, through the gills (*above, left*), then cross the two ends of the string over the snout and tie them under the mouth. If the fish has been gutted through the belly cut a piece of string long enough to encircle the fish's girth. Tie it round loosely (*above, right*).

A Neat Fitting Trick

Eviscerate and scale the fish—here, a whiting—but do not truss it. Curl it into a ring shape, fixing its tail in its mouth (*above*). Place it in a shallow, straight-sided pan just large enough to maintain the tail-in-mouth position. The fish should be put in the pan belly-up, so that it will lie on its underside when it is tipped out. Cover it with hot, but not boiling, court-bouillon and poach it, covered. Cook until tender when tested with a needle (*Step 2, right*). Pour out the liquid and turn the fish on to a serving dish.

2 Using a fish kettle. Place the fish on the rack of the kettle and lower it into the empty pan (*above, left*). Cover with cold, strained court-bouillon (*page 34*). Put the lid on the kettle (*above, centre*), and heat the court-bouillon until the liquid begins to stir, but not boil; in boiling liquid the fish would overcook and begin to fall apart. Poach the fish, allowing 10 minutes' cooking time for every 2.5 cm (1 inch) of its thickness. The fish is done when a trussing needle, inserted in the thick flesh behind the gills, meets almost no resistance. Carefully lift out the rack and slide the fish on to a platter (*above, right*).

3 **Skinning.** It is easy to remove the skin while the fish is still hot and wet. Cut the trussing string and pull it free. With a small knife, cut out the fins (*page 19*). Slit the skin from head to tail along the back and the belly, then pull away the skin from the exposed, upper side of the fish with your fingers (*above*).

4 **Dividing the top fillets.** With a flexible, long-bladed knife, cut down one side of the fish along the line of the backbone (*above*). Then, turning the blade of the knife so that it is almost flat, reinsert it in the incision. Work down the length of the fish, easing the flesh of the top fillet away from the bones.

5 **Serving the fish.** When half the fillet has been freed, divide it into serving portions. Lift the servings on to plates (*above*). Detach and serve the second half of the upper fillet in the same way.

6 **Final division of the fish.** When the entire upper fillet has been removed, pull the tail forward (*above*) to free the attached backbone and head from the lower fillet. Divide the lower fillet also into two segments, and lift these away from the underskin with a fish slice.□

A Range of Sauces from Mild to Pungent

Many sauces are suitable for poached fish. Some complement or accentuate the fish's flavour subtly. Others have acidic, aromatic or other assertive ingredients that provide a contrast to the flavour of the fish. The four sauces shown here (*recipes, pages 172-173*) illustrate this diversity of tastes and enrichments.

The mildest of the sauces is a *sabayon* (*right*)—a perfect partner, like the closely related hollandaise (*recipe, page 172*), for all hot, poached, white fish dishes. A *sabayon* is begun by whisking egg yolks into an equal volume of reduced fumet in a saucepan set in a water bath—a larger pan partly filled with simmering water. At first the mixture of eggs and fumet will be thin, but with whisking it will become frothy and slightly thickened. Butter is incorporated in batches and the sauce whisked constantly until it becomes the consistency of a light custard.

Beurre blanc (*below, right*), a shallot-flavoured combination of butter, wine and vinegar, is an excellent accompaniment to any hot poached fish. Since butter is the only thickener, many cooks think that the sauce requires some special skill. But the trick is simply to keep the heat very low and whisk continuously so that the butter forms a smooth emulsion with the reduced wine and vinegar instead of separating into oil and butter solids. To control the heat, use chilled butter and a heavy saucepan on a fireproof mat.

Montpellier butter (*opposite page, above*) is a purée of herbs, spinach, watercress, capers, gherkins, anchovies, shallots and garlic, all bound together and mellowed by butter, egg yolks and oil. Usually served with cold poached fish, Montpellier butter is especially good with salmon; it may also be served with hot grilled fish. The classic herb mixture is parsley, chervil, chives and tarragon, but this can be varied according to taste.

Aïoli (*opposite page, below*) is simply a mayonnaise that incorporates pounded garlic. It can be served with hot or cold poached fish. In Provence *aïoli* is the almost invariable accompaniment to hot, poached salt cod. The sauce is thickened by blending oil with egg yolks in the proportions of 15 to 20 cl (6 fl oz) to 1 yolk. For a successful mayonnaise, the oil and egg yolks must be at room temperature.

Sabayon: a Blend of Egg Yolks and Butter

1 Mixing eggs and fumet. Boil some fumet in a small pan until it has reduced to a few tablespoons. Put the pan in a water bath and whisk in 2 or 3 egg yolks.

2 Thickening the sauce. When the mixture starts to thicken, add butter chunks, a handful at a time, whisking constantly between each addition.

3 Achieving the right consistency. Continue adding the butter, whisking constantly, until the sauce coats the sides of the pan (*above*).

4 Finishing the sauce. Take the pan off the heat. Continue whisking for about 30 seconds as it cools. Pour the sauce into a warmed sauceboat to serve.

Beurre Blanc: Wine and Shallots Bound with Butter

1 Reducing the liquid. Boil white wine and vinegar with chopped shallots (*above, left*) until the liquid just moistens the shallots (*above, right*).

2 Whisking. Take the pan off the heat to cool, then put it on a fireproof mat over a very low heat. Whisk in butter chunks until the sauce has a mayonnaise texture.

Montpellier Butter: Flavour and Colour from Herbs

1 **Blanching.** Boil herbs—here, parsley, tarragon and chives—with stemmed spinach and watercress for 2 minutes. Drain, refresh in cold water and dry.

2 **Pounding.** Put the herbs in a mortar with chopped gherkins, chopped and parboiled shallots, anchovy fillets, capers, a clove of garlic and salt (*above, left*). Pound to a paste. Pound in hard-boiled egg yolks (*above, centre*) and butter (*above, right*).

3 **Sieving.** When the butter has blended uniformly, rub the mixture through a drum sieve on to a plate. Wipe the mortar and return the mixture to it.

4 **Incorporating oil.** Add a little olive oil, stirring the sauce constantly. To control the flow of the oil, pour it—as shown here—through a slit cut in the cork.

5 **Finishing the sauce.** Continue adding oil until the sauce looks glossy and has a smooth, creamy texture (*above*). The sauce is then ready to serve.

Aioli: Garlic-Flavoured Mayonnaise

  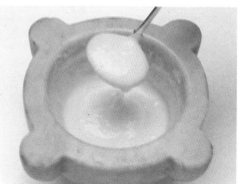

1 **Mixing egg yolks and garlic.** Put peeled garlic cloves and salt in a mortar, and pound to a purée. Add the egg yolks and stir until they lighten in colour.

2 **Incorporating oil.** Add olive oil, drop by drop, stirring briskly all the while. When the sauce starts to thicken, pour the oil in a thin, steady stream.

3 **Finishing.** When the sauce is quite stiff, add lemon juice and a spoonful of warm water. Stir in more oil until the sauce is a thick spooning consistency (*above*).

An Aspic Coating Made with Clear Fumet

A limpid aspic jelly, decorated with a pattern of herbs, or vegetable slices, turns a whole poached fish into a handsome dish to grace a cold buffet. The aspic is made from fumet and may be flavoured with a fortified wine such as Madeira. In addition to contributing its own flavour to the dish, aspic helps to keep the fish moist.

On these pages, aspic is used to coat skinned trout decorated with tarragon leaves, which lend a subtle anise flavour. Other cold whole fish—and moulded dishes, such as the turban on page 87—can be presented in a similar way; and decorations can range from slices of carrot or hard-boiled egg to peeled shrimps.

To make an aspic firm enough to glaze the fish evenly and hold decorations, you must add commercial gelatine to the fumet. Unlike meat and poultry, most fish contain very little natural gelatine. For the correct proportion of gelatine to liquid, follow instructions on the packet, but use slightly less gelatine than indicated to allow for the small amount of natural gelatine already in the fumet.

To make the aspic crystal-clear all solid fragments must be removed from the fumet. The larger particles will form a sediment if the fumet is left overnight in a bowl, and they will be left behind when it is decanted (*page 35*). But small particles will remain in suspension; the only way to extract them is to add an absorbing agent that will bond with the fumet fragments, thus enlarging their size and making it possible to strain them out of the liquid. Egg whites and broken egg shells serve as this agent. After they are added the fumet must be heated for the egg whites to coagulate. The movement of the boiling liquid drives the tiny particles against the solid egg whites, where they adhere. Straining the liquid through a fine cloth removes whites, shell and all impurities.

Once clarified, the liquid must be chilled until close to its jelling point before it can be spooned over the well-chilled fish. Since only a thin film of liquid will set on the fish after a single application, the aspic coating should be built up in layers, with a period of refrigeration after each addition of liquid. Decorations are suspended in the jelly by adding them after the first layer is applied.

1 Mixing in the gelatine. Calculate the volume of fumet required for the aspic (*recipe, page 174*), and warm it in a large saucepan. Take the required quantity of gelatine and leave it to soften for a few minutes in a little cold water. Add some of the heated fumet, and stir until the gelatine melts. Stir the gelatine into the fumet in the saucepan.

2 Adding egg white. Test to make sure that the fumet will gel by refrigerating a spoonful of it. It should set within 10 minutes; if it does not, add more dissolved gelatine to the fumet. Beat 2 egg whites to soft peaks. Add the whites and broken egg shells to the fumet. Place the pan on a high heat and whisk the fumet continuously until it boils.

3 Clarifying the fumet. As the fumet comes to the boil, the egg whites will rise. When they reach the pan's rim, remove the pan from the heat for 10 minutes to allow the foam to settle and form a bond with the particles. Return the pan to the heat and bring the fumet to the boil twice more, again letting it stand for 10 minutes between each boil.

4 Straining the fumet. Place 4 layers of dampened, wrung-out cheesecloth in a fine sieve over a deep bowl and slowly pour in the fumet. Allow the fumet to drip through the cloth, then leave it to cool.

5 **Preparing the fish.** Skin the poached fish while still warm (*page 37*), cover them with a moistened towel, and chill in a refrigerator for at least an hour. Remove them and place them on a rack over a plate. Taste the cooled aspic for salt; add a few tablespoons of Madeira or other fortified wine. Pour a little aspic into a bowl embedded in crushed ice. Stir it, removing it from the ice as soon as it begins to thicken.

6 **Coating the fish.** Working fast before the aspic sets, spoon a thin layer of it over each fish, then add decorations. Here, tarragon leaves are dipped in boiling water, to make them greener, and laid on towels to dry. Dip them in aspic and arrange them on the fish.

7 **Completing the dish.** Refrigerate the fish for 10 minutes before adding another layer of aspic. Apply two or three more coatings in this way, then transfer the fish to a large, chilled platter. Decorate the platter; here, strips of skinned sweet red pepper are used. Cover the entire dish with several more layers of aspic. Refrigerate the dish until you serve it. □

Fillets Twice Enriched by their Cooking Medium

Fish fillets make convenient serving portions, but they lose something in flavour through being cooked off the bone. Because of this, they benefit from a well-flavoured poaching medium. A fumet (*page 35*) meets this requirement admirably. And you can make double use of the fumet's flavour by incorporating it into a sauce to accompany the fillets.

After the fillets are poached, the fumet can be reduced to a syrupy consistency, then enriched and thickened further by the addition of butter (*Step 4, right*). Alternatively, the reduced poaching liquid can be added to a velouté—the term for any sauce made from stock thickened with a flour and butter roux (*box, opposite page, below; recipe, page 173*).

Skinned sole fillets are used in the demonstration here (*recipe, page 124*). Before being cooked, they are prepared so that they will retain their shape when exposed to heat (*box, below*).

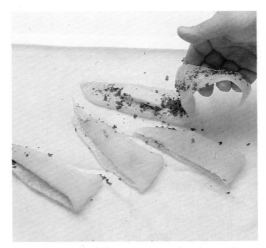

1 **Folding the fillets.** Prepare the skinned fillets (*box, below*) and lay them scored side up on a working surface. Season them with salt and pepper, and sprinkle with chopped parsley. Place a sliver of butter on the wider part of each fillet and fold the fillet over to enclose the butter.

2 **Arranging the fillets in the pan.** Thickly butter a heavy sauté pan, scatter some chopped parsley or other herbs in it, and arrange the fillets compactly in the pan. Sprinkle the fillets with more chopped herbs, salt and pepper. Add enough cold fumet to cover the fillets. Lay buttered, greaseproof paper over the fillets, and place a lid on the pan.

Keeping Fillets Shapely

1 **Rinsing and drying the fillets.** Skin and fillet a flat fish—in this case, sole (*page 20*). Rinse the fillets thoroughly in cold water. Place the fillets on a napkin and gently press another napkin over them to dry them. Use paper kitchen towels instead of napkins, if you prefer.

2 **Flattening the fillets.** With the flat of a wide knife, press each fillet along its length (*above*). The pressure will break down the muscle fibres slightly, which will help prevent the flesh from shrinking and distorting during cooking.

3 **Scoring the fillets.** When flat fish are skinned, a thin layer of membrane remains behind. This can contract during cooking, causing fillets to curl slightly. To prevent curling, score each fillet on the side that formerly bore the skin. With a sharp knife, cut gently through the membrane in three or four places along the length of the fillet.

3 **Cooking.** Heat the fumet gently, lifting the lid and paper occasionally to check when the liquid begins to boil (*above*). Take the pan off the heat and leave it, covered, for up to 10 minutes, until the fish fillets are tender. Remove the fillets, drain them and place them between two heated plates to keep warm.

4 **Making a butter sauce.** Over a high heat, boil the cooking liquid until it has been reduced to a few syrupy tablespoons. Take the pan off the heat and whisk cubes of unsalted butter—about 30 g (1 oz) of butter for each fillet—into the liquid (*above, left*), adding about 60 g (2 oz) at a time and introducing more as each batch is incorporated. The butter will emulsify the liquid to form a light, rich sauce. Pour over the fish and serve (*above, right*). □

A Velvety Sauce Thickened with Flour

1 **Combining the ingredients.** Begin the sauce about 30 minutes before poaching the fish. Melt 30 g (1 oz) butter in a saucepan. Add 2 tablespoons flour, stir it into the butter and cook the mixture for a minute or two without letting it brown. Pour 60 cl (1 pint) of fumet into the pan, whisking as you pour (*above*).

2 **Reducing the sauce.** Bring the sauce to the boil over a high heat, whisking constantly. Lower the heat to simmering point and move the pan half off the heat. A skin of impurities will form on the cooler side; remove this skin periodically with a spoon. Cook the sauce for 45 minutes to reduce its volume and eliminate any floury taste.

3 **Finishing the sauce.** When the velouté has been reduced to half its original volume, stir the syrupy poaching liquid into it. Taste for salt. Finish the sauce, if you like, by stirring into it some double cream and chunks of butter off the heat. Serve it poured over the fillets.

Steaming Shellfish in Their Own Liquid

With bivalves (*page 30*) the main steaming medium is their own abundant liquid, which they release as they are heated. You can, in fact, steam them without supplementing this liquid; simply place the shellfish in a deep, thick-bottomed pan, cover it, and heat. But adding a little white wine, together with herbs and finely chopped aromatic vegetables, flavours the liquid and transforms it into a fragrant broth that can be served with the shellfish—either as it is or reduced by boiling, enriched with butter chunks and flavoured with lemon (*recipe, page 166*).

Steaming with a little wine—a style termed *à la marinière*—is demonstrated below with mussels and, on the right, with cockles. The procedure is essentially the same for both species.

The steaming serves to open bivalves as well as to cook them. They are ready to eat when the shells gape apart; longer cooking would wither and toughen them. They should be steamed over a high heat and shaken vigorously in the pan so that all the shellfish cook evenly. Before cooking, always check that the bivalves are alive (*page 30*); if any dead specimens were to find their way into the pan, the whole dish would have to be discarded.

Steaming is both a complete cooking process and the first step in the preparation of more elaborate dishes. The liquid can be added to a velouté sauce (*page 43*) for example, or used to supplement a fumet for poaching fish, when the shellfish themselves are used as a garnish. The steamed bivalves can be dipped in batter and deep fried (*page 78*); or you can bake them in a gratin, covered with a crust of breadcrumbs (*page 68*).

Mussels with a Wine-Seasoned Broth

1 **Steaming.** Clean the mussels (*page 30*). Put them in a large, heavy pan with chopped onions or shallots, crushed garlic cloves, bay leaves, parsley, thyme, a knob of butter and pepper. Pour in a small amount of white wine. Cover the pan and place it over a high heat to cook. At intervals, lift the pan and shake it to redistribute the mussels.

2 **Serving.** After about 3 to 5 minutes, depending on the size of the mussels and their number, their shells will open. Use a slotted spoon to transfer them to soup plates. Pour the cooking liquid over the mussels. Eat the mussels, prising them from their shells with a fork, then spoon up the broth—with a mussel shell instead of a spoon if you like. □

Cockles Served in Their Half Shells

1 **Cooking the cockles.** Clean the cockles (*page 30*) and put them into a heavy pan, together with flavourings—here, a sliced onion, garlic cloves, bay leaves, chopped parsley, pepper and a sprig of thyme. Add a knob of butter, if you like, and pour in a glass of white wine. Set the pan over a high heat and cook the cockles for 5 to 10 minutes, until all the shells have opened.

2 **Straining off the liquid.** Drain the cockles into a colander set over a deep bowl (*above*). Strain the abundant liquid they have produced through a sieve lined with muslin. Discard the sliced onion, garlic cloves and herbs used for flavouring, then remove and throw away the top shell from each cockle.

3 **The finished dish.** Serve the cockles, still attached to their bottom shells, in soup dishes. Their cooking liquid may be salty. If it is, save it for a sauce, such as a velouté (*recipe, page 173*). Otherwise, serve it as a broth with the cockles.□

2
Stewing and Braising
Assemblages for a Mingling of Flavours

Onions that have been simmered in a mixture of red wine and fumet are poured into a pan containing skinned eel segments, pieces of carp and a bouquet garni. The resulting *matelote*, traditionally an angler's stew, can be made with any freshwater fish.

Both stewing and braising are elaborations of the simple method of poaching fish gently in a liquid. The fish—often an assortment of species, and perhaps shellfish as well—are cooked with vegetables and herbs, and the cooking liquid is always served as part of the finished dish.

In a fish or shellfish stew, the fish cooks in copious liquid that is served as a broth with the fish—and, in some stews, as a preceding course as well (the dividing line between a fish stew and a soup is vague). Fish or shellfish braises, by contrast, involve cooking in a small amount of liquid that is reduced or thickened to make an accompanying sauce.

Traditionally, stews make use of inexpensive and readily available ingredients. *Bouillabaisse*, for example, the famous speciality of Marseilles (*page 48*), includes a wide selection of locally caught fish and the olive oil, garlic and tomatoes of Provence. Like the many other Mediterranean seafish stews, it is thickened slightly by boiling—rather than simmering—the liquid to break up the softer fish and emulsify the olive oil. Other notable stews include the chowders of New England, traditionally made from the locally abundant clams, potatoes and milk; *waterzooi*, a Flemish dish of freshwater or seafish enriched with cream (*recipe, page 149*); and *matelote*, a hearty French stew of freshwater fish cooked in red wine and fumet (*left and page 50*).

Braised fish dishes are also derived from regional cooking, but the inclusion in many of them of ingredients such as lobster or crayfish, an egg yolk and cream liaison, or brandy puts them into a more sophisticated category. Often, the fish or shellfish is sautéed to bring out its flavour before any liquid is added.

The main purpose of braising is to produce a concentrated exchange of flavours between the various ingredients. Among the dishes that typify this aim are *l'anguille au vert* (*page 51*), which counterbalances the richness of eel and yolk-thickened sauce with the acerbity of herbs, spinach and sorrel; lobster *à l'américaine* (*page 55*), which pairs the sweet-fleshed crustacean with a tart tomato and brandy sauce; and a gratin of braised crayfish tails (*page 56*), which makes use of the pounded crayfish shells to give an intense flavour to the accompanying brandy and wine-enriched velouté sauce.

Sea Fish Stews with a Mediterranean Flavour

Any discussion of sea fish stews must include a mention of *bouillabaisse*—a legend even to many people who have never tasted it. Thousands of words have been written about the dish, but there is no definitive recipe for *bouillabaisse* nor for most of the other seafood stews from France, Italy, Spain and Greece.

All these Mediterranean stews share certain distinctive characteristics, however. They invariably include a selection of very fresh fish—and sometimes shellfish as well. The fish are boiled in olive oil mixed either with water or a fumet flavoured with onions, garlic, and the local herbs and spices.

The stew shown here (*recipe, page 168*) is one variation on this theme. The inclusion of pastis—an anise-flavoured spirit—plus orange peel, fennel, thyme and savory, distinguish the dish as peculiar to Provence. But the stew can be made wherever such ingredients are available.

A Mediterranean stew mixes both delicate and firm-fleshed species. Delicacy is provided here by John Dory and red mullet; you could substitute whiting and brill. Baby squid, conger eel, angler-fish and wrasse have been chosen for their compact flesh; among the alternatives are small octopus, sea bass, weaver, gurnard and the sea breams. Include shellfish—mussels, prawns and spiny lobster, for example—if you like. Avoid oily fish, such as sardines and herrings, whose strong flavours would dominate the dish.

The stew shown is started by preparing a fumet from the fish trimmings, while the fish themselves are marinated in olive oil, pastis, herbs and saffron; and a mixture of chopped leek, onion, tomatoes, saffron and orange peel is gently fried in olive oil. Sliced raw potatoes—which help give body to the liquid—can be added to the vegetables before the fumet is poured over the mixture. After the liquid has been brought to the boil, the fish are added at intervals: large, firm-fleshed species first, then smaller, delicate fish.

Broth and fish are presented at table together; the soup is used both as a first course and as an accompaniment to the fish. Both courses can be served with toasted garlic bread and *rouille*, a fiery paste of red chili peppers, garlic, olive oil and breadcrumbs (*box, opposite page*).

1 Preparing the fish. Clean, trim and marinate a selection of fish. Keep the small fish whole; cut up the larger ones, saving their heads and tails for a fumet. Here, clockwise from top right, are an angler-fish, being beheaded, conger eel steaks, wrasse, red mullet and some small squid, another wrasse and two John Dory.

2 Making a fumet. Remove the outer leaves of a few leeks, wash and chop the green parts of the stems, and put them in a large pan of water with bay leaves, fennel and sprigs of thyme. Add the fish trimmings and heads (*above*), a strip of dried orange peel, chopped onion and garlic cloves. Add salt and simmer, covered, for about 30 minutes.

3 Straining the fumet. Pour the fumet through a colander, pressing the solids with a pestle to extract flavour (*above*). Meanwhile, gently stew chopped leek whites and finely chopped onions in olive oil for 10 minutes; add skinned, halved and seeded tomatoes, saffron and a strip of dried orange peel and cook for 5 minutes more.

4 **Combining vegetables and fumet.** If you like, add thickly sliced raw potatoes to the vegetables, adding a welcome contrast to the highly flavoured fish. Season with salt and pepper. Pour on the fumet (*above*) and a dash of pastis.

5 **Stewing the fish.** Bring to the boil and add the firmer fish: squid, conger eel (*above, left*), angler-fish and wrasse. Boil, uncovered, for 5 minutes. Add the delicate-textured John Dory (*above, right*). Cook for another 5 minutes. Then add the even more delicate red mullet and cook for 5 minutes more. Depending on the fish used, the total cooking time will vary from 10 to 20 minutes.

Rouille: a Fiery Sauce

Prepare the *rouille* in advance by pounding seeded red chili peppers to a paste with peeled garlic cloves, salt and pepper (*above, top*). Gradually stir in olive oil, and add breadcrumbs as necessary to give the mixture the consistency of a light-bodied sauce (*above*). Serve the *rouille* in a bowl so that guests can spread it on the garlic bread or put it into their soup.

6 **Serving the stew.** While the fish are cooking, dry some thin slices of bread in an oven set at a low heat, rub them with garlic, and place a bread slice in each soup bowl. When the stew is ready, arrange the fish and potatoes on a hot serving platter. Moisten the fish with some broth; pour the rest into the soup bowls. □

Setting Off the Rich Taste of Eel

Fresh eel should be bought alive and killed at the time of cooking. The fatty skin can then be peeled off like a tight stocking (*box, opposite page*).

The affinity of eel with tart, strongly flavoured sauces is celebrated by two dishes popular in northern France and Belgium—*matelote d'anguilles* and *l'anguille au vert*. The word *matelote* in culinary terms simply means a stew of one or more freshwater fish. Eel is almost always included, but carp—used here—perch, pike, or barbel can be added in any combination, according to preference and availability. The dish's venerable ancestry is vouchsafed by a number of old recipes, among them one for a carp *matelote* dating from 1746 (*recipe, page 103*).

The preparation of a traditional French *matelote* starts with gently sautéing small onions in oil or butter and coating them in flour. After red wine—for its robustness—and herbs have been mixed with the onions, the onions and liquid are poured into a separate pan, already packed with the cut-up fish. As the stew simmers, the flour disperses through the liquid, thickening it. Simmering also evaporates most of the alcohol content—and mellows the slightly bitter, tannic taste—of the raw wine.

L'anguille au vert (*recipe, page 105*) epitomizes the mingling of concentrated flavours typical of braises. The term *au vert*—"with greenery"—refers to the mixture of herbs and green leaves that, together with white wine, gives the dish a hint of sharpness. Parsley, mint, sage, chervil, tarragon, spinach and sorrel are used here. The slight astringency of the herbs balances the mellowness of the egg yolks used to thicken the braising liquid.

A Freshwater Fish Stew Made with Red Wine

1 Preparing the fish. Kill and skin the eel (*box, opposite page*). Cut it into 7.5 cm (3 inch) pieces. Clean, scale and slice the other fish—here, a carp. Put the fish, including the flavour-giving carp's head, in a pan with a bouquet garni.

2 Preparing the onions. In a separate pan, melt some butter and sauté peeled onions over a low heat until they are lightly coloured. Sprinkle enough flour into the pan to coat the onions. Cook until the flour turns yellow, then pour on the wine (*above*) and add salt.

3 Cooking the fish. Bring the wine to the boil, then pour the contents of the pan over the fish. Add an equal quantity of warm fumet. Simmer the fish, covered, for about 30 minutes until tender. Towards the end of cooking, pour most of the sauce into a separate pan and reduce by boiling to half its original volume, skimming off its skin. Pour it back over the fish. Serve the dish garnished with croûtons and parsley (*above*).□

A Braise of Eel and Herbs in an Egg-Thickened Sauce

1 Assembling the ingredients. Melt some butter in a heavy pan and add to it about half of the chopped, fresh herbs and stemmed and chopped leaf vegetables. Spinach, used here, is first parboiled; if you use onions, briefly sauté them. Add the eel pieces (*above*), then the rest of the greenery. Cook, covered, for about 5 minutes. Pour in white wine to cover.

2 Thickening the sauce. Cover the pan and simmer for 10 to 15 minutes, until the eel is tender. Beat the egg yolks with a little lemon juice—some recipes also call for cream—and warm the mixture with some cooking liquid. Remove the pan from the heat, and add the warmed egg yolk mixture (*above*), stirring until the sauce has thickened.

3 Serving. You can eat the dish warm, served straight from the pan, or cold (*above*). To chill the eel, arrange the pieces in a serving vessel, pour over the sauce, leave the dish to cool, and then refrigerate it, covered, for a few hours. Serve it straight from the refrigerator.☐

How to Kill and Skin an Eel

1 Killing the eel. Stun the eel by knocking its head against a hard surface. Holding its slippery body in a cloth, pierce the head with the tip of a small, sharp knife (*above*). The eel will continue to twitch for several minutes after it is dead.

2 Skinning. Grasp the eel's head in a cloth, and cut the skin behind the gills, circling the body. Separating the skin from the flesh is difficult. To start the process, use pliers to loosen a tag of skin large enough to grip (*above*).

3 Cleaning the eel. Grasp the tag of skin in a cloth and, holding the eel's body in another cloth, pull back the skin firmly (*above*). Decapitate the eel, cutting about 7.5 cm (3 inches) behind the head. Discard the head section, which also contains the viscera.

Stuffing and Slicing Squid

The flesh of squid, cuttlefish and octopus has a spicy sweetness that marries well with strong flavourings, such as garlic, capers, anchovies, tomatoes and the cephalopods' own ink (*opposite page*). Most recipes for all three cephalopods are interchangeable, with the proviso that a large, tough octopus needs preliminary beating (to tenderize its flesh) and blanching (to remove its skin), and also requires longer cooking than the other species.

Squid lends itself to a unique presentation. After it has been prepared for cooking, its tapering body makes an ideal pouch for stuffing (*right; recipe, page 157*). Squid with bodies about 15 to 20 cm (6 to 8 inches) long are just the right size for individual portions.

For the stuffing, you can use the squid's chopped tentacles and wings, plus vegetables, herbs and a binding agent. Whatever the choice of flavourings, enough eggs and breadcrumbs—or other binding agents—must be added to ensure that the stuffed squid is firm enough to cut into neat slices after cooking.

To keep the stuffing inside the pouch, the mouth of the pouch should be stitched shut with kitchen string. Here, the stuffed squid is briefly sautéed to soften it and release its flavour, then braised in a rich mixture of brandy and white wine. After cooking, the braising liquid can be reduced, if necessary, and served as an accompanying sauce.

1 Stuffing the squid. Clean and trim the squid (*page 24*). Chop the trimmings into 5 mm (¼ inch) pieces, and sauté with chopped onion until golden-brown. In a bowl, blend the sautéed squid and onion with chopped garlic and parsley, skinned, seeded and chopped tomato, breadcrumbs and egg yolks. Stuff each pouch with the mixture (*above*).

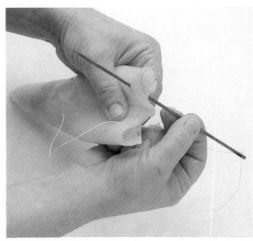

2 Securing the stuffing. Fill each pouch loosely: the stuffing will expand during cooking, while the pouch will shrink slightly. Thread a trussing needle with kitchen string, and sew up each pouch, inserting the needle no closer than 1 cm (½ inch) to the mouth of the pouch (*above*) to avoid tearing the pouch open.

3 Sautéing the squid. Gently stew more chopped onion in oil, lay the squid on top of the onion and sauté until the squid turn opaque. Pour over a generous dash of brandy, and ignite it to burn off the alcohol. Add a glass of white wine and a mixture of chopped parsley, filleted and diced anchovies and capers (*above*).

4 Braising and serving. Cover the pan, and braise the squid over a low heat for about an hour. Remove the squid with a large spoon to a heated platter (*above*). Reduce the braising liquid to a syrupy consistency. Remove the string from each pouch, pour over the sauce and serve whole or cut into thick slices (*right*). □

Gaining an Added Dimension from Ink

The ink secreted by the cephalopods to cover their flight from predators can impart a smooth texture and a deep jet colour to a braising liquid. The ink is stored in a small internal sac, which must be carefully removed from the body when a cephalopod is prepared for cooking (*page 24*). If a cephalopod is frozen, its ink will coagulate; to liquefy the ink, dissolve the granules in a little boiling water.

Cuttlefish is used in this demonstration. Squid is cooked in like manner to make the popular Spanish dish *calamares en su tinta* (*recipes, pages 157-158*). Small octopus can be prepared similarly, with the proviso that their pungently flavoured ink should be used sparingly.

Here, the cleaned cuttlefish are sliced into large pieces, and sautéed in olive oil with onions. Garlic, parsley and tomatoes are added, together with breadcrumbs, which serve to thicken the finished sauce. Wine—preferably red, for its robust flavour—is poured into the pan and then the ink from the cuttlefish is added.

1 **Sautéing the ingredients.** Finely chop onions and sauté them in a heavy pan. Add sliced cuttlefish. Sauté over a high heat until the flesh turns opaque. Toss in finely chopped garlic and parsley, and breadcrumbs. Stir in skinned, seeded and chopped tomatoes.

2 **Preparing the ink.** Break open the ink sacs, and pour the black liquid into a bowl. If the ink is from fresh cuttlefish it will have a viscous texture and glossy blue-black highlights; if it has been frozen, add a tablespoonful of boiling water to dissolve the granules.

3 **Completing the sauce.** Pour about a glass of red wine into the pan, then pour in the ink. Mix the liquids and cover the pan. Stirring occasionally, braise for 45 to 60 minutes, or until the cuttlefish is tender. The sauce will reduce and cling to the cuttlefish as the slices cook.

4 **Presenting the dish.** Taste the sauce, adding salt and pepper, if necessary. Serve the cuttlefish on a hot platter, surrounded—if you like—by a ring of cooked rice (*right*). Sprinkle chopped parsley over the cuttlefish.☐

Cutting up an Uncooked Lobster

To prepare lobster for braising, the crustacean should be killed not by poaching it live (*page 26*), but by halving it from head to tail, then cutting it into pieces. This method ensures that the flesh will stay moist and tender during braising, and that the sauce will pick up additional flavour from the shell and juices.

Many well-known lobster dishes call for raw, cut-up pieces. Among these braises are lobster *à l'américaine*, shown opposite, and lobster Newburg, which is served in a sauce of brandy, sherry and cream (*recipe, page 150*). The technique of splitting a lobster in half is used in the preparation of lobster thermidor (*recipe, page 150*). The spiny lobster and flat lobster are prepared in the same way as the larger European species. All three contain a greenish tomalley, or liver, which can be used to enrich an accompanying sauce (*box, opposite page*). Some female lobsters also contain undeveloped eggs, the coral, that can be incorporated in a sauce to add flavour.

1 Severing the spinal cord. Keeping your hands clear of the claws, hold the lobster underside down on a work surface. With the tip of a heavy knife, pierce the shell firmly in the centre of the cross-shaped mark behind the head. Save any liquid that runs out for cooking.

2 Halving the lobster. Exerting a firm pressure on the knife, cut along the body and tail to divide the lobster into two (*above*). You will see the white gravel sac near the head, the thread-like intestinal canal, the grey-green tomalley beneath the canal, and—if you have a female lobster, as here—the blackish coral.

3 Cleaning the lobster. Pull out and discard the gravel sac (*above*), and the intestinal canal. With a spoon, carefully remove the tomalley and coral, and reserve them; they can be added to a sauce, as demonstrated opposite.

4 Dismembering the lobster. Twist off the claws and reserve them. With the heavy knife, split each lobster half crosswise between the tail and body sections. Twist off the legs and reserve them.

5 Dividing up the tail. Cut the lobster's tail between every two segments of the shell. Do not remove the meat, which will be protected and flavoured by the shell during cooking. Save any liquid from the carcass for incorporation into the braising liquid.

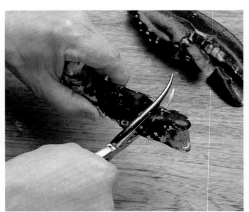

6 Cracking the claws. In order to extract the meat more easily when the lobster is served, crack the claws with a wooden mallet or—as demonstrated here—a pair of pincers. Do not extract the meat.

A Classic Lobster à l'Américaine

The origins of the recipe *à l'américaine* are disputed. Some claim it is a Breton invention that should be spelled *armoricaine*, after the ancient name of the region; others say it was created by a chef in Provence in honour of an American client. Whatever the truth, the rich sauce *à l'américaine*, made from tomatoes, wine and brandy, complements the dense, sweet flesh of lobster (*recipe, page 151*); and it also suits squid, scallops or prawns.

The shellfish is first sautéed with chopped onion and garlic. Brandy and white wine are then added. Additional liquid and flavour are provided by the tomatoes. After the lobster is cooked, the liquid is reduced, then thickened with a paste of tomalley and butter (*box, right*).

The Tomalley Enrichment

The special attraction of lobster *à l'américaine* is that the lobster's uncooked tomalley—and coral, if the lobster is female—can be combined with butter and incorporated into the reduced tomato sauce to give it more body, a smooth texture and added flavour. If you are serving hot poached lobster (*page 26*), eat the cooked tomalley and roe with the flesh or invite your guests to mix it with an accompanying sauce.

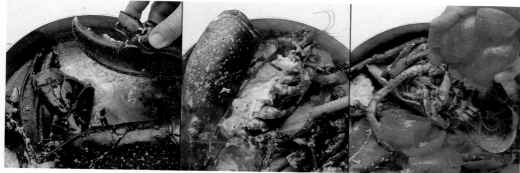

1 **Braising the lobster.** In a heavy pan, sweat chopped onion and garlic in a little butter and olive oil until soft. Add the lobster (*above, left*), raise the heat and turn the pieces with a spoon (*above, centre*) until they begin to redden. Pour in a generous dash of cognac and a glass or two of dry white wine; if they catch fire, stir until the flames die. Add the reserved liquid from the carcass, and the tomatoes and flavourings (*above, right*).

1 **Making the paste.** While the sauce is reducing, mash some softened butter—and, if you like, chopped herbs such as chervil and tarragon —into the tomalley and coral until you obtain a smooth paste.

2 **Finishing the dish.** Cover the pan tightly, lower the heat and simmer for about 15 minutes. Remove the lobster pieces to a hot serving dish. Over a high heat, reduce the sauce to a syrupy consistency, add the tomalley mixture, correct the seasonings, and pour the sauce over the lobster (*above*). □

2 **Finishing the sauce.** When the braising liquid has reduced to a coating consistency, stir in the tomalley and butter mixture. The coral will turn red on cooking. Do not let the sauce come to the boil again, or the mixture will separate.

A Purée of Crayfish Shells to Enhance a Braise

Crayfish are a great delicacy, and because these small, freshwater crustaceans lend themselves to handsome presentations, they are worth buying when available.

In France, crayfish are associated with the elaborate *grande cuisine* of the 19th century, with its garnishes of aspics, truffles, pastry shells and mousses. Although those dishes were unnecessarily complicated and display-conscious, many of them began with a simple braising process, known as *à la bordelaise*, which is unexcelled at bringing out the flavour of the crayfish. This process can also be applied to prawns, and to lobster that is cut up raw (*page 54*).

The technique of cooking *à la bordelaise* is demonstrated here to produce a dish that needs no further elaboration (*recipe, page 156*). Live crayfish are rapidly sautéed in butter with a mixture of carrots and onions finely chopped to yield maximum flavour; the high heat kills the crustaceans quickly. The crayfish are then flamed in brandy and simmered for a few minutes in white wine. Their fleshy tails are served with a sauce which incorporates their braising liquid.

In some versions of the *à la bordelaise* method, the braising liquid is simply reduced and finished with butter or egg yolks before being poured over the crayfish. Here, however, the liquid derives a delicious flavour, grainy texture and delicate golden colour from the parts of crayfish that would otherwise be discarded: the shells, legs, claws and eggs. All these elements are pounded in a mortar to reduce them to a grainy consistency and release their flavour. Next, they are simmered with a velouté (*page 43*) and then puréed in a food mill. Any oversized shell fragments are removed by sieving the sauce. The shellfish are arranged in a serving dish and the sauce poured over. The finished dish may be heated through in the oven or placed under a hot grill to produce an appetizing golden crust.

1 Braising the crayfish. Make a *mirepoix* by first finely chopping a mixture of carrots and onions. Cook the vegetables in olive oil or butter over a low heat until they are soft, but not coloured; then turn up the heat and add the live crayfish. Sauté the crayfish over a high heat until they turn pink. Add and flame a little brandy, then pour in enough white wine to cover the crayfish. Season, bring the liquid to the boil and simmer, covered, for about 10 minutes. Remove the crayfish (*above*) and let them cool.

2 Peeling the crayfish. With a twisting motion, snap the tail from each crayfish body and peel off the shell, legs, claws and any eggs attached to the underside of the shells (*above*). Reserve the shells. Tear off and discard the dark, thread-like intestine that runs down the underside of each crayfish tail. Reserve the tails.

3 Pounding the shells. Add the crayfish shells, legs, claws and any eggs to a mortar and moisten with braising liquid. With a pestle, pound them to a fine, grainy consistency. This will take up to 20 minutes. Alternatively, purée them in an electric food processor.

4 **Blending the shells in a sauce.** Add the pounded shell mixture to a thin velouté (*above*), incorporating enough to bring the sauce to the consistency of a thick soup; discard the rest of the paste. Simmer the mixture for about 10 minutes to extract flavour from the shells and soften them slightly.

5 **Puréeing the shells.** Pass the sauce and shell mixture through a food mill fitted with a fine blade (*above*). Add the mixture a little at a time to avoid forcing the blade upwards, which would reduce the efficiency of the process.

6 **Sieving the purée.** Using a pestle with a broad head, press the puréed shells and sauce through a fine sieve (*above*) to eliminate any remaining large fragments of shell. The texture of the sauce should be slightly grainy.

7 **Finishing the dish.** Arrange the shelled crayfish tails in a buttered serving dish. Gently heat the sauce; whisk in double cream, if you like; adjust the seasonings and ladle the sauce over the fish (*left*). Heat the dish through in the oven or place the dish under a hot, preheated grill for about 10 minutes, or until the surface turns golden (*below*).□

3
Baking

Dishes to Serve
Straight from the Oven

Larding with anchovies
Protective coverings and wrappings
Stuffings for baked fish
Boning for extra stuffing space
Seafood baked and served in their shells

Fish cooked in the oven are said to be baked rather than roasted, although the simplest form of baking fish—subjecting them to dry heat and basting them with fat—is identical to the technique used to roast meat.

Most fish would parch if exposed to the oven's heat without some means of moistening them. One way of adding moisture is to cook the fish in an appropriate liquid—water, wine or fumet (*page 34*)—which can also be used to baste the fish at intervals. (Medium-sized fatty fish, such as mackerel, herring and shad, give off a certain amount of moisture from their gelatine-rich skins and thus need less basting than lean-fleshed fish.) Another method is to enclose the fish so as to prevent its own moisture from escaping. A thick covering of vegetables (*page 62*) or a wrapping of leaves (*page 64*) contribute their own moisture while conserving that of the fish. If the fish is enclosed in a sealed wrapper, such as a bag of aluminium foil, it will cook in the steam from its own juices and that from any added liquid.

Baking lends itself to some particularly attractive presentations: for example, a trout or sole, boned and generously stuffed (*page 66*), a brown gratin topping a dish of fish (*page 62*), or shellfish in their shells (*page 68*). And by baking a whole fish covered with vegetables you can produce a complete and appetizing course in a single dish. If you choose a handsome cooking vessel, you can serve the fish directly from the pot, ensuring that it comes to table oven-hot, with its skin and flesh intact.

Because fish are naturally tender, they generally do not need long cooking to break down tough fibres. The higher the temperature at which they cook, the shorter the cooking time will be. Of course, temperatures differ from recipe to recipe according to such variables as the size of the fish and whether or not it is covered. As a rule of thumb, however, cook large fish at around 180°C (350°F or Mark 4), and small fish at around 200°C (400°F or Mark 6)—though small fish can be cooked at temperatures up to 230°C (450°F or Mark 8) if desired, since the time they take to cook is so short that a hot oven will not dry them out. A very hot oven preheated to at least 230°C (450°F or Mark 8) is essential for a gratin, since the crust would form too slowly at a lower temperature.

A sea bream, nearing the end of its baking time, is basted with cooking juices—wine and olive oil enriched by the liquids exuded by the fish and vegetables. The onions, tomatoes, peppers and olives accompany the fish to table.

Long Cooking for Firm-Fleshed Steaks

A few fish—among them tuna, swordfish, bonito and some sharks—lend themselves to long, gentle braising in the oven. Cut up into large steaks and arranged in a snug-fitting vessel with vegetables and a little liquid, they can be cooked for one hour or more without drying up, and their dense-textured, meaty flesh will not flake or crumble. During the protracted cooking, the flavours of all the ingredients blend together.

In texture, if not in flavour, these fish are not unlike veal. Indeed, the French nickname for the porbeagle shark is *veau de mer*, "sea veal", and some French recipes for braised tuna call for larding the raw flesh with strips of pork fat—a technique often employed to prevent veal and other meat from drying out during long cooking. All these fish, however, contain enough oil to make them, in effect, self-basting provided they are cooked in a moist atmosphere. Larding them with preserved anchovies, as demonstrated here with a tuna steak, introduces extra flavour to the finished dish.

The rich flesh of tuna, swordfish, shark and bonito is best complemented by rather acidic vegetables. Here, sorrel, lemon, and tomatoes provide a foil for tuna; onion adds flavour, and lettuce leaves supply moisture. A 19th-century version of the dish (*recipe, page 134*) substitutes carrots for the tomato and lemon slices, and recommends blanching the tuna in salted water to remove oil, a step that would not be considered necessary today. Spinach or chard can also be substituted for the lettuce and sorrel, or served with the fish, as in the Tunisian recipe on page 135.

Cut up or shredded, and arranged in layers above and below the fish, the vegetables also provide a shield that keeps moisture from escaping. And a little wine poured over the dish guarantees that the fish remains succulent during cooking.

1 **Larding with anchovies.** Choose a large steak—in this case, tuna—weighing from 1.5 to 2.5 kg (3 to 5 lb). With the blade of a small knife, separate two of the concentric rings of flesh just deeply enough to slip in a salted anchovy fillet. Repeat at intervals of 2.5 to 5 cm (1 to 2 inches) on one side of the steak only.

2 **Preparing a bed of vegetables.** Pour a little olive oil into a casserole just large enough to hold the steak. Line the bottom with whole lettuce leaves, then add a layer of skinned, sliced and seeded tomatoes, onion rings and peeled lemon slices. Season with salt and mixed herbs, add a layer of shredded sorrel and put the steak on top (*left*). Moisten it with olive oil.

3 **Covering the tuna with vegetables.** Place another layer of tomatoes, onions and lemon over the tuna, season, then cover them with more sorrel (*above, left*). Arrange lettuce leaves on top, tucking each leaf down the side of the casserole (*above, centre*). Pour in a little white wine (*above, right*) and for extra protection cover the casserole with its lid or aluminium foil.

4 **Cooking the tuna.** Bake the dish in an oven preheated to 170°C (325°F or Mark 3) for at least an hour. By the end of the cooking time, the upper layer of lettuce leaves will be dry (*above*), but the fish itself and the vegetables underneath will be moist. Serve the steak directly from the dish, as shown right.□

Simple Strategies for Whole Fish

A large fish baked with vegetables or as a gratin makes an inviting whole course on its own. The cooking is uncomplicated: it involves laying the fish in an ovenproof dish with the vegetables and herbs—and, in the case of the gratin, breadcrumbs— then putting the assembled dish in the oven to cook. When the fish is done, it can be served straight from its baking dish.

Vegetables with a high water content will help keep the fish moist. Cut up and piled on top of the fish, they will baste it with their own juices. In the demonstration here (*above, right*), a sea bream is baked with sweet green peppers and tomatoes; additional flavour is provided by onions, garlic, black olives, parsley and other herbs. Hake, haddock, sea bass and grey mullet are among the many firm, white-fleshed species that could be substituted for the sea bream.

Delicately flavoured white fish—sole, trout and turbot, for example—would be overwhelmed by strong-tasting vegetables such as green peppers. The gratin shown here (*below, right*), is a much better way to treat them (*recipe, page 126*); a mushroom and shallot base and a breadcrumb crust do not compete with the fish's flavour. These ingredients also flatter more everyday fish, such as plaice, flounder or the whiting used here.

The breadcrumb crust must, however, present a level surface if it is to brown evenly. If round fish are chosen for the dish, they should be filleted or—as here— boned (*page 22*) and flattened. Flat fish are best not filleted; however, to make them more succulent, you may loosen the upper fillets from the backbone along the lateral line sufficiently to insert a strip of butter under each. The dish can be cooked at a very high temperature, since the fish is completely shielded from direct heat by the mushroom and shallot mixture. If the assembled dish is placed in an oven preheated to 230°C (450°F or Mark 8), the fish will cook through in the time it takes the breadcrumb topping to brown.

A Vegetable Garnish to Keep a Fish Moist

Adding flavourings. Season a prepared fish inside with salt and a mixture of herbs; marjoram, savory, thyme and oregano complement the Mediterranean vegetables used here. Oil a large ovenproof dish and sprinkle it with roughly chopped onion, garlic, parsley and the same herb mixture used inside the fish. Lay the fish on top of the vegetables and herbs.

A Gratin Topping to Protect Delicate Flesh

Layering the ingredients. Finely chop mushrooms, shallots and parsley and mix them together. Butter a gratin dish generously and spread half the mixture in the dish. Season with salt and pepper. Lay a boned round fish—a whiting, in this case—or a whole flat fish with the dark skin removed (*page 19*) flat in the dish.

2 **Moistening the fish.** Scatter more chopped onion, garlic and parsley over the fish. Pile wedges of skinned, seeded tomatoes, strips of green pepper and more chopped onion on its back. If tomatoes are out of season, use a purée of canned plum tomatoes instead. Scatter stoned black olives around the fish. Pour olive oil and about one-third of a bottle of white wine over it.

3 **Cooking and serving.** Cook in a hot oven, preheated to 220°C (425°F or Mark 7). Baste the fish at 15 to 20 minute intervals with the liquid in the dish. A 3 kg (6 to 7 lb) fish may take an hour or more to cook. When it is done, remove the vegetables from the top of the fish, then cut down its lateral line and, using a fish slice or spatula, lift out portions of the fish (*above*) and serve.☐

2 **Covering with breadcrumbs.** Salt and pepper the upper side of the fish, cover it with the rest of the mushroom and shallot mixture and season once more with salt and pepper. Add just enough white wine to moisten the ingredients. Scatter fresh breadcrumbs evenly over the surface of the dish (*above*). Melt a generous quantity of butter and spoon it over the breadcrumbs.

3 **Baking the fish.** Put the fish in a very hot oven and leave it for 15 to 20 minutes, without basting, until the breadcrumbs have browned. The fish and the mushroom and shallot mixture will be cooked by this time. If you have cooked a whole flat fish, lift off the upper fillets and remove the backbone before serving.☐

Cooking Under Wraps

Enclosing a fish in layers of vegetable leaves keeps it succulent during baking: the leaves help retain the fish's moisture and also contribute some of their own liquid. Lettuce is used here to wrap a boned and stuffed sea bass (*recipe, page 143*), but chard or spinach leaves, if large and tender, could be used instead. The leaves, made supple by brief parboiling, are spread out and applied to the fish in an overlapping pattern. They adhere naturally to the fish and need not be tied.

Alternatively, the fish may be wrapped in aluminium foil (*below, right*), a modern variation on the traditional technique of cooking in buttered parchment paper. Though the aluminium must be sealed tightly, it should be folded loosely enough to allow steam to circulate around the fish. Technically, the fish—a sea trout, in this case—is steamed rather than baked.

A stuffing is a delicious supplement to fish cooked in these two ways. Any white fish, such as the sea bass (*right*), is flattered by a mildly astringent mixture of spinach, sorrel and herbs. In this case, the bass has first been boned (*page 22*) to permit the flavours of the stuffing to penetrate the flesh more easily. Boning also simplifies serving and allows fish and stuffing to be scooped up together.

Sea trout—or any other pink-fleshed member of the salmon family—benefits from the inclusion of aromatic ingredients in its body cavity. Chopped fennel is used here to perfume the sea trout; dill could be used with equal success. Additional flavour can be provided for either fish by garnishing it with finely chopped onions or shallots and by moistening it with dry white wine, supplemented, if you like, by fish fumet.

The sea trout is served with its cooking liquid alone, but a rich sauce completes the sea bass. Based on the liquid from the baking dish, the sauce is reduced by boiling, enriched with cream, reduced again, then thickened by the inclusion of butter.

A Natural Envelope of Leaves

1 **Wrapping the fish in leaves.** Fill the body cavity of the boned fish with a moist stuffing. Blanch and drain the leaves of a large lettuce. Wrap the leaves around the fish in an overlapping pattern, first down its belly, then down its back. Sprinkle chopped shallots on the bottom of a buttered baking dish and lay the wrapped fish on top. Add salt and pepper, and enough dry white wine to cover generously the bottom of the dish (*above*). If you like, dribble two or three tablespoons of dry vermouth over the fish.

A Foil Package to Keep in Steam

1 **Flavouring from within.** Eviscerate the fish through its gills (*page 19*). Finely chop some fennel—either bulb fennel, as here, or fennel leaves. Season with salt and pepper and insert it into the fish's cavity through the gill openings.

2 **Preparing additional flavourings.** Fold double a large piece of aluminium foil to make a rectangle half as long again as the fish. Finely chop some carrots, onions and fennel leaves. Scatter them on the foil, lay the fish on them and sprinkle the fish with more of the vegetables.

2 Cooking the fish. Place pieces of butter on the lettuce. Cover with foil and bake for about 30 minutes in a hot oven, preheated to 220°C (425°F or Mark 7). In the last 15 minutes baste the sea bass regularly. When done transfer the fish to a hot dish (*above*). If you like, garnish with sautéed cucumber chunks.

3 Transforming the juices into a sauce. Pour the liquid left in the baking dish into a saucepan, and boil rapidly until it has reduced to a syrupy consistency. Add cream and continue boiling until the liquid reaches a coating consistency. Take the pan off the heat and whisk in small pieces of cold butter, which will thicken the sauce. Pour the sauce over the fish (*above, left*). Cut the boned fish into steaks for serving (*above, right*).□

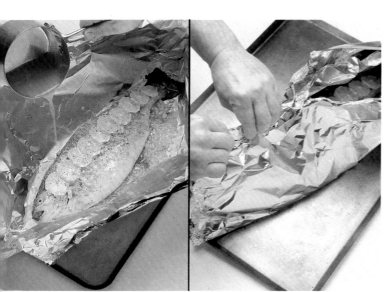

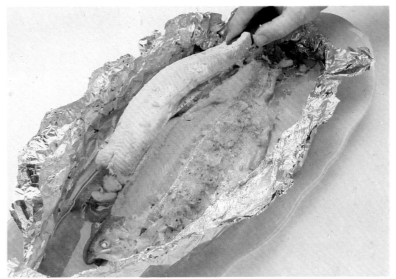

3 Parcelling up the fish. Lay slices of peeled lemon on top of the fish. Season with salt and pepper. Raise the two long edges of the foil and pinch together the shorter edges so that liquids will not run out. Pour in some olive oil, a little dry vermouth and (*above, left*) a little concentrated fish fumet. Fold and double fold together the long edges of the foil to seal it in a loose parcel (*above, right*).

4 Cooking and serving. Place the fish in an oven preheated to 240°C (475°F or Mark 9); lower the heat to 190°C (375°F or Mark 5) after 10 minutes. A 1.5 kg (3 lb) fish will take 45 minutes to cook. When the fish is done, transfer the parcel to a dish and unwrap it carefully. To serve, skin the fish and divide each fillet into two portions by cutting along the lateral line (*above*).□

Capacious Pouches for Stuffing

Boning a fish through the back creates an open pouch, or pocket, which can be heaped with more stuffing than the confines of the body cavity could hold. Because the pouch is on the top side, the fish can be baked lying on its underside—making for a particularly attractive presentation at table.

The technique of boning through the back differs according to the shape of the fish. A round fish should be boned through a cut along the line of the dorsal fins; a flat fish, along the dark, upper side above its backbone. Obviously, if a round fish has already been gutted through the belly, it will separate into halves should the back also be cut open. A round fish should, therefore, be bought whole and its viscera removed at the same time that its backbone and ribs are taken out. Fortunately, a number of round fish—trout (*above, right*), whiting and small sea bass, for example—are usually sold intact, in sizes appropriate for individual portions. A flat fish, which is gutted through a slit behind its gills, does not need to be cleaned and boned in one operation. It may be bought cleaned and then boned through the back at home, as demonstrated here with a sole.

Because the stuffing is a visible feature of the finished dish, it should be a mixture that will contribute to the appearance as well as the flavour of the fish. You can use vegetables alone, or combine them with chopped fish, shellfish or fish roe. In the demonstration above, right, the trout is stuffed with a mixture of spinach, butter and chopped onions, then garnished with pieces of raw salmon and cooked on a bed of onions moistened with white wine; sorrel can be used instead of the spinach (*recipe, page 99*). But the most elegant stuffing of all—used with the sole (*right*)—is a mousseline (*page 84; recipe, page 174*): a purée of fish, bound with egg white and cream.

Boning Round Fish Through the Back

1 Freeing the backbone. Place the round fish—here, a trout—on its belly. Using a small, sharp knife, cut down past each side of the dorsal fin and along the backbone to free the two fillets from the central skeleton (*above*). Do not pierce the fish's belly. Work the backbone and ribs free of the flesh, from the head to within 2.5 cm (1 inch) of its tail.

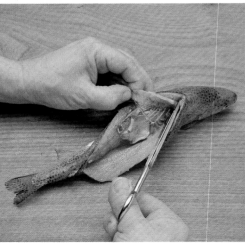

2 Removing the backbone. Using a pair of kitchen scissors, sever the backbone at the head (*above*) and tail. Pull out the backbone. Some of the fish's viscera will probably come out with the backbone; remove the rest with your fingers.

A Boning Variation for Flat Fish

1 Separating fillets from bones. Skin the dark, upper side of the flat fish (*page 19*)—here, a sole. Using a sharp, flexible knife, cut along the length of the backbone. With the knife blade at a slight angle, cut away one fillet almost to the edge of the fish. Then repeat with the other fillet so that the ribs on both sides of the backbone are exposed.

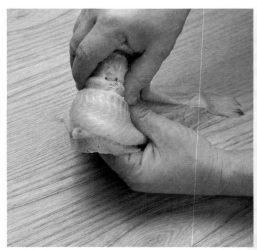

2 Breaking the backbone. It is easier to remove the backbone in sections than to remove it in one piece. Bend the middle section of the fish until the backbone snaps in the middle. Alter your hold on the fish and bend it once more to break the backbone in a different place, repeat this procedure two or three times.

3 **Removing the gills.** Pull back the fish's head so that you can insert your thumb and forefinger into the gill opening on one side and grasp the gill. Tear out the gill with your fingers. Repeat on the other side. Rinse and dry the fish.

4 **Stuffing the fish.** Stuff the empty space, pushing in the stuffing as far as the head. Arrange the fish on a bed of chopped shallots or onions in a baking dish. Place pieces of raw salmon and slivers of butter on top of the fish and pour over a little white wine (*above*).

5 **Cooking the fish.** Cover the dish with buttered aluminium foil. Bake in an oven preheated to 200°C (400°F or Mark 6) for about 15 minutes. If you like, pour a tablespoon of double cream over the fish before serving direct from the dish.□

3 **Removing the bones.** Remove all the broken sections of backbone together with the ribs that are attached to them (*above*). Leave the fins in place in order to give support to the fish.

4 **Stuffing the fish.** Lift back the upper fillets and salt and pepper the resulting pocket. Fill the pouch with the stuffing— in this case, a mousseline. Pour a little fish fumet into a shallow baking dish, place the stuffed fish in the dish and cover it with buttered greaseproof paper or a piece of aluminium foil.

5 **Cooking and garnishing the fish.** Bake the fish in an oven preheated to 200°C (400°F or Mark 6) for about 15 minutes. During cooking, the mousseline will swell. With a broad spatula, transfer the fish to a hot serving dish. If you like, garnish the dish with vegetables. Here, sautéed mushrooms and grilled tomato halves are served with the fish.□

Seafood Gratins Served in Their Own Shells

Crab and Mussels Under a Breadcrumb Topping

The shells of lobsters, crabs and most large bivalve shellfish make attractive and ovenproof individual gratin dishes. Used primarily as cooking and serving vessels for the creatures that formerly inhabited them, such shells may also be used for any fish gratin—for example, one made with leftover cooked fish.

The opening on the underside of a crab shell from which the meat has been extracted (*page 28*) must be enlarged before the shell can be used as a dish. Simply break the shell along a natural cleavage line (*Step 1, right*). In this demonstration, the shell is filled with crab meat mixed with chopped mussels and bound by a flour-thickened sauce based on the mussels' cooking liquid (*recipe, page 155*). Each serving is topped with breadcrumbs and baked in a hot oven to achieve the brown crust that characterizes gratins.

The scallop shell, symbol of St. James, was worn in the Middle Ages by pilgrims journeying to his shrine in northern Spain. The French, therefore, call the shellfish *coquilles Saint-Jacques*, a name that is also universally applied to dishes such as the one on the opposite page, in which scallops are baked in their shells with a sauce. For this gratin (*recipe, page 164*), the scallops are poached briefly, sliced, and then layered in the shells with sautéed mushrooms and a velouté sauce made with the scallops' cooking liquid and an enrichment of egg yolks, to which cream can be added. Since the scallop gratin, like the crab, contains pre-cooked ingredients, it needs to be baked only long enough to heat through thoroughly and acquire a brown crust on top.

A lobster gratin can be prepared like the crab gratin and served in its half shell. Oysters, too, can be gratinéed in their shells with a topping of buttered breadcrumbs or a mixture of parboiled spinach, chopped shallots and mushrooms. However, oysters should not be pre-cooked, since any cooking process that goes beyond warming them will toughen them.

1 Making the shell into a dish. Poach the crab and remove its flesh (*page 28*), separating the white and dark meat. Enlarge the opening on the underside of the shell by breaking it with your fingers along the line of weakness that runs round the shell's rim (*above*). Pound a garlic clove with fennel. Add lemon juice and the dark crab meat.

2 Preparing a sauce. Cook mussels *à la marinière* (*page 44*) and chop them; add the white crab meat and the seasoned dark meat. Make a velouté (*page 43*) with the mussels' strained cooking liquid and an equal volume of milk. Cook the sauce until it reaches a binding consistency, then pour over the crab meat and mussels (*above*).

3 Filling the shells. With a wooden spoon, blend together the sauce, crab meat and chopped mussels. Season the mixture with salt, pepper and cayenne pepper. Spoon it into the shells. Smooth the surface of the filling with a spoon and cover it with a generous layer of fine breadcrumbs.

4 Warming and browning the gratin. To keep the mixture moist and help the crust brown, top the breadcrumbs with thin slices of butter or moisten them with olive oil. Preheat the oven to 240°C (475°F or Mark 9) and put in the crab shells for 10 minutes. If, after this time, the surfaces have not browned, put the shells under a hot grill for a few seconds.□

Scallops and Mushrooms Layered in a Creamy Sauce

1 **Poaching the scallops.** Prepare the scallops (*page 31*) and scrub the shells. Make a white wine court-bouillon (*page 34*) and simmer the scallops' white muscle and coral in it for about a minute (*above*); the brief cooking will firm the meat, making it easy to slice, and will impart flavour to the liquid.

2 **Slicing the scallops.** With a slotted spoon, lift the scallops out of the liquid and slice them thinly (*above*). Prepare a thin velouté with the scallops' cooking liquid, and leave it simmering on a low heat while you prepare the mushrooms.

3 **Cooking mushrooms.** Wipe small mushrooms clean and slice them thinly. Gently stew them in butter to release their juices, then add the scallops (*above*). Cover the pan and put it aside while you complete the sauce.

4 **Preparing the gratin.** Mix 2 or 3 egg yolks with two tablespoons of court-bouillon or cream, and stir them into the velouté sauce. Reheat the sauce gently, but do not let it boil, lest the eggs scramble. Season the sauce with salt and pepper, and spoon some into each scallop shell. Add some scallop pieces (*above, left*), then a little more sauce, some mushroom slices and a final spoonful of sauce (*above, centre*). Cover thickly with breadcrumbs and pour on some melted butter (*above, right*).

5 **Browning the surface.** Put the scallop shells in a very hot oven, preheated to its highest setting, for 10 minutes. If the breadcrumb crust has not browned after this time, complete the gratin by putting the shells under a hot grill. □

4
Frying and Grilling
High Heat Judiciously Applied

A fillet of cod inside a coat of batter is lifted from hot oil, while a second piece cooks in the pan. The batter holds in the fish's natural juices and protects its flesh from drying at the high temperature required for deep frying.

Although fish that are poached or braised are cooked at a mere simmer, fish that are fried or grilled must be exposed to temperatures about twice that of boiling water. At such a high heat, the albumen in the exposed flesh coagulates to form a seal that preserves the flavour of the fish. The cooking then proceeds so rapidly that a minute or two may make the difference between a perfectly cooked fish and a dry one. For this reason, the cook should be ready to remove the fish from the frying pan or grill the moment it is done: to avoid distractions while cooking the fish, any accompanying sauces should be made beforehand.

All fish and many firm-fleshed shellfish can be pan fried or deep fried. Pan frying is cooking in a shallow layer of oil or fat, a method particularly suitable for whole medium-sized fish, fillets and steaks. Deep frying, which calls for immersion in very hot oil or fat, is best suited to whole small fish and thin fillets; because of the high temperature at which fish are deep fried, larger fish and thick fillets would dry and scorch on the outside before being cooked within. Vegetable oils are the best general purpose frying medium, since they can be heated to the required temperatures without burning, and most of them have neutral flavours that will not mask the flavour of the fish.

Whether pan fried or deep fried, fish are almost always coated before being placed in the fat—both to help shield the flesh from the searing heat and to provide a delicious crust. In pan frying, where the coating also helps to prevent the fish from sticking to the pan, fish may be dusted with nothing more elaborate than flour or coarsely ground meal; in deep frying, the fish may be enveloped in batter or egg and breadcrumbs.

Grilling, which dates back to the discovery of fire, is the oldest method of cookery—and the most radically simple. The fish, perhaps flavoured with herbs or a marinade, are laid over a bed of hot embers or under a gas or electric grill. In each case, the fish are cooked by radiant heat; a wood or charcoal grill will, in addition, affect the taste of the fish, imparting an extra flavour lent by the embers themselves. As a way of cooking freshly caught sweet-fleshed fish, this method has no equal.

A Straightforward Sauté for Fine Fish

French by name but a universally adopted method, cooking *à la meunière*—literally, "miller's wife style"—involves coating a fish with flour, sautéing it rapidly and serving it sauced with hot butter. In the pan, the flour forms a crisp, golden crust around the moist, tender flesh.

Cooking *à la meunière* is closely associated with sole, shown here; but any firm, white-fleshed fish with a good flavour is suitable (*recipe, page 128*). For easy filleting at table (*box, opposite page*), flat fish can be skinned beforehand on their dark upper side (*page 19*). Round fish, however, can either be cooked whole and unskinned, or in fillets.

For best results, fry small fish over a high heat so that the flour coating sets firmly, locking in the juices. Start large fish and thick fillets over a high heat until the coating has sealed, then cook them over a reduced heat to doneness.

Fry the fish either in a vegetable oil, such as the olive oil used here, or in clarified butter. At the high temperature required for frying *à la meunière*, unclarified butter would smoke and burn. To clarify butter, warm the desired quantity gently until it melts and separates into a clear, golden liquid and a whitish deposit, then decant the clarified liquid.

The unclarified butter used for saucing should be prepared in the same pan as the fish. Pour it over the fish immediately before serving: if the sauced fish stands for more than a few seconds, the butter will begin to congeal and will turn the coating soggy. The finished dish should simply be garnished with parsley and slices of lemon; any other garnishes would detract from the finely balanced flavours of fish and butter.

1 **Coating the fish with flour.** If the flesh of the fish—here, a sole—is dry, moisten it with milk or water so that the flour will adhere. Season the fish with salt and pepper. Cover a plate with flour, then dip both sides of the fish in the flour (*above*). Lay the coated fish on a pastry grill for a few minutes to allow the flour to dry, in order to form a more adhesive coating.

2 **Heating the pan.** Pour oil or clarified butter into a large frying pan to a depth of about 5mm (¼ inch). Heat the pan; it will be hot enough when a corner of the fish dipped into the oil or butter sizzles. Gently lay the fish (marked here by the pattern of the pastry grill) in the pan.

3 **Frying the fish.** Cook the fish until the underside has turned golden-brown—about 3 to 5 minutes for a whole sole, depending on size. Carefully turn the fish over (*above*), and fry the second side. Lift the cooked fish on to a hot serving dish. Garnish it with lemon and parsley.

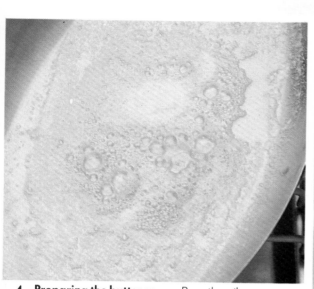

4 **Preparing the butter sauce.** Pour the oil or butter out of the frying pan. Put a generous knob of butter in the empty pan, and heat it until it begins to froth (*above*) and turn golden-brown. Pour over the fish (*right*) and serve at once. □

How to Serve Flat Fish Off the Bone

Holding the fish steady with the back of a fork, cut away the fins on each side (*above, left*). Do not discard the fins; the crisp flesh, which is easily scraped from between the bones, is delicious. Cut along the length of the backbone (*above, centre*) to separate the two upper fillets, and lift them away from the bone. Peel the backbone from the lower fillets (*above, right*) and discard it.

Robust Coatings of Coarse Grain

To pan fry sole with anything other than a flour coating (*pages 72 and 73*) would detract from the flavour and texture of the fish. Most other fish, however, can be fried in a variety of coatings, including coarse-ground grains that have robust flavours and their own crunchy textures.

Yellow cornmeal, for example, has a somewhat sweet flavour. Associated with the cooking of America's southern states, it complements most white fish—such as catfish (*recipe, page 107*) or the cod steak shown here. Oatmeal, a grain with a nutty taste, balances the richness of herring, its traditional partner in Scottish cookery, or other fatty fish.

To give extra flavour, fry the grain-coated fish in lard or bacon fat rather than oil or butter. Use a generous quantity of fat to allow for the amount that will be absorbed by the coating.

Steaks in Cornmeal: an American Favourite

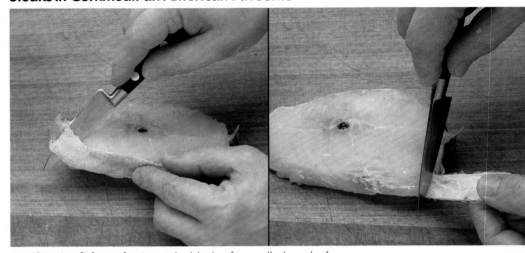

1 **Skinning fish steaks.** Insert the blade of a small, sharp knife between skin and flesh. Angle the blade against the skin (*above, left*) and cut through it to leave a small tag of skin. Holding the skin by one end, cut it away from the flesh, keeping the blade of the knife against the skin to avoid damaging the flesh (*above, right*).

2 **Coating with cornmeal.** Fill separate dishes with milk and coarsely ground cornmeal. Dip each side of the steaks first in the milk then in the meal (*left*). Sprinkle more meal on any uncovered areas and pat the coating with the palm of your hand to help it to adhere.

3 **Frying the steaks.** In a heavy skillet, melt enough fat—here, lard—to cover the bottom to a depth of about 5 mm ($\frac{1}{4}$ inch). Heat the fat so that it sizzles as the steaks are placed in it. Fry the steaks for about 6 to 8 minutes on each side, until they are golden-brown; remove them with a spatula and drain on paper towelling before serving. □

Herring in Oatmeal: a Scottish Speciality

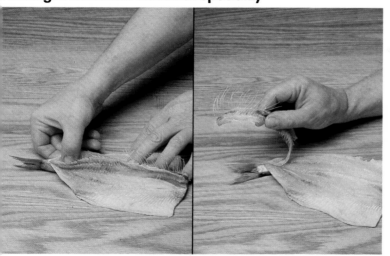

1 **Boning the herring.** Herring is easier to coat if it is first boned and flattened. Gut the fish, remove its head and cut open its belly to the tail. With your fingers, ease the bones from the flesh (*above, left*), then pull the backbone free. Extract any remaining small bones with tweezers.

2 **Coating with oatmeal.** Season the fish with salt and pepper. Its own moisture will make the meal stick to it, so do not dip the fish in a liquid. Cover a dish with coarse-ground oatmeal and put some more meal in a cup. Place the fish, flesh-side down, on the dish. Pour the oatmeal from the cup over the back of the fish (*above, left*); and pat it firmly into place with the palm of your hand (*above, right*) to produce a firm and even coating.

3 **Frying and serving.** Heat enough fat— here, bacon fat—to cover the bottom of a heavy pan. When it is hot, add the fish. Fry over a moderate heat for about 6 minutes each side, until the coating has browned evenly. Remove the fish with a spatula and drain. Garnish with parsley and lemon (*above*). □

Deep Frying Small Fish

Whitebait, smelt, anchovies and similar-sized fish can be deep fried whole, unlike the larger species, which have to be cut into fillets or steaks if they are to cook through evenly. Coated with flour or breadcrumbs, small fish cook to doneness in the same brief time that it takes for their coatings to brown.

For deep frying them, the correct vessel is a heavy round or oval metal pan. Choose one deep enough for the fish to be completely immersed in fat when the pan is no more than half full; deep-frying pans, of course, should never be filled beyond that point, because of the danger of hot fat bubbling over when the fish is added.

The oil must be preheated for the coating of the fish to seal crisply. The ideal cooking temperature is 190°C (375°F). If the oil is hotter, the coating may brown too rapidly and burn; if cooler, it will not seal properly. Use a vegetable oil that can be heated to the necessary high temperatures without the oil itself burning. Test the temperature with a deep-fat thermometer, or throw in a small cube of white bread—at 190°C (375°F) the bread will brown in about one minute.

Remember that the temperature of the oil will drop substantially when food is placed in it. Since very small fish cook in little more than a minute, you can minimize the cooling effect by cooking them a handful at a time. Keep each batch warm in a low oven until all the fish are fried and you are ready to serve them.

Small fish to be deep fried can simply be coated with flour, as shown here with whitebait (*recipe, page 111*). More elaborate dishes can be prepared by stuffing the fish before cooking them. Examples of this technique include southern Italy's stuffed sardine rolls (*recipe, page 110*), and Sardinia's fresh anchovies stuffed with white cheese and preserved anchovy fillets (*opposite page; recipe, page 112*).

Whitebait Filmed with Flour

1 Flouring the fish. Fill the bottom of a large paper bag with flour, seasoned with salt, pepper and cayenne. Drop the whitebait into the bag a handful at a time. Shake the bag to coat the fish.

2 Removing excess flour. Transfer the coated fish to a sieve and toss them gently to shake off any surplus flour. Repeat this process until all the whitebait have been coated with flour.

3 Deep frying. Drop the fish a handful at a time into a deep-frying pan half filled with hot oil. Cook briefly until the fish are lightly browned. Lift them out with a skimmer and drain on paper towels.

4 Frying parsley. After cooking all the fish, drop a handful of parsley into the oil which will sizzle violently. Cook it for a few seconds, then lift it out with a skimmer and drain it on paper towelling.

5 Serving the dish. Garnish the whitebait with the fried parsley and some lemon halves or wedges. Traditionally, whitebait are served on a white cloth napkin, which helps to absorb any remaining oil. Brown bread and butter can be eaten with the dish □

Anchovies with an Unexpected Filling

1 Gutting. Wash the fresh anchovies in cold water. Eviscerate each fish by holding it at the back of the head and pressing a thumb into the underbelly. Run the thumb along the belly to open it.

2 Removing the head. Pull the head—together with the gills and the stomach sac that lies between the gills—away from the body, pinching it loose where it connects with the backbone.

3 Boning. Open the fish out flat. Hold the backbone at the head end and peel it away from the flesh, together with the small bones attached to it (*above*). Pinch it loose at the tail. Rinse the fish.

4 Preparing preserved anchovies. Soak the preserved anchovies in cold water for a few minutes to remove excess salt, then split them in two and discard the backbones. Pick out any small bones.

5 Beginning the stuffing. Open out the fresh anchovies. Spoon into each one a generous filling of a soft, white cheese—such as the *ricotta* used here. Add a preserved anchovy fillet (*above*).

6 Completing the stuffing. Reshape the fish (*above*); the sides need not close fully around the stuffing, which will be secured in place by breading (*Step 7*). Season the fish with salt and pepper.

7 Breading. Dip the fish successively in separate dishes of flour, beaten eggs, and stale white breadcrumbs. Leave them on a wire rack for a few minutes while the coatings set.

8 Deep frying. In a heavy skillet, heat enough cooking oil to cover the fish. The stuffed fish are fragile, so add them one at a time to the pan. Cook for about 4 minutes until golden-brown.

9 Serving. Lift the fish out of the pan with a skimmer, drain them on paper towelling, and serve them at once, on a warmed platter. Garnish the fish with lemon cut into slices or wedges.□

A Mixed Fry of Batter-Sealed Seafood

A batter coating for deep-fried fish does double duty: it both protects the fish against the searing heat of the oil during cooking and becomes a crunchy golden crust for the finished dish. All firm, white fish and shellfish can be coated and deep fried. Small specimens may be cooked whole; larger fish, of course, must first be filleted or cut into steaks.

In Britain, batter-coated fillets of cod, haddock or plaice, served with potato chips, are a national institution. In the Mediterranean countries, a variety of deep-fried fish and shellfish are served together, the flavour of each one locked in by its batter casing. One example of such a dish is the Italian *fritto misto di mare*, shown here with squid, oyster and prawns. It can also contain tiny sole, sardines, soft-shelled crabs, shrimps, cuttlefish or red mullet and be cooked coated in batter or flour (*recipe, page 168*). The popular Japanese delicacy tempura (*recipe, page 152*) is made with shrimps, prawns or other seafood plus various vegetables, all coated with a thin batter, deep fried and served straight from the pan.

Batter mixtures are made from seasoned flour, beaten eggs, and a liquid, often water or milk. In the batter used here (*box below; recipe, page 175*), beer adds a faintly bitter tang that brings out the flavour of the fish—and beaten egg whites are folded into the batter at the last moment to give a light, airy texture.

Whatever batter you use, make it thick enough to provide an even covering. Beat the mixture only long enough to eliminate lumps, then leave it to stand before using it. During the resting period, the flour loses some of the elasticity it acquired in the beating and the batter will cling better to the fish.

The coated fish may then be deep fried in the same way as fish in other coatings (*pages 76 and 77*). Serve them immediately, while the batter is at its crispest.

1 Preparing the ingredients. Open the oysters (*page 30*). Clean and skin the squid (*page 24*); then slice the body pouch into rings, leaving the tentacles joined together. Shell the prawns (*above*), starting at the seam in the underside of the shell—but leave the fan-shaped tail attached, to serve as a handle for lowering the prawns into a pan.

2 De-veining the prawns. Inside the body of each prawn lies a dark, vein-like intestine that has a bitter taste. Remove it before cooking. To locate the intestine, make a shallow incision with a sharp knife along the centre of the back. Pull out the intestine and discard it.

Making Light Batter with Beer and Egg Whites

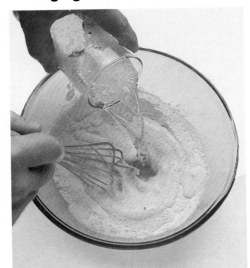

1 Mixing the batter. Sift the flour into a mixing bowl and season it with salt and pepper. Make a well in the centre of the flour, add oil and, working from the centre outwards, whisk beer into it until the mixture is smooth and has a light, pouring consistency. Leave to stand for at least 30 minutes at room temperature.

2 Adding egg whites. Shortly before you intend to use the batter, beat egg whites in a separate bowl until they form soft peaks. Transfer them to the batter bowl (*above, left*) and fold into the mixture with a wooden spoon (*above, right*).

3 **Testing the oil.** Make a batter (*box, opposite page, below*). Heat a deep pan half-filled with cooking oil until the oil reaches a temperature of 190°C (375°F) on a deep-frying thermometer. Alternatively, test the temperature of the oil by dropping a spoonful of batter into it (*above*). If the temperature is right for cooking, the batter will sizzle on contact with the oil.

4 **Deep frying.** Hold each piece of seafood in your fingers and dip it in the batter to coat it. Using tongs or a wire scoop, or holding each morsel by a corner, lower the seafood very carefully into the oil. To avoid reducing the temperature of the oil, which would make the batter soggy, fry only a few pieces at a time.

5 **Draining and serving.** The pieces will be done after 3 to 5 minutes, when they are crisp and golden-brown on all sides. Lift them out of the pan with a wire scoop (*left*), and place them on paper towelling to drain off excess fat. Keep warm in the oven until they have all been cooked and drained. Serve them on a napkin (*above*), and garnish them with wedges of lemon.□

Tactics for Coping with a Grill's Intense Heat

A Double-Sided Rack to Handle Large Fish

Although gas and electric grills have now come to supplement, if not supplant, traditional wood or charcoal fires, grilling fish still demands a critical eye and undivided attention if overcooking is to be avoided. Properly applied, however, grilling is unsurpassed as a way of bringing out the flavour of fresh fish.

When subjected to the intense heat of a grill, fattier fish—salmon, mackerel and herring, for example—are kept from drying out by their natural oils. Some firm-fleshed ones, such as tuna, swordfish, bonito and salmon can even be grilled *en brochette*—cut into chunks and skewered together with vegetables (*opposite page, below; recipe, page 101*). But lean fish, such as the sea bream, right, can also be grilled with excellent results if they are frequently basted with oil or an oil-based marinade. Indeed, basting adds extra succulence and flavour to any grilled fish.

Most fish should be grilled whole and unskinned, to shield the flesh and conserve its moisture. Small fish can be further safeguarded against drying by wrapping them in leaves (*opposite page, above; recipe, page 110*). Vine leaves, fresh or preserved, make good wrappings, since they do not shrivel quickly when exposed to high heat.

Before grilling fish, preheat the grill and oil its rack (which need not be preheated) to prevent the fish from sticking to it. Cooking time will depend on the size of the fish and the distance it is placed from the heat source. The smaller the fish, the closer it should be to the heat—about 5 cm (2 inches) for sardines. Larger fish should be about 10 cm (4 inches) away, so that they cook through without burning on the outside. To allow heat to penetrate them, score their sides with a knife (*above, right*). Any fish is cooked if its flesh separates easily from the bone; test whole fish by inserting a skewer or knife behind the gills.

To avoid breaking a large fish when turning it, use a double-faced grill of the type shown here, which will allow you to turn the fish without actually touching its skin. Turn smaller fish in a hinged rack or with the aid of two spatulas—one placed under the front of the fish, the other under the tail end.

1 **Preparing the fish.** Place the scaled, eviscerated fish—here, a sea bream—on a dish. Cut two or three diagonal slits in each side (*above, left*). Rub chopped herbs into the slits and stuff the body cavity with sprigs of herbs (*above, centre*); fennel—the choice here—complements fish particularly well. Rub the fish with olive oil to coat it thoroughly on both sides (*above, right*) and, if you like, sprinkle it with a few drops of aniseed-tasting liquor.

2 **Grilling and serving.** Lay the fish on a well-oiled, double-sided grill and cook until done, turning the grill once and basting the fish frequently with oil. To serve, slip the fish out of the rack on to a hot serving dish. Cut away the fins, and cut the flesh down the backbone to separate the fillets. With a fish slice, cut each fillet into serving portions (*right*). □

Vine-Leaf Jackets for Small Fish

1 Wrapping the fish. Place the prepared fish in a dish; red mullet, used here, should not be eviscerated since their livers are a delicacy. Sprinkle herbs—such as chopped fennel, dill or *fines herbes*—over the fish, then marinate them in olive oil for up to an hour. Lay each fish across the bottom of a vine leaf and roll the leaf around it. Arrange the fish on an oiled grill rack, with the loose ends of the leaves underneath to prevent them from unrolling.

2 Grilling and serving. Grill the wrapped fish for about 3 minutes on each side. When the vine leaves begin to char and the exposed flesh at the head and tail crisps, remove the fish from the grill. Serve the fish immediately in their wrappings, garnished with lemon wedges. Each guest can then peel away the leaves at table.□

Skewering Firm-Fleshed Fish with Vegetables

1 Preparing the ingredients. Choose a steak about 4 cm (1½ inch) thick, cut from a large, firm-fleshed fish, such as the tuna used here. Cut the steak into 4 cm (1½ inch) cubes. Prepare vegetables to accompany the fish; here, cucumbers have been peeled, halved, seeded and cut into 2.5 cm (1 inch) square segments.

2 Marinating and skewering. Put the cubed fish and vegetable pieces in a dish and pour over them a marinade—here, melted butter, white wine, herbs and lemon juice. Coat the pieces evenly, letting them steep for at least 1 hour. Impale alternate pieces of fish and vegetable on skewers (*above*) and place them on an oiled pan or grill rack.

3 Grilling the brochettes. Place the pan under a preheated grill. Cook for about 10 minutes, occasionally turning the skewers. Baste the fish frequently with the remaining marinade. Serve from the skewers, pressing the pieces free with the back of a fork.□

Miscellaneous Preparations
New Textures and Combinations

Special preparatory techniques make it possible to prepare unique seafood dishes—while still using familiar cooking methods. On the following pages you will learn how to purée raw fish and combine it with egg whites and cream to make a mousseline; how to reconstitute cod that has been cured by salting and drying; how to flake and mould leftover cooked fish to make new dishes; and how to prepare mussels for stuffing.

Because of the time and effort involved in puréeing fish by hand, mousselines were once considered preparations to be attempted only by professional chefs. Nowadays, an electric food processor can relieve you of the labour; if you do use the manual technique, you will need a large, heavy mortar (a marble mortar is ideal) and a heavy pestle with which to pound the flesh to the required degree of smoothness.

When cooked, mousselines rise slightly and have a light, airy texture. They can be used as a stuffing or prepared as dishes in their own right. An especially striking way to cook a mousseline is to pack it in a mould lined with fish fillets and then poach the assembled dish in a water bath. The turban shown opposite is one such creation.

Uncooked salt cod looks so irredeemably leathery that the uninitiated may be forgiven for doubting its culinary value. But if salt cod is soaked for about a day, it will be restored to its former plumpness and be freed of excess salt. The taste and texture of the reconstituted fish remain different from those of fresh cod, but the flesh can be cooked in any of the ways suitable for the fresh fish. Among the range of salt cod dishes, most call for a three-stage cooking process: the fish is poached, then flaked and combined with other ingredients before being reheated.

Flaking is also a preliminary step in the creation of most dishes made with leftover fish. Prepared in this way, the leftovers can be mixed with moistening, binding and flavouring agents—such as butter, cream, fumet, eggs or breadcrumbs—and moulded into cakes, balls or puddings. The decorated fish pudding on page 88 is an example of how humble ingredients can be transformed into eye-catching and delicious dishes.

Mussels are frequently used in rapid preparations—such as the *marinière* shown on page 44—or as garnishes. But by forcing apart the mussels and then poaching them in a sauce, you produce a distinguished dish that does full justice to the flavour of these shellfish.

The first slice is lifted from a turban of overlapping salmon and sole fillets that enclose an airy mousseline made of whiting studded with pistachios. Cooked in a mould, the turban has been left to set for a few minutes so that it retains its perfect form on being turned out for serving.

Making a Basic Mousseline

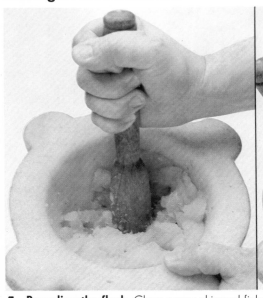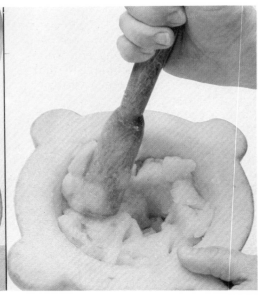

1 **Pounding the flesh.** Chop some skinned fish fillets—here, whiting—and pound them into a purée with a pestle (*above, left*). Season with pepper and any flavourings your recipe calls for. Add egg whites little by little (*above, centre*), pounding between each addition (*above, right*); or use an electric food processor to purée the fish and egg whites.

2 **Sieving the purée.** To make the purée very smooth, rub the mixture through a fine-meshed nylon drum sieve a little at a time, using a plastic pastry scraper, or push it through a stainless steel wire sieve with a wooden pestle. Pack the purée into a glass or metal bowl. Press plastic film over the surface of the purée. Place the bowl inside a larger bowl containing crushed ice, and refrigerate for at least an hour.

3 **Adding cream.** Take the two bowls out of the refrigerator, and replace the ice in the large bowl to keep the purée chilled. Add a little double cream to the purée and work it in with a wooden spoon. Use unwhipped cream at this stage, since whipped cream would be impossible to incorporate into the purée.

4 **Mixing in the cream.** Continue stirring in small quantities of cream, returning the mixture to the refrigerator for 15 minutes between each addition. Beat the mixture vigorously as soon as it becomes soft enough. When you have used up half the cream, season the mixture with salt, then return it to the refrigerator again for a few minutes. Finally, lightly whip the remaining cream and fold it in. Keep in the refrigerator until ready to use.

A Sublime Purée with Multiple Uses

The magical transformation of a fish into the smooth, light purée known as a mousseline is achieved by pounding the flesh and patiently incorporating egg whites and cream into it. The technique for making the basic mixture is demonstrated on the opposite page.

Cooked by itself, a mousseline makes a dish of great delicacy. It is often formed into quenelles (*right*)—light dumplings that are poached in water or fish fumet and served with a sauce. You can also use a mousseline as a stuffing (*page 67*) or else as an ingredient in a decorative moulded dish (*page 87*).

Most fish with firm, non-oily flesh will make a good mousseline. Pike is traditional for quenelles, but you can also use salmon or sole for luxurious purées, and economical whiting or hake for dishes where mousseline is combined with fillets or whole fish, or else with highly flavoured seasonings.

The proportions of fish, egg white and cream (*recipe, page 174*) can be varied, depending on what you intend the mousseline for. Extra egg whites strengthen the mixture; quenelles and mousseline cases (used to enclose pre-cooked fish fillings) need a larger ratio of egg whites to fish than other preparations to prevent them from collapsing during cooking. But whites tend to make the mixture rubbery. For a stuffing, where strength is not important, use a minimum of egg whites and as much cream as the fish will absorb.

Adding whipped cream to the mixture at the last moment will make it lighter. The mousseline can then be stored in a refrigerator, covered with plastic film, for up to 24 hours. Better still, blend all the ingredients except the cream in advance, and refrigerate the mixture; then add the cream immediately before using.

Some of the many combinations of mousselines with other forms of fish are shown on page 86. For example, one mousseline is flavoured with saffron and used as a casing. On the same page, sole fillets spread with a salmon mousseline are wrapped up to form pink and white rolls, or paupiettes. For the exquisite moulded turban on page 87, a mousseline filling studded with pistachios is enclosed by alternating fillets of sole and salmon.

Shaping and Poaching Quenelles

1 Moulding with spoons. Place a bowl containing a firm mousseline (*recipe, page 174*) in ice. Dip two large spoons in cold water. Scoop up spoonfuls of the mousseline and use the second spoon to smooth the mixture into egg shapes.

2 Poaching the quenelles. Gently place the quenelles in a buttered sauté pan, leaving plenty of space between them. Pour in enough boiling water just to cover them. Simmer them for about 10 minutes: when they float, they are fully cooked. Lift them out of the water with a perforated spoon.

3 Finishing in the oven. Arrange the quenelles in an ovenproof dish. Cover them with a sauce—here, a velouté (*recipe, page 173*) with cream added. Sprinkle with cheese and cook in an oven preheated to 200°C (400°F or Mark 6) for 15 to 20 minutes, or until the cheese has browned (*right*).□

Zephyrs: Airy Fillings for Individual Moulds

1 Filling the moulds. Make a firm saffron-flavoured mousseline (*demonstration, page 84, recipe, page 174*). Butter some moulds and line their bases and sides thickly with the mousseline. Spoon in a cooled prepared filling—here, squid cooked *à l'américaine* (*recipe, page 151*) whose sauce has been reserved. Top the filling with more mousseline.

2 Cooking the zephyrs. Cover each mould with buttered, greaseproof paper. Place the moulds on a wire rack in a pan, pour warm water into the pan to two-thirds the depth of the moulds—turning it into a bain-marie—and cover it with a lid. Cook in an oven preheated to 180°C (350°F or Mark 4) for 20 to 30 minutes, until the zephyrs are firm to the touch.

3 Serving the zephyrs. After removing the zephyrs from the oven, leave them to stand, out of the water, for 6 or 7 minutes to settle. Unmould them on to a dish or individual plates. Spoon over the zephyrs the filling's cooking liquid—here, *américaine* sauce—reduced and finished with double cream. Sprinkle with chopped parsley. □

Paupiettes: Fillets Rolled Around a Mousseline

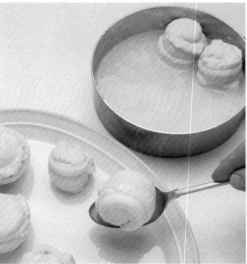

1 Rolling up the fillets. First make a rich mousseline (*recipe, page 174*) with salmon, and spread it thickly on to the lightly scored skinned sides of sole fillets. Then roll up the fillets (*above*), and pack them in a buttered sauté pan that is just wide enough to hold all the *paupiettes*. The close contact will prevent them from unrolling as they cook.

2 Cooking the paupiettes. Gently pour a concentrated fumet (*page 35*) between the *paupiettes* to avoid disturbing them; add enough fumet almost to cover them, as shown above. Place buttered greaseproof paper over the *paupiettes* and poach, covered, for about 12 minutes until the fillets are cooked.

3 Serving. Using a spoon, transfer the cooked *paupiettes* to a warm serving dish. Reduce by rapid boiling the fumet left in the pan until it reaches a syrupy consistency. Take it off the heat and rapidly whisk in enough butter to give the sauce a velvety texture, then pour it over the *paupiettes*. □

The Turban: a Spectacular Mousse Steamed in a Mould

1 **Lining the mould.** Lay equal-sized fish fillets, prepared as for poaching (*page 42*), across a buttered border mould; let their ends hang over the rim. Here, sole and salmon fillets alternate. Pack a rich, chilled mousseline into the mould (*left*); the mixture here contains chopped pistachios (*recipe, page 126*). Fold over the ends of the fillets (*above*).

2 **Cooking.** Cut a circle of greaseproof paper a little larger than the mould and make a hole in the centre for steam to escape. Butter and place over the fish. Put the mould on a wire rack set in an ovenproof pan; add hot but not boiling water to come half-way up the mould. Cook in an oven preheated to 170°C (325°F or Mark 3) for 35 to 40 minutes, until the turban is springy to the touch. Remove, and lift out the mould (*above*).

3 **Draining the mould.** Leave the turban to rest for 10 minutes. Remove the paper, place the wire rack over the mould and turn both over smartly so that the turban rests on the rack but is still enclosed by the mould (*above*). Set the rack in a shallow pan to catch the liquid that will run out of the mould. When drained, turn the mould over again so that the turban is once more resting in it.

4 **Unmoulding the turban.** Unmould the turban on to a plate. Soak up any water on the plate with paper towels. Brush the top of the turban with melted butter to make it glisten, and use the brush to pick up any small loose pieces of fish. Serve the turban hot with a separate sauce, such as a velouté (*recipe, page 173*); or serve it cold—as it is or covered in aspic, as described on page 40.☐

Leftovers with a New Look

Since fish requires only brief cooking in the first place, any subsequent reheating of leftover cooked fish must be as gentle as possible to prevent it from drying up. And since leftovers will have lost their fresh and attractive appearance, they need to be given a new look.

One way to solve these problems is to skin, bone and flake the fish, moisten it with melted butter or perhaps a white or velouté sauce, and heat it in the oven or under the grill beneath a topping of mashed potato or buttered breadcrumbs.

Another possibility is to use the fish for a kedgeree (*recipe, page 119*), a traditional English breakfast dish made by gently heating in butter a mixture of fish, seasoned rice and boiled eggs. The dish is Anglo-Indian in origin, and can be made with leftover smoked fish and enlivened by curry spices.

A more formal dish, worthy of the dinner table, can be made by pounding flaked fish to purée consistency, mixing it with a binding agent, and then heating the mixture in a mould to create a fish pudding. In the demonstration on the right (*recipe, page 171*), red mullet, whiting and conger eel left over from a Mediterranean stew (*page 48*) are bound with egg yolks, breadcrumbs and grated Parmesan cheese. Beaten egg whites are folded into the mixture to give it lightness, then the mixture is turned into a decorative mould lined with a pattern of sliced vegetables—in this case, strips of sweet red pepper and blanched leeks. To make the pudding set without overcooking the fish, and to give it a moist, homogeneous texture, it is cooked in a bain-marie.

The same basic fish, egg and bread mixture can also be blended with mashed potato, moulded into cakes and fried; or it can be flavoured with herbs, shaped into balls and fried or poached. In the Spanish dish demonstrated on the opposite page (*recipe, page 149*), the balls are first fried to give them a crisp coating, then simmered in a fish fumet thickened and flavoured with ground almonds.

A Moulded Pudding Made from a Stew

1 **Boning the fish.** Peel the skin from the leftover fish and separate the flesh from the bones (*above*). Check whether any small bones remain embedded in the flesh; if so, remove them. Put the fish in a mortar, pound it to a smooth paste with a pestle, and put it in a mixing bowl.

2 **Binding the mixture.** Soak fresh breadcrumbs in milk, then squeeze out excess liquid. Add the breadcrumbs to the fish and blend them together in a mortar. Mix in egg yolks, finely chopped parsley, and grated Parmesan cheese; season with salt and pepper. In a separate mixing bowl, beat the egg whites until they form peaks, then fold them into the mixture (*above*).

3 **Filling the mould.** Liberally butter an ovenproof mould and decorate it with vegetable strips. Spoon in the fish mixture (*above*), tap the mould to settle the contents, cover with a piece of greaseproof paper to prevent the top overcooking and place in a bain-marie. Cook in an oven preheated to 170°C (325°F or Mark 3) for about 40 minutes.

4 **Serving.** When the pudding is firm to the touch, remove it from the oven and let it settle for 5 minutes. Peel off the paper and lay an inverted serving dish over the top. Turn dish and mould over together, then remove the mould. If you have any leftover fish broth, reduce it by two-thirds, thicken it with breadcrumbs, and ladle it over the pudding (*above*).□

Fish Balls for Frying and Poaching

1 Assembling the ingredients. Pound the fish flesh and put it in a bowl. Add the breadcrumbs, beaten eggs, olive oil, chopped parsley and very finely chopped onions. Season with salt, pepper and, if you like, dried oregano. If your oregano is in a bunch, crumble the leaves and flowers by rubbing it between your hands (*above*).

2 Shaping the fish balls. Blend all the ingredients together. Shape the mixture into balls about the size of small eggs. Moisten your hands with water, then roll each fish ball between your palms, pressing gently to compact it (*above*). Dip the balls in flour, then in lemon juice, and give them another coating of flour.

3 Browning the fish balls in oil. Warm some oil in a frying pan over a moderate heat, then lower the fish balls into the pan with a spoon. Shake the pan gently as the fish balls fry, so that they brown evenly. When they are nicely coloured, remove them with a spatula or spoon.

4 Cooking the fish balls in a sauce. Place the fish balls in a shallow cooking pot and pour in fish fumet to half cover them. Add salt, parsley and finely chopped onion. Simmer the fish balls for 15 minutes, thickening the sauce with ground, toasted almonds (*left*). Serve straight from the pot (*below*).□

Salt Cod: a Lovingly Preserved Tradition

Although fresh fish is available all year round, salt cod—a heritage of the days when fish had to be cured to survive long journeys from fisheries to the markets—remains firmly entrenched in the regional cuisines of Europe and the United States. Indeed, the concentrated, briny flavour of the fish and its firm, almost chewy, texture, make fresh cod seem insipid by comparison. And salt cod, unlike most fish preserved by smoking or pickling, can be cooked in any of the ways that are suitable for the fresh fish.

Most of the salt cod eaten in Europe is prepared in Scandinavia. Freshly caught fish are eviscerated, opened out flat, layered with salt and then stored in a dry place for several weeks. The salt inhibits the action of harmful bacteria and also draws off moisture, so that the flesh becomes firmer and shrinks to about half of its original volume. Salt cod should be off-white or greyish in colour; a dull yellow colour indicates that the fish has been left in salt for too long. Soaking the fish in fresh, cold water will restore its original plumpness, tenderness and white colour.

To remove almost all of the salt, the fish must be soaked for at least 48 hours in three or four changes of cold water. You can, however, shorten the soaking time if you prefer a salty taste. Some addicts grill salt cod without any soaking at all—an old French treatment.

After soaking, the simplest treatment is to cut the fish into serving portions and poach it. Served with a pungent *aïoli* sauce (*recipe, page 173*), poached salt cod is one of the great delights of Provence, often served at festive gatherings.

Or, the poached cod can be broken into large flakes and mixed with other ingredients. The three finished dishes shown here suggest some of the ways in which salt cod may be prepared.

1 Cutting up whole salt cod. Eviscerated and opened out before preserving, whole cod has a kite-like shape. Slice each fillet (*above*) into two or more sections that will fit into a bowl large enough to add water for soaking.

2 Soaking the cod. Put the cod sections in the bowl and cover them with cold water. Leave them to soak for at least 24 hours or more, pouring off and replacing the water at least three times. The fish will be ready for cooking when it has roughly doubled in volume, but you can leave it soaking for up to 48 hours if you want a fish with only a mildly briny taste.

Elaborations on a Theme

Combining salt cod with potatoes and eggs. The bland flavour of potatoes and eggs is a good foil to the saltiness of preserved cod. To make the French dish shown here (*recipe, page 118*), poach and flake the cod, boil and slice the potatoes, and hard-boil and halve the eggs. To add flavour, pound some garlic to a purée, mix it with finely chopped parsley and add the eggs and some olive oil. Sauté the cod and potatoes in oil, add the egg mixture (*above, left*) and heat the assembled dish through in a frying pan (*above, right*), stirring gently.

3 **Poaching the cod.** Transfer the cod to a pan full of fresh, cold water. Add a sprig of thyme and a bay leaf. Heat the water gently until it approaches a boil, ladle off the scum that forms on the surface (*above*), then lower the heat until the surface of the water barely trembles.

4 **Removing skin and bones.** Continue poaching the fish until the thickest part of the flesh flakes apart easily when it is probed with a knife—about 10 minutes. Drain the fish and discard the poaching water—unless your recipe calls for it. Peel off the fish's fatty skin (*above, left*). Separate the fish into large flakes (*above, right*). Remove the exposed bones with your fingers. □

Baking salt cod in a vegetable sauce. Onions, tomatoes, garlic, leeks and sweet red pepper give this Spanish dish (*recipe, page 116*) a characteristically Mediterranean flavour. Poach and flake the cod. Meanwhile, fry the vegetables then add white wine and some of the fish cooking liquid and simmer until cooked to a sauce-like consistency. Mix the fish and the vegetables together in an ovenproof dish (*above, left*). Bake in an oven preheated to 180°C (350°F or Mark 4) for 20 to 30 minutes (*above, right*).

Making a gratin of salt cod. This dish (*recipe, page 117*) contrasts the saltiness of the cod with the richness of cream. Poach and flake the cod. Stew chopped leeks and onions in butter, heat parboiled spinach in butter and combine with cream. Mix the vegetables together and line a gratin dish with half the mixture. Add the fish, cover with the rest of the vegetable mixture and place halved, hard-boiled eggs on top. Decorate with anchovies (*above, left*), sprinkle with grated cheese and breadcrumbs and bake until the top browns (*above, right*).

Stuffed Mussels: a Surprise Package

By cooking mussels with their shells filled with stuffing, you transform them from plain fare into an epicurean treat. In the dish demonstrated here (*recipe, page 167*), the stuffing is made of chopped cooked mussels, parboiled and chopped spinach and a hard-boiled egg (breadcrumbs soaked in milk can be substituted for the egg, if preferred). The stuffed shells are then simmered in a tomato and onion sauce. You could also stuff the mussels with a mixture of finely chopped mushrooms, shallots and breadcrumbs, gently sautéed, and you could simmer them in mussel liquid or a fumet.

The important thing is that the mussels be stuffed while still alive, so that the flesh will contract during cooking, neatly enclosing the stuffing. Only the largest mussels will do, and they must be opened with a knife (*Step 1, right*) since steaming—the conventional opening method—would kill them. After they have been stuffed, the mussels must be tied shut (*Step 3, below*) to prevent sauce from soaking into the stuffing as they cook.

1 Opening the mussels. Clean all the mussels (*page 30*) and steam the smallest ones open (*page 44*), saving their juices for the sauce. Holding the large live mussels one at a time over a bowl—to reserve their liquid—force the blade of a sharp knife between the curved edges of the shells (*above*). Prise apart but do not separate completely.

2 Stuffing the mussels. Chop the flesh of the steamed mussels and mix it with the other stuffing ingredients. Pack the stuffing into the opened large mussels; press the shells together and remove any surplus stuffing that squeezes out.

3 Arranging the mussels in a pan. Tie each mussel with a piece of twine. Pack the mussels firmly in a pan with their hinged edges down, so that the stuffing stays in place during cooking. Scatter any unused stuffing over them (*above*).

4 Adding the sauce. Make the tomato and onion sauce, incorporating the liquor collected from the mussels and the steaming juices. Sprinkle any remaining stuffing over the mussels and pour on just enough sauce (*above*) to cover them, then put the lid on the pan and simmer them for about 15 minutes.

5 Serving the stuffed mussels. Divide the mussels into serving batches and accompany each portion with some of the sauce. If you provide your guests with sharp-bladed knives, they can cut and remove the twine from the mussels themselves at table (*above*). □

Anthology
of Recipes

Drawing upon the cooking literature and culinary traditions of more than 40 countries, the Editors and consultants for this volume have selected 207 of the best published fish and shellfish recipes for inclusion in the Anthology that follows.

The selections range from the classic and traditional to the exotic and contemporary—from lobster thermidor and mackerel with gooseberry sauce to a Vietnamese dish of shark with tomato and citrus sauce and a baked trout recipe created by the French chef Michel Guérard.

The Anthology spans more than two centuries and includes recipes by 138 writers, many of them distinguished exponents of the culinary art. But there are also recipes by little-known authors of now rare and out-of-print books held in private collections. A number of these recipes—including some from the most popular cook books of pre-revolutionary and Stalinist Russia—have never before been published in English.

Since many early recipe writers did not specify amounts of ingredients, these have been judiciously added; and where appropriate, introductory notes in italics have been supplied by the Editors. Modern terms have been substituted for archaic language, but to preserve the character of the original recipes, and to create a true anthology, the authors' texts have been changed as little as possible. Some instructions have been expanded for clarity, but in cases where cooking instructions may seem somewhat abrupt, the reader has only to refer to the appropriate demonstration in the front of the book to find the technique explained in words and pictures. Cooking terms and ingredients that may be unfamiliar to the reader are explained in the combined Index and Glossary at the end of the book.

For ease of use, the Anthology is organized in the same way as the Guide to fish and shellfish on pages 8-17; recipes that call for the same species are grouped together. Since the Anthology is international in scope and includes recipes for types of seafood that may not be available in all markets, a list of suitable options is given at the beginning of each recipe where relevant. Recipes for sauces and standard preparations—court-bouillons, fumet, pastry and batter, for example—appear at the end of the Anthology. The serving suggestions that have been included in some recipes are, of course, optional.

In each recipe, the principal ingredients are listed first, and the other ingredients in order of use, with both metric and imperial weights for each ingredient in separate columns. The two sets of figures are not exact equivalents, but are consistent for each recipe. Working from either metric or imperial weights and measures will produce equally good results, but the two systems should not be mixed. All spoon measures are level.

Freshwater Fish

Stuffed Pike

Täytetty Hauki

(Options: pike-perch, grey mullet)

This recipe goes back to the turn of the century. The prunes in the stuffing may seem surprising, but they are very good and very nutritious.

In Finland the stuffed fish is often arranged in a circle, tail in mouth and cooked in a round casserole.

To serve 4 to 6		
1.5 kg	pike, cleaned, head left on	3 lb
	Prune stuffing	
60 g	brown rice, cooked	2 oz
2	eggs, hard-boiled and chopped	2
15g	butter, softened	½ oz
6 to 8	prunes, soaked in warm water until plump, stones removed	6 to 8
	Breadcrumb topping	
1	egg white, lightly beaten	1
2 tbsp	dry breadcrumbs	2 tbsp
½ tsp	sea salt	½ tsp
⅛ tsp	white pepper	⅛ tsp
	butter, cut into small bits	

Dry the fish well. Mix together the rice, chopped eggs and softened butter. Loosely fill the cavity of the fish with this mixture. Arrange the prunes on top of the filling. Sew up the opening of the cavity with strong thread.

Preheat the oven to 180°C (350°F or Mark 4). Butter the bottom and sides of an ovenproof casserole that will hold the fish snugly and put the fish in it. Brush the top of the fish with the egg white; sprinkle with the breadcrumbs, salt and pepper. Dot with bits of butter and bake the fish for 1 to 1½ hours. Test for doneness by pulling a fin. If the fin feels loose, the fish is done. Remove the sewing thread and serve the fish from the casserole, accompanied by a light salad.

ULLA KÄKÖNEN
NATURAL COOKING THE FINNISH WAY

Pike with Horseradish and Soured Cream Sauce

Hecht mit Saurer Sahne und Meerrettich

(Options: pike-perch, redfish, wolf-fish, ling)

To serve 4		
1 kg	pike, cleaned	2 to 2½ lb
	Court-bouillon	
2 litres	water	3½ pints
	salt	
4 tbsp	lemon juice	4 tbsp
1 each	stick celery, carrot, leek and Hamburg parsley root or parsnip, all sliced	1 each
	Horseradish and soured cream sauce	
2 tbsp	grated horseradish	2 tbsp
1 tbsp	flour	1 tbsp
40 cl	soured cream	¾ pint
30 g	butter	1 oz

Put the court-bouillon ingredients into a large pan and cook for 10 to 15 minutes. Add the pike and poach for 25 to 30 minutes. Meanwhile, put the horseradish in a saucepan, sprinkle the flour over it and add the soured cream. Bring to the boil, stirring. Then whisk in the butter and 1 tablespoon of the fish broth. Drain the fish, place it on a warmed plate and pour the sauce over it. Serve immediately.

ELEK MAGYAR
KOCHBUCH FÜR FEINSCHMECKER

Grilled Pickerel with Mint

(Options: perch, pike, pike-perch)

In Canada and the United States, pickerel is a name applied to several members of the pike family. In England it simply means a young pike.

To serve 6		
1 kg	pickerel fillets	2 to 2½ lb
	salt and pepper	
60 g	butter, melted, or 4 tbsp oil	2 oz
4 tbsp	lemon juice	4 tbsp
2 tbsp	chopped fresh mint	2 tbsp
6	sprigs mint	6

Season the fillets with salt and pepper. Mix the melted butter or oil, lemon juice and chopped mint. Brush the fillets with this mixture, and grill them under a medium heat for 5 minutes. Turn the fish over, brush again with the mint mixture and grill for another 5 minutes, or until cooked. Serve decorated with the sprigs of mint.

GOVERNMENT OF CANADA, FISHERIES AND OCEANS
THE CANADIAN FISH COOKBOOK

Gefillte Fish

Kimsta Žuvis

(Options: pike, pike-perch, carp)

This famous Jewish dish originated in Lithuania. If desired, instead of slicing the fish, skin it whole; then stuff and shape it to give the appearance of a whole fish. Tie the stuffed fish in a cloth before cooking.

The fish flesh can be pounded in a mortar or put through a food processor with the onion.

To serve 6

1 kg	fish, heads removed, gutted without breaking the skin, cut into 5 cm (2 inch) slices	2 to 2½ lb
	salt	
2	large onions, sliced	2
2	eggs	2
4 tbsp	matzo meal or cracker crumbs	4 tbsp
	pepper	
1	stick celery, diced	1
1	large carrot, sliced	1
2 to 3 tbsp	chopped parsley	2 to 3 tbsp

Carefully remove the flesh and bones from the fish without breaking the skin. Sprinkle the skin, heads and bones with salt and place them, covered, in the refrigerator while you are preparing the filling.

Put the fish flesh and one of the onions through a mincing machine, then place the mixture in a wooden chopping bowl and chop until smooth. Add the eggs, matzo meal or cracker crumbs, season with salt and pepper, and add about 2 tablespoons of cold water—enough to make a light, soft mixture—then blend them well together.

Wet your hands with cold water and form the mixture into oval cakes that will fit into the bands of fish skins. Fit these cakes into the fish skins. Rinse the fish heads and bones and place them in the bottom of a deep, heavy fish kettle or saucepan. Add the remaining onion, the celery, carrot, fish cakes and just enough cold water to cover.

Put the lid on the kettle and bring to a quick boil, then remove the lid and reduce the heat. Simmer very slowly for 1½ to 2 hours, by which time the liquid should be reduced by half.

Serve the fish cakes warm or thoroughly chilled, garnished with the sliced, cooked carrot and chopped parsley. If served cold, use the strained jellied sauce as a garnish.

JOSEPHINE J. DAUZVARDIS
POPULAR LITHUANIAN RECIPES

Braised Pike

Brochet à l'Étuvée

(Options: pike-perch, burbot)

To serve 4

1 kg	pike, cleaned, scaled and cut crosswise into 2.5 cm (1 inch) thick steaks	2 to 2½ lb
60 g	butter	2 oz
2 tbsp	flour	2 tbsp
60 cl	red wine	1 pint
1	bouquet garni, including tarragon	1
3 or 4	cloves, tied in muslin	3 or 4
12	small onions, parboiled	12
125 g	button mushrooms	4 oz
4	artichoke bottoms, parboiled and quartered	4
	salt and freshly ground pepper	
4	anchovy fillets, soaked, drained and chopped	4
1 tbsp	capers	1 tbsp
	croûtons, fried in butter	

In a fireproof casserole over a low heat, make a roux with half the butter and the flour. Whisk in the wine, bring to the boil, then add the bouquet, cloves, onions, mushrooms and artichoke bottoms, and season with salt and pepper. Add the fish pieces, cover, and simmer gently for about 15 minutes.

Transfer the fish pieces to a warmed serving dish and keep them hot. Discard the bouquet and cloves, then reduce the cooking liquid slightly over a brisk heat. Off the heat, whisk in the remaining butter, then add the anchovies and capers. Garnish the dish with croûtons, and pour over the sauce.

OFFRAY AINÉ
LE CUISINIER MÉRIDIONAL

Pike with Currant Sauce

Hecht mit Rosinensosse

(Options: pike-perch, burbot)

To serve 6

1 kg	pike, cleaned	2 to 2½ lb
½ litre	vinegar	18 fl oz
¼ litre	water	8 fl oz

Sauce

100 g	butter	3½ oz
2 tbsp	flour	2 tbsp
30 g	currants	1 oz
50 g	raisins	2 oz
40 g	almonds, chopped	1½ oz
¼ tsp	grated nutmeg	¼ tsp
¼ litre	white wine	8 fl oz
1 tbsp	lemon juice	1 tbsp
1	sugar lump	1
	salt and pepper	
2	egg yolks	2

Poach the pike either whole or in pieces, as preferred, in the vinegar and water until done. Drain the fish and keep it warm. Meanwhile, for the sauce, make a light-coloured roux with the butter and flour, and then add the remaining ingredients, with the exception of the egg yolks. Bring to the boil, reduce the heat, and cook over a low heat for 20 to 30 minutes. Bind the sauce with the egg yolks. Serve the sauce separately.

MARIA ELISABETH STRAUB
GRÖNEN AAL UND RODE GRÜTT

Pike-Perch with Chanterelle Sauce

Ugnstekt Vänergös med Kantarellsås

(Options: pike, burbot)

To serve 5

1 kg	pike-perch, filleted	2 to 2½ lb
	salt and white pepper	
2	eggs, beaten	2
100 g	dry breadcrumbs	3½ oz
75 g	butter, melted	2½ oz
1 tbsp each	finely chopped parsley and chives	1 tbsp each

Chanterelle sauce

250 g	chanterelles, finely chopped	8 oz
40 g	butter	1½ oz
2 tbsp	flour	2 tbsp
45 cl	single cream	16 fl oz
	salt and white pepper	

Season the fish with salt and pepper. Preheat the oven to 200°C (400°F or Mark 6). Dip the seasoned fish in the beaten eggs, then in the breadcrumbs. Put the fish in a buttered shallow baking dish. Bake in the oven, basting often with the melted butter, for 20 minutes or until the fish is done and the coating crisp. Transfer the fish to a heated serving dish and keep it warm.

To make the sauce, sauté the chanterelles in the butter over a high heat. When their liquid has evaporated, sprinkle on the flour. Pour the cream into the dish used for baking the fish. Bring to the boil and strain the cream on to the chanterelles, stirring. Cook over a low heat for about 10 minutes. Season with salt and white pepper. Sprinkle the parsley and chives over the fish, and pour the sauce into a warmed gravy boat. Serve with boiled new potatoes garnished with dill.

OSKAR JAKOBSSON
GOOD FOOD IN SWEDEN

Sweet-Sour Fish

(Options: pike-perch, pike, burbot, barbel)

The technique of making shallow slashes on each side of a whole fish is demonstrated on page 80.

To serve 8

1.5 to 2 kg	fish	3 to 4 lb
1 tbsp	flour	1 tbsp
	oil for frying	
1	spring onion, including the green top, cut into 2.5 cm (1 inch) sections	1
4 or 5	slices fresh ginger root	4 or 5
125 g	sugar	4 oz
10 cl	vinegar	4 fl oz
3 tbsp	dry sherry	3 tbsp
4 tbsp	cornflour	4 tbsp
½ litre	water	18 fl oz
1 tsp	salt	1 tsp
4 tbsp	soy sauce	4 tbsp

Clean the fish and make 3 or 4 slashes on each side. Rub the outside of the fish with flour. In a large frying pan, heat about 2.5 cm (1 inch) of oil, until very hot. Fry the fish over a high heat for 2 minutes on each side. Reduce the heat to medium and fry the fish for 4 minutes longer on each side. Then turn the heat up again and fry for 1 more minute on each side. The outside of the fish will be very crisp while the inside will be soft. Take the fish out of the pan, put it on a warmed platter and keep it hot while making the sauce.

Pour off all but about 1 tablespoon of oil from the pan. Put in the spring onion and ginger first. Lightly cook them, stirring all the time. Then add the remaining ingredients. When the mixture becomes translucent, pour it on the fried fish and serve. If you like, you can add some shreds of sweet green pepper or sweet pickle with the seasonings.

BUWEI YANG CHAO
HOW TO COOK AND EAT IN CHINESE

Fish Baked in Soured Cream

Rȳba Zapechennaya v Smetane

(Options: pike-perch, perch, powan, cod, haddock, redfish)

This is a Russian recipe taken from the best-selling cook book of Stalin's era.

To serve 3 or 4

500 g	fish fillets	1 lb
	salt and pepper	
	flour	
150 g	butter	5 oz
200 g	button mushrooms, chopped	7 oz
850 g	potatoes, cut into 5 mm (¼ inch) slices	1¾ lb
2	eggs, hard-boiled and sliced	2
3 to 4 tbsp	grated Cheddar cheese	3 to 4 tbsp
2 to 3 tbsp	finely chopped parsley	2 to 3 tbsp
	Soured cream sauce	
¼ litre	soured cream	8 fl oz
1 tbsp	flour, worked with 15 g (½ oz) butter to make *beurre manié*	1 tbsp
	salt	

Season the fish fillets with salt and pepper and coat them with flour. Sauté them in 60 g (2 oz) of the butter for 8 to 10 minutes, or until golden on both sides.

In separate frying pans, sauté the mushrooms in 15 g (½ oz) of the butter over a high heat until their liquid has evaporated, and fry the potato slices in 60 g (2 oz) of the butter until they are soft and pale golden on both sides.

Arrange the fish in a buttered fireproof casserole. Place a

few slices of hard-boiled egg and a spoonful of mushrooms on each fillet. Cover the fish with the potato slices.

To make the sauce, bring the soured cream to the boil over a low heat. Mix in the *beurre manié*. Simmer for a minute or two, add salt to taste, then strain the sauce over the fish.

Sprinkle the cheese over the top, dot with the remaining butter, and put the casserole in an oven preheated to 230°C (450°F or Mark 8) for 5 to 10 minutes, or until brown on top. Just before serving, sprinkle with the chopped parsley.

O. P. MOLCHANOVA
KNIGA O VKUSNOĬ I ZDOROVOĬ PISHCHE

Perch in Waterfish Sauce

Waterfish de Perches

(Options: burbot, pike, pike-perch, trout)

"Waterfish" or, more correctly, "waterfisch", is a Dutch word adopted by the French to describe a sauce served with fresh-water fish, particularly perch. The technique of scoring whole fish is demonstrated on page 80.

To serve 6

Two 750 g	perch, cleaned and trimmed, flesh slit at regular intervals	Two 1½ lb
1	large onion, finely sliced	1
60 g	celeriac, cut into *julienne* strips	2 oz
60 cl	white wine	1 pint
2	cloves	2
	salt	
2	chili peppers, stemmed and seeded	2
1 tbsp	flour	1 tbsp
30 g	butter	1 oz
1 tbsp	chopped parsley	1 tbsp

Line a large pan or oval flameproof casserole with the onion and celeriac, and arrange the fish on top. Pour on the wine and add the cloves, salt and chili peppers. Bring to the boil, cover and simmer for 10 minutes. Transfer the fish to a warmed serving dish. Continue to cook the vegetables if necessary; when done, drain them and keep them warm with the fish, discarding the cloves and chili peppers.

Reduce the cooking liquid to one-third of its original quantity. Make a *beurre manié* with the flour and half the butter; whisk it into the reduced liquid to make a thin, light sauce. Add the parsley. Off the heat, whisk in the remaining butter. Pour the sauce over the fish and vegetables and serve.

URBAIN DUBOIS
ÉCOLE DES CUISINIÈRES

Perch Fillets with Lemon

Filet de Perche Citronelle

(Options: grayling, trout)

To serve 4

Four 400 g	perch, filleted, skinned and lightly flattened with a meat bat	Four 14 oz
	salt and pepper	
3	lemons, pith and skin peeled, knife slipped between flesh and membrane to extricate each segment	3
1 tbsp	sugar	1 tbsp
3 tbsp	wine vinegar	3 tbsp
½ litre	fish fumet (page 174)	18 fl oz
50 g	butter, cut in small chunks	2 oz

Season the fish fillets with salt and pepper. Roll each fillet round a lemon segment and secure with a cocktail stick.

In a small, enamelled or stainless steel saucepan, dissolve the sugar in the vinegar, and cook very gently to a very pale caramel colour. Pour in the fish fumet, bring to the boil, then set aside until tepid.

Butter a shallow-sided pan. Arrange the perch fillets in it, and cover them with the fish fumet. Add the rest of the lemon segments, cover, and simmer gently for 15 minutes.

Remove the fillets and lemon segments and arrange them in a warmed serving dish, covered to keep them hot.

Over a brisk heat, reduce the fumet to about 6 tablespoons of syrupy sauce. Off the heat, add the butter, whisking all the time. Correct the seasoning. Remove the cocktail sticks and coat the fish with the hot sauce. Serve immediately.

JEAN AND PIERRE TROISGROS
CUISINIERS À ROANNE

Char Mousse

Mousse d'Omble

(Options: sea trout, brown trout)

The famous omble chevalier *of the Lake of Geneva,* Salvinus alpinus, *closely resembles the sea trout. It also occurs in Canadian and other northern waters where it is known as the Arctic char. This recipe is from Alain Chapel, chef-proprietor of the restaurant La Mère Charles at Mionnay, near Lyon.*

To serve 2

200 g	char fillets	7 oz
15 to 20 cl	milk	6 fl oz
2	eggs	2
1	egg yolk	1
	salt and pepper	

	Sauce	
1	preserved truffle, liquor reserved	1
10 cl	fish fumet (page 174), reduced to 1 to 2 tbsp	4 fl oz
15 g	butter	½ oz
	freshly ground pepper	

Pound the char in a mortar, then press it through a very fine sieve. Add the milk, eggs and extra egg yolk, and season with salt and pepper. Mix together thoroughly. Pour the mixture into a buttered mould, filling it to just below the brim. Set the mould on a trivet or rack in an ovenproof pan partly filled with hot water. Cover and bake in an oven preheated to 170°C (325°F or Mark 3) for about 30 minutes, or until the centre of the mousse is dry to the touch.

Meanwhile, prepare the sauce. In a small saucepan, bring the truffle liquor to a simmer, stir in the reduced fumet and reduce until the liquid has a syrupy consistency. Melt the butter in a small pan. Slice the truffle fairly thickly, add the slices to the butter and sweat them over a low heat for a few minutes until they are heated through. Toss the truffle slices and the butter into the reduced sauce.

Unmould the char mousse and coat it with the sauce. A sprinkling of freshly ground pepper gives the final touch to this delicate, easily prepared dish.

LES PRINCES DE LA GASTRONOMIE

Sea Trout in Red Wine

Truite Saumonée au Vin Rouge

(Option: salmon)

To serve 10

2 kg	whole sea trout, cleaned	4 lb
90 g	butter	3 oz
	beurre manié, made from 30 g (1 oz) flour, kneaded with 30 g (1 oz) butter	
2	anchovy fillets, pounded to a paste	2

	Fumet	
30 g	butter	1 oz
1	small carrot, thinly sliced	1
1	small onion, thinly sliced	1
1 litre	red wine	1¾ pints
½ litre	water	18 fl oz
1	bouquet garni	1
	salt and pepper	

To prepare the fumet, melt the butter in a saucepan. Add the vegetables, stirring briskly over a low heat, then leave to simmer for a few minutes. Add the wine, water and bouquet garni and season with salt and pepper. Bring to the boil, cover and simmer gently for 30 minutes. Set the fumet aside to cool.

Put the prepared trout on the rack of a fish kettle. Strain the cooled fumet through a fine sieve over the fish. Put the fish kettle on the stove; bring to the boil, cover, and simmer over a very low heat for about 40 minutes. Remove the trout, still on the rack, and slide it gently on to a very hot serving dish. Keep the fish hot.

To make the sauce, strain the cooking liquor through a fine sieve into a saucepan; bring it to the boil over a high heat and continue boiling until its volume is reduced by a third. Off the heat, whisk the *beurre manié* into the sauce. Correct the seasoning and add the rest of the butter, cut into small pieces, and the anchovy paste.

Remove the skin from the top of the trout, coat the fish with the hot sauce and serve.

ODETTE KAHN
LA PETITE ET LA GRANDE CUISINE

Baked Trout Stuffed with Sorrel

Truites à l'Oseille au Four

(Options: powan, whiting, small sea bass)

The technique of boning a trout through the back is demonstrated on page 66. If sorrel is not available spinach may be substituted.

To serve 4

4	medium-sized trout, boned through the back, cleaned, rinsed and sponged dry with paper towels	4
500 g	sorrel, stems and fibrous veins removed, coarsely chopped	1 lb
125 g	butter	4 oz
	salt and pepper	
1	small onion, finely chopped	1
4 tbsp	dry white wine	4 tbsp
4 tbsp	double cream	4 tbsp

Melt half the butter in a saucepan and gently stew the sorrel leaves, seasoned with salt and pepper, stirring frequently until they have "melted" to a near purée.

Spread the onion over the bottom of an ovenproof earthenware or enamelled, cast-iron baking or gratin dish just large enough to hold the fish comfortably. Season the fish, inside and out, with salt and pepper, and arrange them in the dish, belly-side down. Place a small piece of butter inside each fish and stuff the cavities with the sorrel purée. Place a thin slice of butter on top of each and sprinkle white wine over and around the fish. Gently press a piece of buttered greaseproof paper, cut slightly smaller than the top of the baking dish, on

the surface. Bake in a fairly hot oven, preheated to 200°C (400°F or Mark 6), for about 15 minutes. Upon removing the fish from the oven, pour a tablespoon of double cream over each and serve the fish immediately in their baking dish.

RICHARD OLNEY
THE FRENCH MENU COOKBOOK

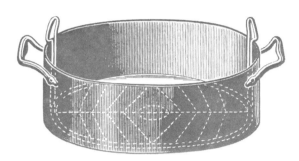

Trout Cooked in Foil with Dill and Lemon

Truite en Papillote à l'Aneth et au Citron

(Options: small sea trout, burbot, powan)

The technique of wrapping fish in aluminium foil is demonstrated on page 64.

To serve 4

Four 200 g	trout, cleaned and fins removed	Four 7 oz
	salt and pepper	
4	sprigs dill or fennel	4
1	shallot, chopped	1
1 tbsp	dry vermouth	1 tbsp
4 tbsp	fish fumet (*page 174*)	4 tbsp
2 tsp	olive oil	2 tsp
1	lemon, peel and pith removed, thinly sliced	1

Wipe the trout thoroughly with paper towels. Season the cavities and stuff them with the sprigs of dill or fennel.

Preheat the oven to 230°C (450°F or Mark 8). Prepare 4 sheets of aluminium foil, cut into 30 cm (12 inch) diameter circles. Fold each piece of aluminium foil into an oval, like a boat, with raised sides. Lay a trout in each, sprinkle it with shallot, vermouth, fish fumet and olive oil, and cover it with slices of lemon. Pleat the foil over at the top to enclose the fish, pinch together carefully and shape the foil wrapping rather like a Cornish pasty.

Put the *papillotes* (little parcels) in an oval, ovenproof gratin dish and cook in the oven for 8 minutes. Serve the *papillotes* just as they are, after first cutting gently through the top pleats to make it easier for your guests to open them.

MICHEL GUÉRARD
MICHEL GUÉRARD'S CUISINE MINCEUR

Barbecued Trout Armenian-Style

Forel'na Vertele

Armenia is famous for the pink-fleshed Ishkhan trout that come from Lake Sevan, but any trout can be used for this recipe. In Armenia, pomegranate seeds are often served as an accompaniment. The technique of gutting fish through the gills is demonstrated on page 19.

To serve 4

Four 250 g	trout, gutted through the gills	Four 8 oz
	salt	
	cayenne pepper or Hungarian paprika	
60 g	butter, melted	2 oz
2	lemons, sliced	2
8	sprigs tarragon	8

With a sharp knife, make a few shallow, diagonal incisions in the skin on both sides of the fish to ensure that the trout will not lose their shape when cooked. Sprinkle each fish inside and out with salt and cayenne pepper or paprika. Roll them in melted butter and cook for 10 to 12 minutes over glowing charcoal or under a hot grill, turning the fish periodically and basting with butter. Serve the cooked trout on a dish decorated with slices of lemon and sprigs of tarragon.

A. S. PIRUZYAN
ARMYANSKAYA KULINARIYA

Blue Trout

Truite au Bleu

It is important to use freshly killed trout for this recipe. Live trout can be kept for several hours in a plastic sack or bucket filled with water. The technique of gutting a fish through the gills is demonstrated on page 19.

To serve 8

Eight 150 g	live trout	Eight 5 oz
About 2 litres	vinegar court-bouillon (*page 174*), made with ½ litre (18 fl oz) vinegar	About 4 pints
6 tbsp	vinegar	6 tbsp
4	lemons, halved	4
6 to 8	sprigs parsley	6 to 8

First prepare the court-bouillon. Ten minutes before serving time, take the trout out of water, kill each of them by a blow on the head on the edge of a table, and quickly gut them through the gills. Sprinkle the vinegar over the trout and drop them into the boiling court-bouillon. Cook for 7 to 8 minutes,

making sure that the liquid is just simmering, not boiling. The trout will turn blue and curl up as they cook.

Drain the fish and arrange them on a heated serving dish. Garnish with the lemon halves and sprigs of parsley. Serve boiled potatoes and melted butter separately. If desired, some of the cooking liquor may be served in a sauceboat.

ACADÉMIE CULINAIRE DE FRANCE
CUISINE FRANÇAISE

Tamar Salmon in Pastry

(Options: sea trout, grayling)

The Tamar is a river in Devon, in the south-west of England.

To serve 6

1 kg	salmon fillet	2 to 2½ lb
2 tbsp	olive oil	2 tbsp
	salt and freshly ground pepper	
1 to 2 tbsp	lemon juice	1 to 2 tbsp
750 g	rough-puff pastry (*page 175*)	1½ lb
250 g	onions or shallots, finely chopped	8 oz
1 tsp	chopped tarragon	1 tsp
125 g	button mushrooms, finely sliced	4 oz
1	egg, beaten	1
90 g	butter, melted	3 oz

Heat 1 tablespoon of olive oil in a frying pan. Season the salmon with salt, pepper and lemon juice. Place it in the hot oil and cook lightly on both sides without colouring. Take out the salmon and allow it to cool.

Roll out the pastry into an oblong, allowing enough width to fold over the salmon and seal it, and enough length for sealing the ends. Heat the remaining oil in a pan and sweat the onions or shallots with half the tarragon. Allow to cool.

Spread the onions or shallots on the pastry, the width and length of the salmon fillet. Place the sliced mushrooms on top and season with salt and pepper. Then place the salmon on top of this filling. Brush beaten egg on the edges of the pastry and fold them over; seal well. Grease a baking tray, place the pastry-wrapped salmon on it, folded side down, and brush more beaten egg over the top. Bake for 1 hour in an oven preheated to 190°C (375°F or Mark 5). Serve with the melted butter mixed with the remaining tarragon.

CAROL WRIGHT
THE WEST COUNTRY

Salmon Barbecue, Seattle

(Option: sea trout)

To serve 10

4.5 kg	whole salmon, filleted, skin left on	10 lb
125 g	butter, melted	4 oz
4 tbsp	lemon juice	4 tbsp
¼ tsp	dried oregano	¼ tsp
	salt and pepper	

Make a basting sauce with the melted butter, lemon juice and oregano, and brush it over the salmon flesh. Salt the fish fillets heavily and pepper them generously. Let the salmon stand at room temperature for 1 hour or more. Place each fillet, skin side down, on a piece of aluminium foil; crimp up the edges of the foil to form a tray. Place it on a barbecue grill over wood or charcoal embers. Cover with hood or foil. Lift the hood or foil cover, baste, and check for doneness about every 5 to 10 minutes. The fish is cooked when it flakes with a fork (about 25 to 30 minutes). To serve, cut the flesh into serving-size pieces and lift from the skin.

SHIRLEY SARVIS
CRAB AND ABALONE, WEST COAST WAYS WITH FISH AND SHELLFISH

Salmon Cooked in Red Wine

Saumon au Vin Rouge

(Option: sea trout)

To serve 2

Two 250 g	salmon steaks	Two 8 oz
1	medium-sized onion, finely chopped	1
90 g	butter	3 oz
	salt and pepper	
About 35 cl	red wine	About 12 fl oz
1	bouquet garni of 2 sprigs parsley, 1 bay leaf, 1 garlic clove	1
2 tsp	flour	2 tsp

Put the onion into a shallow casserole with 60 g (2 oz) of the butter. Lightly brown the onion, then add the salmon and season with salt and pepper. Pour in enough red wine to cover the fish completely. Add the bouquet of herbs and garlic, cover the casserole and simmer for 15 to 18 minutes, depending on the thickness of the salmon steaks. When the salmon is cooked, remove it to a very hot serving dish. Discard the bouquet, bind the sauce by mixing the remaining butter with the flour and adding it little by little to the cooking juices,

blending well. Check the seasoning, pour the sauce over the salmon, and serve at once.

You can vary this dish by lightly frying some thinly sliced mushrooms at the same time as the onion.

The salmon steaks can also be served on slices of bread which have been fried in butter.

White wine may be used instead of red wine.

I should also point out that this very simple recipe, intended for household cooking, can be refined: the sauce can be strained and the fish can be garnished with little onions glazed in butter and with mushroom caps. Carp's roe and crayfish tails may also be used as garnish.

AUGUSTE ESCOFFIER
LE CARNET D'ÉPICURE

Salmon and Cucumber Kebabs

(Options: sea trout, tuna, swordfish)

To serve 5 or 6

1 kg	centre-cut salmon steaks, 4cm (1½ inches) thick, bones removed	2 to 2½ lb
3	cucumbers, peeled, halved lengthwise and seeds removed	3
10 cl	dry white wine	4 fl oz
3 tbsp	soy sauce	3 tbsp
1 tsp	sugar	1 tsp
30 g	butter, melted	1 oz

Cut the salmon into 4 cm (1½ inch) chunks and the cucumbers into 2.5 cm (1 inch) chunks.

Combine the wine, soy sauce, sugar and melted butter. Pour the mixture over the salmon and cucumber chunks. Mix and allow to marinate in the refrigerator for at least an hour.

Just before serving, thread alternate pieces of salmon and cucumber on skewers. Grill, preferably over charcoal, turning the skewers, until the salmon is lightly browned all over. Brush occasionally with the marinade while grilling.

PAULA PECK
PAULA PECK'S ART OF GOOD COOKING

Salmon Escalopes with Sorrel

Escalopes de Saumon à l'Oseille Troisgros

It is important that this dish be prepared at the last moment.

To serve 4

850 g	middle cut of salmon, filleted, skin removed and trimmed	1¾ lb
15 cl	fish fumet (*page 174*)	¼ pint
6 tbsp	dry white wine, preferably Sancerre	6 tbsp
3 tbsp	vermouth	3 tbsp
2	shallots, finely chopped	2
40 cl	double cream	¾ pint
90 g	sorrel, ribs removed, washed and large leaves torn up into 2 or 3 pieces	3 oz
40 g	butter	1½ oz
1 tbsp	lemon juice	1 tbsp
	salt and pepper	
4 tbsp	groundnut oil (optional)	4 tbsp
	fine sea salt	

With the aid of tweezers, pick out any small bones embedded in the salmon; they can be felt by running the fingers over the fish against the grain. Split each fillet horizontally into 2 equal escalopes of about 150 g (5 oz) each. Slide the escalopes between 2 sheets of oiled greaseproof paper, and flatten them gently with the side of a large knife blade. This is to ensure that the escalopes are of an even thickness.

Put the fish fumet, white wine, vermouth and shallots into a sauté pan. Place over a high heat, and reduce almost to a glaze—that is to say until the liquid becomes syrupy and shiny. Add the double cream, bring to the boil and cook until the sauce thickens slightly.

Toss in the sorrel. After 25 seconds, remove the pan from the heat and swirl in the butter, cut into small knobs, by rotating the pan. Do not use a whisk as this would tear the sorrel leaves. Add the lemon juice, salt and pepper.

Heat a very large frying pan, dry if it has a non-stick lining, or with a very little oil if it is an ordinary frying pan. If you do not have a pan large enough to hold the salmon escalopes, use two frying pans. Season the salmon escalopes with salt and pepper on the least presentable side, and lay them in the pan, seasoned side down. Leave them for 25 seconds, turn and cook them for 15 seconds on the other side. The salmon has to be barely cooked so that it stays soft and juicy.

Spoon equal amounts of the sauce on to 4 large, warmed plates. Press gently with a cloth to remove any excess fat from the salmon escalopes, and put one on each plate. Sprinkle each lightly with fine sea salt on the unseasoned side, which is now uppermost, and serve.

JEAN AND PIERRE TROISGROS
CUISINIERS À ROANNE

Carp Budapest-Style

Karpfen auf Budapester Art

(Options: bream, perch, pike, pike-perch)

To serve 4

1 kg	carp, cleaned and cut into serving pieces	2 to 2½ lb
30 g	butter	1 oz
2	carrots, cut into *julienne* strips	2
2	sticks celery, cut into *julienne* strips	2
1 each	Hamburg parsley root, and kohlrabi or turnip, cut into *julienne* strips	1 each
1	small onion, finely sliced	1
	salt	
1 litre	white wine	1¾ pints

Melt the butter in a large saucepan and cook the vegetables over a low heat. When they are softened add the carp. Season with salt. Pour the wine into the pan, bring to the boil, and simmer for 15 minutes, or until the carp is cooked. Remove the carp to a heated serving dish. Boil the contents of the pan until the liquid has reduced by about half. Pour the cooking liquid and vegetables over the fish, and serve with toasted bread.

ELEK MAGYAR
KOCHBUCH FÜR FEINSCHMECKER

Poached Carp with Raisins and Almonds

Carpe à la Juive

This recipe from Lorraine uses Malaga raisins. These partially dried Muscat grapes are much larger and sweeter than the ordinary type of raisins.

To serve 6

2.5 kg	carp, cleaned, whole or cut into large pieces	5 lb
¼ litre	oil	8 fl oz
250 g	small onions	8 oz
2 tbsp	flour	2 tbsp
1 tbsp	sugar	1 tbsp
1 tbsp	vinegar	1 tbsp
125 g	Malaga raisins	4 oz
125 g	almonds, blanched and sliced lengthwise	4 oz
	salt	

Heat the oil in a saucepan (or in a fish kettle, if you want to cook the fish whole). Put in the onions and cook them until softened. Add the flour and half the sugar and cook, stirring, without letting the mixture brown. Add the vinegar, the remaining sugar, the raisins and almonds, and enough water just to cover the fish. Bring to the boil, add salt, and lower the heat. Put in the fish and simmer for 10 to 15 minutes if cut into slices, or up to 45 minutes for a whole fish.

Place the cooked fish in a deep serving dish and pour over the sauce, arranging the onions, raisins and almonds around the fish. Allow to cool. The fish is served cold in its jelly.

E. AURICOSTE DE LAZARQUE
CUISINE MESSINE

Fish Stuffed with Buckwheat Porridge

Rȳba, Farshirovannaya Kasheĭ

(Options: carp, freshwater and sea bream, cod, pollack)

	To serve 3 or 4	
750 g	whole fish, head removed, gutted through the gills, washed and dried	1½ lb
100 g	buckwheat groats	3½ oz
About 20 cl	boiling water	About 7 fl oz
	salt	
60 g	butter	2 oz
1	medium-sized onion, chopped	1
2	hard-boiled eggs, chopped	2
	pepper	
1 tbsp	flour	1 tbsp
¼ litre	soured cream	8 fl oz

The first step is to prepare the buckwheat porridge. Roast the groats in a frying pan over a low heat without using any fat, stirring continuously, until they begin to turn brown. (If you have bought roasted buckwheat groats, this step is unnecessary.) Transfer the groats to an ovenproof casserole and pour on the salted boiling water: this should just cover the groats. Add 15 g (½ oz) of the butter, stir well, cover tightly and put in a moderate oven, preheated to 180°C (350°F or Mark 4), for 20 minutes or until all the water is absorbed and the porridge has a light and fluffy consistency.

Fry the onion in another 15 g (½ oz) of the remaining butter and combine it with the buckwheat porridge and hard-boiled eggs. Sprinkle a little salt into the inside of the fish and then put in the stuffing.

Dust the stuffed fish with pepper and the flour, and fry it on both sides in the remaining butter until lightly browned. Place the fish in a shallow ovenproof dish, then put it in a moderate oven, preheated to 180°C (350°F or Mark 4), for 5 minutes. Remove the fish from the oven and pour the soured cream over it. Return it to the oven and continue cooking, basting it with the liquid, until the fish is cooked right

through. This is likely to take a further 20 to 25 minutes, depending on the size and shape of the fish. Serve the fish in the dish in which it has been cooked.

Pickled cucumber, a vegetable and fruit salad of your choice, or marinated apple slices may be served with the fish.

O. P. MOLCHANOVA
KNIGA O VKUSNOĬ I ZDOROVOĬ PISHCHE

Freshwater Fish Stew

Carpe en Matelote

(Options: pike, perch, eel, crayfish, barbel, gudgeon)

Menon's instructions for this classic dish are refreshingly flexible and practical as regards the choice of fish. The carp is obligatory, but the other freshwater fish can be selected from the options given above, or, as Menon obligingly remarks, can be "any river fish that are conveniently to hand". The more kinds of fish the better, but carp and one other will do very well. An alternative method of cooking, which keeps the fish pieces intact, is demonstrated on page 50.

	To serve 6	
1 kg	carp, cut into thick slices	2 to 2½ lb
750 g	freshwater fish (not carp), prepared according to type and cut into pieces	1½ lb
60 g	butter	2 oz
2 tbsp	flour	2 tbsp
12	small white onions (or 3 large onions, quartered)	12
40 cl	red wine	¾ pint
40 cl	fish fumet (*page 174*)	¾ pint
	salt and pepper	
1	bouquet garni	1
	croûtons	

Make a roux in a saucepan with half the butter and all the flour. When it has turned golden-brown, add the onions and cook them gently in the roux for about 10 minutes, adding the remaining butter. Then add the red wine and the fish fumet, bring the sauce to the boil and simmer for about 30 minutes.

Put the prepared fish in a large saucepan. Pour the sauce over the fish, season with salt and pepper, add the bouquet garni, then cook, uncovered, over a high heat for 30 minutes. When you are ready to serve the dish, remove the bouquet garni and scatter the croûtons over the stew.

MENON
LA CUISINIÈRE BOURGEOISE

Carp with Saffron

Carpe au Safran

To serve 6

2 kg	carp, cleaned and cut crosswise into 1 cm (½ inch) slices	4 lb
400 g	onions, very finely chopped	14 oz
4	garlic cloves, very finely chopped	4
2 tbsp	vegetable oil	2 tbsp
1 litre	water	1¾ pints
½ litre	white wine	18 fl oz
	salt	
½ tsp	powdered saffron	½ tsp

Lightly brown the onions and garlic in the oil. Add the water and wine, and season with salt. Add the saffron and boil for 30 minutes. Reduce the heat to a simmer, put the carp portions into this court-bouillon and cook them for 30 minutes. Remove the fish and arrange the slices on a serving dish.

Reduce the court-bouillon by two-thirds, strain it and pour it over the fish. Allow to cool and set before serving.

ÉDOUARD DE POMIANE
CUISINE JUIVE: GHETTOS MODERNES

Carp Flemish-Style

Vlaamse Karper

To serve 6

1.5 kg	carp, cleaned and scaled	3 lb
10 cl	vinegar	4 fl oz
90 g	butter	3 oz
250 g	onion, sliced	8 oz
30 g	gingerbread, coarsely crumbled	1 oz
	salt and pepper	
1	sprig thyme	1
1	bay leaf	1
1	Hamburg parsley root, sliced	1
2	sticks celery, sliced	2
About 60 cl	lager	About 1 pint
2 tbsp	flour	2 tbsp
	sprigs parsley	

Steep the carp for 30 minutes or more in water to which the vinegar has been added.

Heat 60 g (2 oz) of the butter, add the onion and cook very gently until softened, about 15 minutes. Add the gingerbread and transfer the mixture to a deep ovenproof dish large enough to hold the carp. Drain the carp and put it in the dish. Season it with salt and pepper. Add the thyme, bay leaf, parsley root and celery, and pour on enough lager to cover the fish. Bake, uncovered, basting regularly, in an oven preheated to 180°C (350°F or Mark 4), for about 1 hour, or until the fish is cooked through.

Transfer the fish to a warmed serving dish and strain the cooking liquid through a fine sieve into a saucepan. Work the remaining butter and the flour together to make a smooth paste, and whisk this *beurre manié* into the cooking liquid. Cook for a few minutes to thicken slightly, and pour the sauce over the fish. Garnish with parsley sprigs before serving.

FONS VERMEERSCH
OP ZOEK NAAR SPIJS EN DRANK

Poached Bream with Horseradish and Apples

Leshch, Varenÿĭ s Khrenom i Yablokami

(Options: sea bream, redfish)

A recipe from the classic pre-revolution cookbook of Russia. The parsley root called for is Hamburg parsley, a variety of parsley with a large parsnip-like root. If unavailable, substitute a small turnip and a parsnip.

To serve 6 to 8

1.5 to 2 kg	bream, cleaned, rubbed inside and out with salt and cut into 6 to 8 pieces	3 to 4 lb
25 to 30 cl	vinegar	8 to 10 fl oz
1	parsley root, cut into pieces	1
1	heart celery, cut into pieces	1
1	leek, sliced	1
2	medium-sized onions, sliced	2
	salt	
12 to 15	peppercorns	12 to 15
2 or 3	bay leaves	2 or 3
1	lemon, thinly sliced	1
	Sauce	
3 to 4 tbsp	freshly grated horseradish	3 to 4 tbsp
4 to 6	cooking apples, peeled and freshly grated	4 to 6
2 to 3 tsp	cider vinegar	2 to 3 tsp
	sugar	

Place the pieces of bream in a dish. Bring the vinegar to the boil and pour it over the fish.

After a few minutes, remove the fish from the vinegar and transfer it to a fireproof casserole.

In a saucepan, put the vegetables to boil in about ¾ litre (1¼ pints) water with the salt, peppercorns and bay leaves. After about 15 to 20 minutes, when the vegetables are well cooked, strain off the liquid and pour it over the fish. Set the fish to cook over a fairly high heat for about 15 minutes.

To prepare the sauce, mix together the horseradish, apple, vinegar and sugar to taste, and add about 5 tablespoons of the fish cooking liquid, strained.

Transfer the pieces of fish to a warmed serving platter and garnish with the lemon slices. Serve the sauce separately.

ELENA MOLOKHOVETS
PODAROK MOLODỸM KHOZYAĬKAM

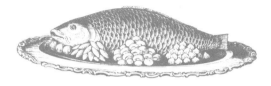

Eel Cooked with Greenery

L'Anguille au Vert

The technique of skinning an eel is demonstrated on page 51.

	To serve 6	
2 kg	eels, 2.5 cm (1 inch) thick, skinned, heads cut off, cut into sections 5 cm (2 inches) long	4 lb
125 g	butter	4 oz
2	large onions, chopped	2
125 g	sorrel, stems removed	4 oz
125 g	watercress, large stems removed	4 oz
50 g	white nettle, stems removed	2 oz
50 g	tarragon (optional)	2 oz
30 g each	parsley and chervil	1 oz each
1 each	sprig mint, sage, and savory or rosemary, stems removed	1 each
1	stick celery, finely chopped	1
2 or 3	shallots, chopped and pounded	2 or 3
	zest of 2 lemons (optional)	
	salt and pepper	
About ½ litre	dry white wine	About 1 pint
15 cl	double cream	¼ pint
2	eggs, beaten	2
About 5 tbsp	lemon juice	About 5 tbsp

In a large sauté pan, heat the butter until it is foaming, then toss in the pieces of eel and the onions. Meanwhile, finely chop the sorrel, watercress, nettle and other herbs. This must be done at the very last moment, or they will lose their freshness.

Add the greenery, celery, shallots and lemon zest, if used, to the eels and leave to sweat, covered, for 5 minutes. Season with salt and pepper. Pour in enough white wine to cover the contents of the pan, adding a little water if necessary, and simmer, covered, for 10 to 15 minutes.

Mix the cream with the eggs, the lemon juice, salt and pepper. Remove the pan from the heat and pour in the cream mixture; blend it gradually with the greenery, rotating the pan. Transfer to a serving dish and serve either hot or cold.

CLAUDIAN
À TABLE

Eel-Pie Island Pie

Eel-Pie Island, near Richmond, on the Thames, achieved its name from the famous pies that for nearly two centuries drew visitors from far afield, there to savour eels from the river and to argue whether the pies were better hot or cold.

The technique of skinning an eel is demonstrated on page 51.

	To serve 6 to 8	
1.5 kg	eels, skinned, cut into 4 cm (1½ inch) pieces and bones removed	3 lb
125 g	butter	4 oz
2	shallots, chopped	2
2 tsp	chopped parsley	2 tsp
	grated nutmeg	
	salt and pepper	
30 cl	dry sherry or white wine	½ pint
30 g	flour	1 oz
2 to 3 tbsp	lemon juice	2 to 3 tbsp
3	eggs, hard-boiled and sliced	3
600 g	rough-puff pastry (*page 175*)	1¼ lb
1	egg, beaten with a little milk or water	1

Melt the butter in a saucepan and cook the shallots for a few minutes without letting them colour, then add the parsley, nutmeg, salt, pepper and the sherry or white wine. Put the eels into this mixture, with just enough water to cover; bring slowly to the boil. When boiling point is reached, remove the eels and place them in a 1.5 litre (2½ pint) pie dish. Strain the cooking liquid and reserve it.

Melt the remaining butter in a clean saucepan; stir in the flour and gradually add the reserved cooking liquid. Bring to the boil, stirring. Add the lemon juice, correct the seasoning and pour the sauce over the fish. Arrange slices of hard-boiled egg on top, cover with the pastry and brush the top with the beaten egg mixture. Bake in a very hot oven, preheated to 230°C (450°F or Mark 8), for 15 minutes. Then reduce the heat to 180°C (350°F or Mark 4) and bake for 45 minutes.

LIZZIE BOYD (EDITOR)
BRITISH COOKERY

Baked Eel with Olives

Terrine d'Anguilles

According to the author, this dish is often served in Martigues, a fishing port near Marseilles, for the big supper that precedes Midnight Mass on Christmas Eve. The technique of skinning an eel is demonstrated on page 51.

	To serve 4	
1.5 kg	eel, skinned and cleaned	3 lb
500 g	leeks, finely chopped	1 lb
2	garlic cloves, finely chopped	2
4 tbsp	finely chopped parsley	4 tbsp
	salt and pepper	
1	bay leaf	1
60 g	stoned black olives (or black and green mixed)	2 oz
20 cl	dry white wine	7 fl oz
40 g	dry breadcrumbs	1½ oz
10 cl	olive oil	4 fl oz

Arrange the leeks in a thick layer in the bottom of an oven-proof gratin dish or terrine. Cover with the chopped garlic and parsley. Season with salt and pepper and add the bay leaf. Sprinkle over the olives and moisten with the wine. Place the eel on this bed with its tail in its mouth. Scatter the breadcrumbs over the whole surface and sprinkle with the oil.

Cook in a moderate oven, preheated to 180°C (350°F or Mark 4), for about 1½ hours, basting occasionally.

IRÈNE BORELLI
LA CUISINE PROVENÇALE

Eel Grilled in Vine Leaves

Anguilla ai Ferri con Foglie di Vite

The technique of skinning an eel is demonstrated on page 51.

	To serve 4	
1.5 kg	eel, skinned and cut into 10 cm (4 inch) sections	3 lb
10 to 12	vine leaves	10 to 12
	Marinade	
4 tbsp	olive oil	4 tbsp
2 to 3 tbsp	lemon juice	2 to 3 tbsp
1	small onion, chopped	1
1	small carrot, chopped	1
1	stick celery, chopped	1
1 tbsp	chopped parsley	1 tbsp

Mix the marinade ingredients together in a bowl, add the eel pieces, and leave to marinate for 2 hours, turning the pieces several times. Remove the eel pieces from the marinade, wrap them in vine leaves and tie the parcels with string. Dip the parcels in the marinade, then grill them for 6 minutes on each side on a barbecue grill. Remove the string, and serve the eel with steamed potatoes and tartare sauce.

NINO BERGESE
MANGIARE DA RE

Elvers Bilbao-Style

Angulas Estilo Bilbao

Elvers (baby eels) are usually bought after they have been given an initial cooking, to keep them from spoiling quickly.

	To serve 4	
500 g	cooked elvers	1 lb
4 tbsp	olive oil	4 tbsp
3	garlic cloves	3
1	small chili pepper, seeded and chopped	1
	salt	

Heat the oil and garlic in a fireproof earthenware casserole and let the garlic turn golden. Remove the garlic and put in the elvers. Give them a quick turn over a high heat, adding the chili pepper and salt, and serve them at once.

ANA MARIA CALERA
LA COCINA VASCA

Eels Volendam-Style

Paling op Zijn Volendams

The technique of skinning an eel is demonstrated on page 51.

	To serve 4	
1 kg	thumb-thick eels, skinned and cut into 9 cm (3½ inch) pieces	2 to 2½ lb
	freshly ground black pepper	
	salt	
60 g	butter	2 oz
3 tbsp	wine vinegar	3 tbsp

Pack the eels, not too tightly, in an upright position in a small, deep, straight-sided saucepan which fits in the oven; the easiest way to pack the eels in is to place the pan on its side. Sprinkle generously with pepper and lightly with salt. Cover the pan and set it over a moderate heat for 20 minutes without adding any liquid. Then lift the lid so that it rests ajar and cook for a further 10 minutes.

Remove the pan from the heat and dot the eels with the butter. Cover the pan and place it in a moderate oven, pre-heated to 180°C (350°F or Mark 4), for 10 minutes. Remove the lid and cook uncovered for another 10 minutes, until the contents start to crackle and splutter. Sprinkle with the vinegar and cook for a further 3 minutes.

Serve with boiled new potatoes, sprinkled with chopped parsley, and provide each diner with a fork and a small dish of melted butter mixed with vinegar and pepper. Take a piece of eel on the fork, dip it in the vinegar-butter and nibble it off. Do the same with the potatoes.

HUGH JANS
BISTRO KOKEN

Eel Stew with Garlic and Red Wine

Catigot d'Anguilles à la Gardiane

The technique of skinning an eel is demonstrated on page 51.

To serve 4 to 6

2	medium-sized eels, skinned and cut into 5 cm (2 inch) pieces	2
4 to 5 tbsp	olive oil	4 to 5 tbsp
10 to 12	garlic cloves, crushed	10 to 12
1	bay leaf	1
1	sprig thyme	1
1	piece dried orange peel	1
	red chili pepper	
	salt	
15 to 20 cl	red wine	6 fl oz

Put the oil into a fireproof earthenware casserole. Add the crushed garlic, bay leaf, thyme, orange peel and a tiny piece of red chili pepper. Sprinkle the pieces of eel with salt. Place them in the casserole, pour the wine over them, and add just enough water to cover. Cook, uncovered, over a moderate heat, for 20 to 30 minutes, depending on the thickness of the eels. Serve them on hot plates.

JEAN-NOËL ESCUDIER
LA VÉRITABLE CUISINE PROVENÇALE ET NIÇOISE

Eel Stew with Prunes

Matelote d'Anguille aux Pruneaux

The technique of skinning an eel is demonstrated on page 51. The marc *called for in this recipe is a type of brandy distilled from grape skins and pips after wine is made. If* marc *is not available, substitute brandy.*

To serve 4

750 g	eel, skinned, head removed, and cut into 6 cm (2½ inch) pieces	1½ lb
50 g	butter	2 oz
12	small white onions	12
½ litre	red wine	18 fl oz
4 tbsp	*marc*	4 tbsp
1	lump sugar	1
1	garlic clove, crushed	1
1	bouquet garni	1
12	prunes, soaked in tea for 3 hours and drained	12

Melt the butter in a fireproof casserole and lightly sauté the eel pieces and the onions. Add the wine and the *marc*, then the sugar, garlic and bouquet garni. Cover the casserole and bring to the boil. Ignite the liquid as you would if making a punch. Cover and simmer gently for 2 hours over the lowest possible heat. Add the prunes, and cook for 1 hour longer.

ROBERT COURTINE
MON BOUQUET DE RECETTES

Pan-Fried Catfish

(Options: cod, dogfish, coley, haddock, gurnard)

Despite the title of this recipe, the cooking method is strictly speaking not pan frying, but semi-deep frying. The catfish family is important in the United States and Asia, but almost unrepresented in Europe, and not at all in Britain.

To serve 4

1 kg	catfish, cleaned, left whole or cut into pieces	2 to 2½ lb
¼ litre	milk	8 fl oz
250 g	fresh breadcrumbs or cornmeal	8 oz
	lard or oil for frying	
	salt and pepper	

Dip the fish in milk, then coat with crumbs or cornmeal. Cook rapidly in a skillet in hot lard or oil about 2.5 cm (1 inch) deep. Drain the fish, season to taste and serve.

JAMES BEARD
JAMES BEARD'S NEW FISH COOKERY

The Herring Family

Fried Herring

(Option: pilchard)

The technique of boning herrings is demonstrated on page 75.

To serve 2

2	herrings, cleaned and boned	2
100 g	fine oatmeal	3½ oz
	salt and pepper	
60 g	lard or bacon dripping	2 oz

Put the oatmeal on a plate and season it well. Dip the herrings in this coating, covering them well, back and front.

Have a frying pan with some hot fat in it. Put the herrings in, back first, and fry over a medium heat for 3 to 5 minutes, depending on the thickness of the fish. Turn them and give them the same cooking on the other side. They should be a light brown and very crisp when ready.

JANET MURRAY
WITH A FINE FEELING FOR FOOD

Salted Herrings with Anchovy Stuffing

Paupiettes de Hareng

To serve 6

6	salted herrings, heads removed, skinned, filleted and soaked in milk overnight	6
16 to 20	anchovy fillets, soaked and drained	16 to 20
150 g	butter	5 oz
2	egg yolks	2
2 tbsp	very finely chopped *fines herbes*	2 tbsp
	cayenne pepper	
4 tbsp	dry breadcrumbs	4 tbsp
2 to 3 tbsp	lemon juice	2 to 3 tbsp

Trim the herring fillets into neat rectangles. Pound the trimmings with the anchovies in a mortar, or chop them together very finely. Add 100 g (3½ oz) of the butter to the anchovy mixture, then mix in the egg yolks, the *fines herbes* and cayenne pepper very thoroughly.

Lay the herring fillets flat. Cover them with a layer of stuffing. Roll them up and arrange them close together in a buttered gratin dish large enough to hold them in a single layer. Sprinkle over the breadcrumbs. Melt the remaining butter and pour a little over each rolled fillet. Bake in an oven preheated to 220°C (425°F or Mark 7) for 15 to 20 minutes, or until the top is golden-brown.

Remove the dish from the oven, pour the lemon juice over the cooked fish and serve.

ALOIDE BONTOU
TRAITÉ DE CUISINE BOURGEOISE BORDELAISE

Herring and Apple Casserole

Sild med Epler

(Options: pilchard, small mackerel)

To serve 4

1 kg	herrings, filleted, roes reserved	2 to 2½ lb
2 tsp	salt	2 tsp
40 g	butter	1½ oz
2	medium-sized onions, finely chopped	2
4	cooking apples, peeled, cored and grated	4
2 tbsp	fresh breadcrumbs	2 tbsp
2 tbsp	grated cheese	2 tbsp

Sprinkle the herring fillets with the salt. Heat 30 g (1 oz) of the butter in a skillet and gently fry the roes and onions.

Cover the bottom of a buttered baking dish with the apples. Sprinkle with the onions and roes and place the herrings close together on top, backs uppermost.

Sprinkle with the breadcrumbs and grated cheese. Dot with the remaining butter. Bake in a very hot oven, preheated to 240°C (475°F or Mark 9), for 15 minutes. Serve the fish hot with mashed potatoes.

BORGSTRÖM AND DANFORS
SCANDINAVIAN COOKBOOK

Grilled Herrings with Mustard

(Options: small mackerel, large pilchard, tuna slices)

To serve 4

4	fresh herrings	4
2 tbsp	flour, seasoned with salt and freshly ground black pepper	2 tbsp
2 to 3 tbsp	olive oil	2 to 3 tbsp
2 to 3 tbsp	French mustard	2 to 3 tbsp
30 g	fresh breadcrumbs	1 oz
60 g	butter, melted	2 oz

Clean and scale the herrings, taking care not to break the delicate skin; cut off the heads; wash and dry the herrings carefully. Make three shallow incisions on both sides of each fish with a sharp knife.

Dip the herrings into the seasoned flour; brush them with olive oil and grill them on a well-oiled baking sheet for 3 to 4 minutes on each side.

Arrange the herrings in a shallow ovenproof gratin dish; brush them with the mustard; sprinkle with the breadcrumbs and melted butter, and put in a very hot oven, preheated to 240°C (475°F or Mark 9), for 5 minutes. Serve in the gratin dish with boiled new potatoes.

ROBERT CARRIER
THE ROBERT CARRIER COOKERY COURSE

Swedish Herring Gratin

Sillgratäng från Gamla Opris

(Options: smelts, small mackerel, salt herring)

This is a speciality of the Opera Cellar restaurant in Stockholm, where Baltic herring are used for the dish. If you use salted herring, soak the fillets overnight in cold water.

To serve 4		
4	herring fillets	4
8	potatoes, thinly sliced	8
2	onions, thinly sliced	2
40 cl	single cream	¾ pint
1	bay leaf, crumbled	1
1 tsp	thyme	1 tsp
	white pepper	
3 tbsp	coarsely chopped fresh dill	3 tbsp
4 tbsp	fresh breadcrumbs	4 tbsp
3 tbsp	grated Cheddar or Gruyère cheese	3 tbsp
60 g	butter	2 oz

Put the potatoes and onions into a saucepan with the cream to barely cover, bay leaf, thyme and white pepper. Cook, covered, until the potatoes are tender, about 20 minutes. Place half of the potato mixture in a buttered gratin dish, and sprinkle with half the dill. Arrange the herring fillets on top and sprinkle with the remaining dill. Cover with the rest of the potato mixture and the cream. Mix the breadcrumbs and cheese and sprinkle over the surface. Dot with the butter. Brown in an oven preheated to 200°C (400°F or Mark 6) for 20 minutes, or until the fish is cooked and the surface is crisp.

TORE WRETMAN
SVENSK HUSMANSKOST

Grilled Kippers

To serve 4		
4	kippers, soaked in milk for 3 hours	4
	dry white breadcrumbs	
	Marinade	
4 tbsp	olive oil	4 tbsp
	pepper	
1 tbsp	chopped parsley	1 tbsp
1	onion, finely chopped	1

Drain and dry the kippers. Mix together the marinade ingredients, and soak the kippers for at least 3 hours in the marinade, turning them several times. Remove the kippers and roll them in breadcrumbs. Grill at a high heat for 7 to 8 minutes on each side, and serve with brown bread and butter.

AMBROSE HEATH
HERRINGS, BLOATERS AND KIPPERS

Stargazey Pie

(Options: herring, small mackerel, sardines)

The design of this dish came about for reasons of economy. It was wasteful to cover the uneatable fish head with pastry, yet if the fish head was cut off, the rich oil in it was lost. The solution was to cover the body of the fish with pastry and leave the head sticking out.

To serve 4		
8	pilchards, cleaned	8
	salt and pepper	
6 tbsp	finely chopped onion	6 tbsp
2 tbsp	finely chopped mixed herbs	2 tbsp
300 g	shortcrust pastry (*page 175*)	10 oz
3 tbsp	warm milk mixed with ⅛ tsp powdered saffron, or 1 egg, beaten (optional)	3 tbsp

Season the fish well. Mix the onion and herbs and put a spoonful of this mixture into the belly of each fish (this improves the flavour and keeps the fish moist while baking).

Divide the pastry into two pieces and roll it out. The underside crust should be rolled out rather more thinly than the top cover. Use the underside piece to line a 23 cm (9 inch) pie plate. Place the fish in the plate, heads resting on the outer rim, tails in the centre. Cover with the pastry lid (this should be the diameter of the plate less the rim, so that the heads are uncovered). Seal the edges of pastry between the heads.

The top may be brushed over with a little saffroned milk, or beaten egg, to give it a golden colour. Bake in an oven preheated to 190°C (375°F or Mark 5) for about 40 minutes.

DOROTHY HARTLEY
FOOD IN ENGLAND

Sardines Stuffed with Spinach

Sardines Farcies aux Épinards

(Options: anchovies, sprats)

The technique of cleaning and boning sardines is the same as for anchovies, demonstrated on page 77.

To serve 4

1 kg	sardines, cleaned, heads removed, and boned	2 to 2½ lb
10 cl	olive oil	4 fl oz
1 kg	spinach, parboiled, squeezed and chopped	2 to 2½ lb
100 g	bread, soaked in milk, squeezed and crumbled	3½ oz
2	garlic cloves, finely chopped	2
2 tbsp	chopped parsley	2 tbsp
	salt and pepper	
60 g	dry breadcrumbs	2 oz

Heat 4 tablespoons of the oil and lightly sauté the spinach in it, then incorporate the soaked bread, the garlic, the parsley, salt and pepper.

Spread half the spinach mixture in an oiled gratin dish. Open out the sardines, skin-side down. Place a spoonful of the remaining spinach on each sardine and roll it up round the spinach from head to tail. Half bury the stuffed sardines in the dish of spinach with the tails pointing upwards. Dust with the breadcrumbs, sprinkle with oil and put in an oven pre-heated to 220°C (425°F or Mark 7), for 10 to 15 minutes.

LOUIS GINIÉS
CUISINE PROVENÇALE

Sardines Grilled in Vine Leaves

Sardines Grillées aux Feuilles de Vigne

(Options: anchovies, sprats, small red mullet)

To serve 2

12	fresh sardines, cleaned and dried with paper towels	12
4 tbsp	olive oil	4 tbsp
2 tbsp	lemon juice	2 tbsp
	salt and pepper	
1	sprig fresh rosemary	1
12	well-shaped fresh vine leaves	12

Mix the oil, lemon juice, salt and pepper in a shallow dish. Quickly roll the sardines in this mixture, and put a little rosemary inside each one. Wrap each fish in a vine leaf, using the stalk of the leaf to secure it. (Alternatively, tie the wrapped sardine rolls with fine string.)

Grill the sardine rolls over glowing embers for about 3 minutes each side, or until the vine leaves start to blacken. Serve immediately. When the rolls are opened, the skin will peel off with the leaves, revealing the delicious fillets.

MICHEL BARBEROUSSE
CUISINE PROVENÇALE

Stuffed Sardine Rolls

Sarde a Beccafico

(Option: anchovies)

The canestrato *and* caciocavallo *called for in this recipe are sharp-flavoured cheeses made in southern Italy. If unavailable, substitute a mixture of half Parmesan and half ricotta. The technique of boning the fish is demonstrated on page 77.*

To serve 6

1 kg	fresh sardines, cleaned, heads removed, scaled and boned but left in one piece	2 to 2½ lb
10 cl	wine vinegar	4 fl oz
3 tbsp	olive oil	3 tbsp
250 g	fresh breadcrumbs	8 oz
100 g	fresh *canestrato* or *caciocavallo* cheese, diced	3½ oz
30 g	pine-nuts	1 oz
60 g	raisins	2 oz
1	garlic clove, chopped	1
40 g	parsley, chopped	1½ oz
	salt and pepper	
	flour	
3	eggs, lightly beaten	3
	oil for deep frying	

Open out the sardines and put them to marinate in the vinegar for 15 minutes. Heat the 3 tablespoons of olive oil in a frying pan over a low heat. Drain 3 of the sardines, add them to the pan and break them up with a wooden spoon. Add 60 g (2 oz) of the breadcrumbs, and cook, stirring, until brown. Off the heat, add the cheese, pine-nuts, raisins, chopped garlic and parsley and season with salt and pepper. Mix thoroughly until the stuffing mixture is smooth.

Drain the remaining sardines, place them skin-side down, spread the stuffing mixture on them and roll them up from head end to tail. Dredge the sardine rolls in flour, dip them in the beaten egg, then coat with the remaining breadcrumbs. Deep fry them in the oil until golden-brown.

As a variation, the sardine rolls can be arranged in an oiled baking dish, separated from each other with bay leaves, sprinkled with lemon juice and olive oil, and baked in an oven preheated to 190°C (375°F or Mark 5), for 30 minutes.

PINO CORRENTI
IL LIBRO D'ORO DELLA CUCINA E DEI VINI DE SICILIA

Sardine Rolls in Marrow Flowers

Sardines à la Niçoise

To serve 4 to 6

12	fresh sardines, filleted	12
24	marrow flowers	24
60 g	butter	2 oz
15 cl	fish fumet (*page 174*)	¼ pint
	salt and pepper	
1 tbsp	flour	1 tbsp
4	anchovy fillets, soaked, drained and pounded or sieved	4
	Duxelles stuffing	
15 g	butter	½ oz
1	onion, finely chopped	1
250 g	mushrooms, finely chopped	8 oz
	salt	
	freshly grated nutmeg	
1 tbsp	chopped parsley	1 tbsp
1 tbsp	lemon juice	1 tbsp

To make the *duxelles* stuffing, melt the butter in a frying pan and sauté the onion until soft but not brown. Raise the heat, add the mushrooms. Season with salt and nutmeg, and cook, stirring occasionally, until the mushroom liquid has evaporated. Stir in the parsley and lemon juice, remove from the heat, and leave to cool.

Spread the sardine fillets with the *duxelles* mixture and roll them up. Put a sardine roll into each marrow flower, folding the tops of the petals over to make closed bundles. Melt 30 g (1 oz) of the butter in a sauté pan and put in the marrow-flower rolls. Sweat, covered, for a few minutes, turning the rolls once or twice. Pour on the fish fumet, season with salt and pepper, and cook, covered, over a low heat for about 15 minutes. Remove the marrow-flower rolls and arrange them in a warmed serving dish.

Make a paste with the remaining butter, the flour and the anchovy purée, and whisk it into the cooking liquid. Heat until thickened, and pour over the rolls. Serve immediately.

A. CAILLAT
150 MANIÈRES D'ACCOMMODER LES SARDINES

Devilled Whitebait

(Options: small smelts, small gudgeon)

Whitebait is the name applied to tiny herring and sprats.

To serve 6 to 8

1 kg	whitebait	2 to 2½ lb
60 g	flour, seasoned with salt and pepper	2 oz
	oil or fat for deep frying	
1 tsp	cayenne pepper	1 tsp

Wash and carefully dry the whitebait; coat them with the seasoned flour. Deep fry in hot oil or fat, at about 190°C (375°F), until crisp. Drain on paper towels and sprinkle with cayenne pepper before serving.

LIZZIE BOYD (EDITOR)
BRITISH COOKERY

Anchovies with Chard Stuffing

Acciughe Ripiene

(Options: sardines, sprats)

To serve 6

1 kg	fresh anchovies, cleaned, heads removed, and boned	2 to 2½ lb
2	egg yolks, lightly beaten	2
100 g	dry breadcrumbs	3½ oz
15 to 20 cl	olive oil	6 fl oz
	Stuffing	
6 to 8	salted anchovy fillets, chopped	6 to 8
1	garlic clove	1
30 g	Parmesan cheese, grated	1 oz
60 g	day-old bread, crusts removed, soaked in milk and squeezed	2 oz
1 tsp	oregano	1 tsp
4	eggs	4
1 kg	chard leaves, ribs removed, parboiled, refreshed in cold water, squeezed dry and chopped	2 to 2½ lb
	salt	

To make the stuffing, pound the anchovy fillets in a mortar with the garlic, then mix in the cheese, soaked bread, oregano and eggs. Combine with the chard, and season with salt.

Stuff the fresh anchovies with this mixture. Dip them in the beaten egg yolks, then in the breadcrumbs. Heat the oil and fry the anchovies until golden-brown.

DARIO G. MARTINI AND MANUELLI FERRER
PESTO E BURIDDA

Stuffed Anchovies

Acciughe Ripiene

(Options: sardines, sprats)

The techniques of gutting, removing the heads and boning the anchovies are demonstrated on page 77.

To serve 6

1 kg	large fresh anchovies, cleaned, heads removed, and boned	2 to 2½ lb
About 125 g	anchovy fillets, soaked and drained	About 4 oz
About 250 g	*Fontina*, *ricotta*, or other soft cheese, cut or formed into thin strips	About 8 oz
75 g	flour	2½ oz
3	eggs, beaten	3
100 g	fine dry breadcrumbs	3½ oz
	oil for deep frying	
1 or 2	lemons, quartered	1 or 2

Stuff each fresh anchovy with an anchovy fillet and a strip of cheese. Close the anchovies and reshape them. Roll them in flour, dip them carefully into the beaten eggs and roll them in the breadcrumbs. Put aside until required.

When ready to serve, heat the oil and fry the anchovies, a few at a time, for about 5 minutes, or until golden-brown. Drain them on paper towels and serve very hot, garnished with the quartered lemon.

ADA BONI
ITALIAN REGIONAL COOKING

Mixed Fried Fish Cake

La Sartagnado à la Toulonnaise

(Options: sardines, anchovies, small sole, red mullet)

The name of this recipe derives from *la sartan*, the Provençal word for a frying pan in which the dish is traditionally cooked.

To serve 2

250 g	mixed very small fish, well washed and dried	8 oz
30 g	flour, seasoned with salt and pepper	1 oz
4 to 5 tbsp	olive oil	4 to 5 tbsp
2 tbsp	vinegar	2 tbsp

Toss the fish in the seasoned flour until they are evenly coated. Heat the oil in a frying pan until very hot, then add the fish. Reduce the heat to medium and fry, without stirring, for

about 6 to 7 minutes, or until the undersides turn golden-brown, like a flat omelette. Turn the fish and cook on the other side. Slide the fish on to a warmed serving platter. Add the vinegar to the pan, and pour the pan juices over the fish.

JOSÉPHINE BESSON
LA MÈRE BESSON "MA CUISINE PROVENÇALE"

Shad Stuffed with Stuffed Dates

Alose Farcie aux Dattes Fourrées

This dish is just as good if prunes are used instead of dates. Rice may be used instead of semolina.

To serve 8 to 10

3 kg	shad, cleaned and washed in salted water	6 to 7 lb
100 g	almonds, blanched and crushed	3½ oz
1 tbsp	sugar	1 tbsp
100 g	butter	3½ oz
	salt and black pepper	
½ tsp	ground ginger	½ tsp
100 g	semolina or *couscous*, boiled or steamed, and cooled	3½ oz
500 g	large dates, washed, if necessary, and stoned	1 lb
¼	onion, thinly sliced	¼
¼ litre	water	8 fl oz
½ tsp	ground cinnamon	½ tsp

First prepare the stuffing for the dates. Pound the almonds in a large mortar, then pound in the sugar, 30 g (1 oz) of the butter, a little pepper, and half the ginger. Mix with the semolina or *couscous* and stuff the dates with this mixture.

Fill the fish with the stuffed dates and sew up the belly carefully with cotton thread. Rub a large gratin dish with half the remaining butter and line the dish with the sliced onion. Put in the fish and dot with the rest of the butter. Add the water and sprinkle with plenty of pepper, a very little salt and the remaining ginger. Bring to a simmer on top of the stove, and cook, covered, either on top of the stove or in an oven preheated to 170°C (325°F or Mark 3) for about 1½ hours.

When the fish is cooked, unstitch the belly and remove the dates. Arrange them in the gratin dish around the fish and pour over the braising liquid. Place the dish in the oven at 220°C (425°F or Mark 7) or under a preheated grill. Cook, basting, for 10 to 15 minutes, or until the liquid has nearly all evaporated, leaving only a syrupy juice, and the skin of the shad is crisp and golden. The dates should be caramelized but still soft. Sprinkle the cinnamon over the fish and serve.

Z. GUINANDEAU
FEZ VU PAR SA CUISINE

Braised Shad with Sorrel

Alose à l'Avignonnaise

(Options: herring, pilchard)

To serve 3 or 4

1 kg	shad, cleaned, scraped and trimmed	2 to 2½ lb
750 g	sorrel, chopped	1½ lb
10 cl	olive oil	4 fl oz
1	large onion, finely chopped	1
3 or 4	tomatoes, skinned, seeded and roughly chopped	3 or 4
1	garlic clove, crushed	1
	salt and pepper	
2 tbsp	chopped parsley	2 tbsp
30 g	fresh breadcrumbs	1 oz

Lightly sauté the sorrel in 3 tablespoons of the oil with the onion, tomatoes and garlic for about 10 minutes. Season, then add parsley and breadcrumbs to bind everything together.

Meanwhile, in a fireproof earthenware casserole with a lid, lightly brown the shad in another 3 tablespoons of the oil. Remove the fish, and line the bottom of the casserole with half of the sorrel mixture. Place the shad on top and cover it with the rest of the sorrel mixture. Sprinkle with the remaining oil, put on the lid, and braise in a very cool oven at 130°C (250°F or Mark ½) for 8 to 10 hours.

At the end of this long cooking period, the sorrel will have lost its slightly bitter taste, the fish bones will have dissolved and you will have a delicious dish.

MICHEL BOUZY
LES POISSONS-CRUSTACÉS-COQUILLAGES

Baked Maine Smelts

(Options: pilchard, sprats)

To serve 4

750 g	smelts	1½ lb
250 g	rashers, streaky green or smoked bacon	8 oz

Preheat the oven to 200°C (400°F or Mark 6). In a flat baking tin, interweave the smelts with rashers of bacon, much as if you were weaving a basket. Bake for 10 to 15 minutes, or until the smelts and bacon are moulded into a crisp cake.

MARJORIE PAGE BLANCHARD
TREASURED RECIPES FROM EARLY NEW ENGLAND KITCHENS

The Cod Family

Fish in Aspic with Lemon Juice

Rȳba Zalivnaya s Limonnȳm Sokom

(Options: cod, haddock, wolf-fish, angler-fish)

Fish in aspic is a traditional and popular dish in the Soviet Union and is usually an item at birthday or party meals. The technique of coating a fish in aspic for a more formal presentation is demonstrated on page 40.

To serve 4

600 to 750 g	filleted white fish, cut into serving pieces	1¼ to 1½ lb
1	carrot, quartered lengthwise	1
1	stick celery, roughly chopped	1
1	onion, roughly chopped	1
1	sprig parsley	1
1 or 2	bay leaves	1 or 2
5	peppercorns	5
	salt	
2 to 3 tbsp	lemon juice	2 to 3 tbsp
	sugar	
2 tsp	powdered gelatine, dissolved in a little water	2 tsp
1	lemon, thinly sliced, pips removed	1
1	stick celery, cut into thin strips	1

Poach the fish with the vegetables, herbs and peppercorns in about 40 cl (¾ pint) salted water. When the fish is cooked, after about 10 minutes, set it in a shallow serving dish to cool. Strain the poaching liquid into an enamelled or stainless steel saucepan, add the lemon juice together with salt and sugar to taste and set the pan over a low heat. Add the dissolved gelatine, bring to the boil, stirring, then remove the pan from the heat and let the liquid cool to room temperature.

Decorate the fish attractively with the lemon slices and strips of celery. Pour half the liquid over the fish, and place in the refrigerator for about 30 minutes. When the liquid has started to set, pour over the remainder. Refrigerate until ready to serve.

The aspic, when set, should have an agreeable sweet-and-sour taste and a flavour of lemon. The use of carrot in the poaching liquid gives the aspic a pleasant amber colour.

L. L. LAGUNOV
RȲBNȲE BLYUDA

Gratin of Cod with Vegetables

Trondhjemstorsk

(Options: haddock, ling, wolf-fish)

A Norwegian fish and vegetable combination from Trondheim.

To serve 4

750 g	cod fillets, cut into 8 equal pieces	1½ lb
About 100 g	butter	About 3½ oz
1	medium-sized onion, grated	1
175 g	carrots, grated	6 oz
175 g	celeriac, grated	6 oz
6	slices bread, crusts removed	6
	salt and pepper	
1 tbsp	chopped parsley	1 tbsp
30 g	dry breadcrumbs	1 oz

Melt half of the butter in a small pan and add the onion and root vegetables. Stir everything together, over a low heat, for 10 to 15 minutes or until "stewed" but not browned.

Butter a large, shallow baking dish and line the bottom with the bread slices. Arrange the fish pieces on top, season with salt and pepper, then spread the vegetables over the fish. Sprinkle with the parsley and breadcrumbs, and dot with the remaining butter. Place in an oven preheated to 180°C (350°F or Mark 4) for about 40 minutes, or until the fish is cooked and the topping is golden-brown.

HROAR DEGE
FRA NEPTUNS GAFFEL

Cod with Saffron Sauce

Cabillaud à la Sauce Jaune

(Options: haddock, hake, halibut)

To serve 4

1 kg	fresh cod, thickly sliced	2 to 2½ lb
4 tbsp	olive oil	4 tbsp
	salt	
2 tbsp	finely chopped parsley	2 tbsp
2	garlic cloves, finely chopped	2
½ tsp	powdered saffron	½ tsp
	flour	
2 tbsp	lemon juice	2 tbsp
About ¼ litre	hot water	About 8 fl oz

Put the oil, salt, parsley, garlic, saffron, a pinch of flour and the lemon juice into a pan large enough to hold the fish slices side by side. Cook, stirring, over a low heat for 2 to 3 minutes.

Add the fish slices, moving them around to coat the underside with the seasoning mixture. Cover and cook gently. When the surfaces of the fish slices turn white, after about 10 minutes, turn the slices over and moisten with the hot water. Bring to the boil and serve.

L. E. AUDOT
LA CUISINIÈRE DE LA CAMPAGNE ET DE LA VILLE

Fish with Walnut Sauce

Satsivi iz rȳbȳ

(Options: cod, hake, grey mullet, turbot)

Satsivi is a famous Georgian sauce served with meat or chicken as well as fish.

To serve 4

1 kg	fish, cleaned	2 to 2½ lb
2	bay leaves	2
8	peppercorns	8
100 g	walnuts, shelled	3½ oz
2 to 4	garlic cloves	2 to 4
	paprika	
	salt	
1 tsp	ground coriander seeds	1 tsp
3 to 4	small onions, finely chopped	3 to 4
1 tsp	ground cinnamon	1 tsp
¼ tsp	ground cloves	¼ tsp
	freshly ground black pepper	
6 tbsp	vinegar, or pomegranate juice, or unripe grape juice	6 tbsp

Cut the fish into portion-sized pieces. Put the fish pieces into a pan with the bay leaves, peppercorns, and just enough salted water to cover. Simmer for 12 to 15 minutes. Remove the fish from the pan and put it on a serving dish. Leave the fish to cool and reserve the cooking liquid.

Pound the walnuts together with the garlic, paprika and salt to taste. Add the ground coriander and mix well. Dilute the mixture to the consistency of single cream by adding some of the cooking liquid. Pour the sauce into a pan, add the onions, and simmer, uncovered, for 10 minutes. Mix the cinnamon, cloves and pepper with the vinegar, or pomegranate or grape juice, and add this mixture to the sauce. Continue to cook for 10 minutes more. Pour the hot sauce over the fish. Leave to cool, then serve, decorated if desired with walnut halves, sprigs of fresh coriander and spring onion stalks.

N. PAKHURIDZE
BLYUDA GRUZINSKOÏ KUKHNI

Fish Pie

(Options: cod, hake, coley, haddock, whiting, dab)

It is important to use a large pie dish for this recipe so that there is ample room for covering the fish with the sauce; otherwise, the sauce may bubble over the edges of the dish.

	To serve 5 or 6	
1 kg	mixed white fish, whole or cut into pieces, depending on size	2 to 2½ lb
1 litre	fish fumet (*page 174*)	1¾ pints
3	eggs, hard-boiled and finely chopped	3
75 g	butter	2½ oz
60 g	flour	2 oz
	salt and black pepper	
2 tbsp	chopped parsley and capers	2 tbsp
750 g	potatoes, boiled and mashed with butter	1½ lb

Poach the fish in the fumet for 5 to 6 minutes. With a perforated fish slice, transfer the fish to a pie dish. Remove the heads, bones and skin from the fish and break the flesh so that it is spread out evenly in the dish. Add the eggs.

To make a thick velouté melt the butter in a saucepan and stir in the flour to make a roux. Pour in the hot fumet, bring to the boil, stirring, and simmer and skim for about 20 minutes. Season and stir in the parsley and capers.

Pour the velouté over the fish. Cover with the mashed potato, and cook at the top of a fairly hot oven, preheated to 190°C (375°F or Mark 5), for 25 minutes. For the last few minutes, raise the heat to 200°C (400°F or Mark 6) to brown the potato. Alternatively, brown under the grill.

GEORGE LASSALLE
THE ADVENTUROUS FISH COOK

Golden Cod

(Options: ling, hake, pollack, large haddock)

	To serve 4	
4	cod slices, 2.5 cm (1 inch) thick	4
2	onions, 1 halved crosswise, 1 finely chopped	2
	salt and pepper	
60 to 90 g	finely ground oatmeal	2 to 3 oz
60 g	butter	2 oz
1	large parsnip or carrot, finely chopped	1
1 tbsp	finely chopped *fines herbes*	1 tbsp

	Fumet	
	cod trimmings	
90 cl	water	1½ pints
1 each	onion and carrot, sliced	1 each
1	bouquet garni	1
¼ tsp	powdered saffron	¼ tsp

Combine the fumet ingredients in a pan, bring to the boil, skim, and simmer for 30 minutes.

Meanwhile, rub the fish slices well with the halved onion. Season the fish with salt and pepper, coat as thickly as possible with the oatmeal, and quickly fry until golden (but not cooked through) in the butter (do not allow the butter to get too hot and darken). Pack the fried slices into a large, flat ovenproof dish. Chop the halved onion and fry with the already chopped onion, and the parsnip or carrot, till golden-brown in the butter used for frying the fish. Pack the vegetables around and over the fish, sprinkling in the herbs.

Strain the fumet, which should be clear gold from the saffron, and pour it over the fish. Cover and bake for 40 minutes in an oven preheated to 180°C (350°F or Mark 4).

ELISABETH AYRTON
THE COOKERY OF ENGLAND

Salt Cod with Spinach

Morue à la Lessiveuse

	To serve 4	
750 g	salt cod, soaked overnight, drained, and cut into 5 cm (2 inch) squares	1½ lb
60 g	flour	2 oz
4 tbsp	olive oil	4 tbsp
500 g	spinach, chopped, salted and squeezed to remove excess water	1 lb
10 cl	boiling water	4 fl oz
2 tbsp	finely chopped parsley	2 tbsp
1	garlic clove, finely chopped	1
1 tsp	finely chopped bitter orange peel	1 tsp
2	anchovy fillets, soaked, drained and finely chopped	2

Flour the pieces of cod and half cook them in the oil over a low heat (allow about 2 minutes on each side). Remove the cod from the pan, then add the spinach and cook over a high heat for 1 to 2 minutes, tossing it frequently. Add 1 teaspoon of flour, the water, parsley, garlic, orange peel and anchovy. Bring to the boil, then reduce the heat to medium. When the spinach is cooked (after about 5 minutes), add the cod, cook for 2 to 3 minutes, shaking the pan vigorously, then serve.

CHARLES DURAND
LE CUISINIER DURAND

Salt Cod with Tomatoes and Peppers

Morue à la Cantabrica

To serve 4 or 5

800 g	salt cod fillets, soaked in water overnight	1¾ lb
2 tbsp	olive oil	2 tbsp
2	large onions, finely sliced	2
6	garlic cloves, crushed	6
2	leeks, white parts only, chopped	2
6	sweet red peppers, seeded and cut into strips	6
6	tomatoes, skinned and seeded	6
1	bouquet garni	1
20 cl	white wine	7 fl oz
	pepper and salt	

Put the cod fillets in a large flameproof casserole and cover them with fresh cold water. Bring to the boil, then remove the casserole from the heat.

Heat the olive oil in a sauté pan. Lightly fry the onions, garlic and leeks in it; then add the peppers, tomatoes and bouquet garni. Leave to simmer for a few minutes, then add the white wine with an equal quantity of the water in which the fish has been boiled. Season with pepper and a very little salt and leave to cook, uncovered, over a medium heat for about 15 minutes.

Drain the fillets of cod; flake them and remove any bones. Mix the fish and the sauce together in an ovenproof dish and cook in an oven preheated to 180°C (350°F or Mark 4) for 20 to 30 minutes. Remove the bouquet garni and serve.

IRÈNE LABARRE
LA CUISINE DES TROIS B

Dutch Mess

This dish, popular among the Germans of Lunenburg, was soon adopted by English-speaking settlers. The "Dutch" in the title is probably a corruption of "Deutsch".

To serve 4

500 g	salt cod, soaked in 1 to 2 changes of cold water for 6 to 10 hours	1 lb
4	large potatoes, cut into large pieces	4
125 g	green bacon, diced	4 oz
1	large onion, chopped	1
¼ litre	double cream (optional)	8 fl oz
	pepper	

Drain the salt cod, reserving the water in which it has been soaked. Flake the fish and discard the skin and bones. Cook

the potatoes in the reserved water. When the potatoes are about half done, after 15 minutes or so, add the fish and simmer for 10 minutes, or until the potatoes are tender. Meanwhile, fry the bacon in a pan until the fat begins to run, then add the onion and cook until both bacon and onion are golden-brown. Drain off excess fat. Add the cream, if desired, and heat through, stirring. Drain the potatoes and salt cod and place on a warmed platter, top with the bacon and onion mixture and season generously with pepper.

MARIE NIGHTINGALE
OUT OF OLD NOVA SCOTIA KITCHENS

Cream of Salt Cod

Brandade de Morue à la Ménagère

To serve 6 to 8

500 g	very white salt cod, soaked in several changes of cold water for 24 hours, and drained	1 lb
20 to 30 cl	olive oil	7 to 10 fl oz
1	garlic clove, crushed	1
6 to 8 tbsp	single cream or milk	6 to 8 tbsp
125 g	potato, boiled or steamed, and mashed	4 oz
	freshly ground white pepper	
	salt (optional)	
2 to 3 tbsp	lemon juice	2 to 3 tbsp
	tiny bread croûtons, fried until golden in oil or butter	

Cut the cod into several pieces and place them in a saucepan with 3 litres (5½ pints) water. Bring to the boil. As soon as the water boils, turn the heat as low as possible and poach the fish for 10 to 12 minutes.

Drain the pieces of cod. Remove the black and white skin, and the bones. Break the flesh into fine flakes.

In a heavy-based saucepan, heat 10 cl (4 fl oz) of the olive oil. Add the cod and crushed garlic. Beat vigorously with a wooden spatula or spoon until the fish is reduced to a fine paste. Lower the heat. Continue to beat the paste without stopping, adding the remaining oil and the cream or milk alternately, in small quantities.

Add the mashed potato and mix thoroughly. Season with white pepper and, if necessary, add a little salt. Finally, mix the lemon juice in well. When finished, the *brandade* should be a smooth paste, light and very white. Serve it in a mound on a warmed serving dish, surrounded with the croûtons.

PAUL BOCUSE
THE NEW CUISINE

Salt Cod with Aïoli

Grand Aïoli

Grand Aïoli is a typical Marseilles dish. The basic *aïoli* is transformed into a celebration spread when served with various boiled vegetables, salt cod and hard-boiled eggs. Snails and squid are often included, as in this recipe. Artichokes, cauliflower and even chick peas may also be used.

If you are using live snails, put them in a bowl with a handful of salt and pour over enough vinegar to cover them. Stir and leave them for 15 minutes. Then wash the snails well in several changes of water. The technique of cleaning and preparing squid is demonstrated on page 24.

To serve 12

600 g	salt cod fillets, soaked overnight in cold water and drained	1¼ lb
36	snails, cleaned	36
About 1 litre	white wine court-bouillon (*page 174*) with fennel added	About 1¾ pints
1 tbsp	olive oil	1 tbsp
750 g	squid, cleaned and cut into pieces	1½ lb
	salt and pepper	
6	carrots	6
6	new potatoes, unpeeled	6
750 g	French beans	1½ lb
6	eggs	6
	Aïoli	
6	garlic cloves, peeled	6
1	egg yolk	1
	salt	
50 cl	olive oil	18 fl oz
2 tbsp	lemon juice	2 tbsp
About 2 tsp	warm water	About 2 tsp

Simmer the snails in their shells, covered, in the court-bouillon for about 2 hours. Meanwhile make the *aïoli*. Crush the garlic in a mortar. Add the egg yolk and salt, then add the oil drop by drop, always turning the pestle in the same direction and with the same rhythm. Do not stop turning until you have a thick paste.

When you have mixed in the equivalent of 3 or 4 tablespoons of oil, add the lemon juice and 2 teaspoons of warm water. Then continue adding the oil, a little at a time, and a few more drops of warm water if the mixture seems too thick.

(If in spite of all precautions the *aïoli* "turns"—that is, the oil separates and rises to the surface—the only remedy is to turn the whole lot out into a bowl so that you can clean the mortar and pestle. Then put another egg yolk into the mortar with a few more drops of lemon juice, and very gradually add the separated mixture, a spoonful at a time, turning the pestle continuously. This is called "saving the *aïoli*".)

Now prepare the remaining accompaniments. Heat the oil in a large saucepan, add the squid, season and cook very gently, covered, for about 30 to 40 minutes, or until tender. Hard-boil the eggs. In separate pans boil the carrots and potatoes for about 30 minutes and cook the French beans in plenty of boiling water for 5 to 6 minutes. Poach the salt cod in barely simmering water for 8 to 10 minutes. Drain.

Serve all the accompaniments very hot and in different dishes, with the *aïoli* at the centre of the table.

IRÈNE BORELLI
LA CUISINE PROVENÇALE

"Grandmother's" Gratin of Salt Cod

Gratin de Morue "Grand-Mère"

To serve 4 to 6

1 kg	salt cod, soaked in water overnight	2 to 2½ lb
500 g	leeks, white parts only, chopped	1 lb
500 g	onions, chopped	1 lb
60 g	butter	2 oz
250 g	spinach, parboiled, squeezed and finely chopped	8 oz
30 cl	double cream	½ pint
4 to 6	eggs, hard-boiled and halved lengthwise	4 to 6
8	anchovy fillets, soaked, drained and halved lengthwise	8
50 g	Parmesan or Gruyère cheese, grated	2 oz
30 g	dry breadcrumbs	1 oz

Poach the cod for 10 to 20 minutes, according to the thickness of the fish. Drain and flake the fish.

Put the leeks, onions and half the butter in a fireproof casserole, cover with a tightly fitting lid and cook over a very low heat for 1½ hours.

Meanwhile, in a large saucepan, heat the spinach in the remaining butter over a low heat for 3 to 5 minutes. When the spinach is cooked, remove the pan from the heat and stir in one-third of the cream. When the leeks and onions are ready, mix them with the spinach and stir in the remaining cream.

Cover the bottom of a gratin dish with half this mixture, add the flaked fish and cover it with the rest of the mixture. Set the halved hard-boiled eggs, yolks facing upwards, in a circle on top of the vegetables. Criss-cross the anchovy fillets between them. Sprinkle all over with grated cheese, then with breadcrumbs and cook in an oven preheated to 200°C (400°F or Mark 6) for 10 to 15 minutes.

MICHEL BARBEROUSSE
CUISINE PROVENÇALE

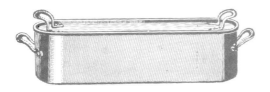

Cod, Potatoes and Eggs

Estofinade à la Rouergatte

Stockfish was originally used for this preparation—but stockfish is cod that has been salted and drained, and requires at least 4 days soaking, with several changes of water. The cod should be poached and the potatoes and eggs boiled so that all are still hot when assembled.

To serve 4

750 g	salt cod, soaked in water for 24 to 36 hours, changing the water at least 4 times	1½ lb
1	bay leaf	1
1	sprig thyme	1
1 kg	firm-fleshed potatoes, unpeeled	2 to 2½ lb
4	eggs	4
2 or 3	garlic cloves, pounded to a purée in a mortar	2 or 3
4 tbsp	chopped parsley	4 tbsp
¼ litre	olive oil	8 fl oz
	pepper	
	salt (optional)	

Drain the cod, place it in a saucepan and cover generously with cold water containing the bay leaf and thyme; bring slowly to a near boil, and remove any scum that forms on the surface. Reduce the heat and poach in the hot but not simmering water for about 10 minutes, depending on the thickness of the fish. When the flesh at its thickest point shows little resistance to the tip of a sharp knife, it is ready. Remove the skin and bones, and flake the flesh into large pieces.

Meanwhile boil the potatoes in their skins and hard-boil the eggs. Then peel and thickly slice the potatoes. Shell the eggs and cut them into pieces.

Mix the garlic purée and parsley together well, add the eggs, and stir gently with half of the olive oil. Add the potatoes to the remaining oil over medium heat, toss with the flaked cod, and gently stir in the egg and parsley mixture, peppering generously. Taste and add salt if needed; the cod may be salty enough. Turn out on to a heated platter and serve.

RICHARD OLNEY
SIMPLE FRENCH FOOD

Fish Pudding from the Azores

Pudim de Peixe dos Açores

(Options: haddock, coley, wolf-fish, ombrine, grouper)

The fish recommended for this pudding is what the Portuguese call cherne, which is known as wreckfish or stone bass in English. The pudding is served cold the day after it is made.

To serve 4

600 g	firm white fish fillets, skinned and cut into almond-sized pieces	1¼ lb
75 g	butter	2½ oz
1	large onion, chopped	1
2	medium-sized tomatoes, skinned, seeded and chopped	2
	salt	
75 g	fresh breadcrumbs	2½ oz
3	eggs, beaten	3
75 g	olives, stoned	2½ oz

Melt the butter in a saucepan, and cook the onion until softened but not coloured, then add the tomatoes, salt and fish. Cook over a moderate heat until the fish is done, about 7 to 8 minutes. Then add the breadcrumbs, eggs and olives. Mix well and pour the mixture into a buttered 1 litre (1¾ pint) oven dish. Cook in a bain-marie in a moderate oven, preheated to 180°C (350°F or Mark 4), for about 1 hour. Leave the mixture to chill overnight in the refrigerator.

On the following day, turn the pudding out into a serving dish, garnish it with olives, lettuce and radishes. Serve cold.

MARIA ODETTE CORTES VALENTE
COZINHA REGIONAL PORTUGUESA

Fish Poached in Milk

(Options: smoked haddock, cod, halibut)

In this recipe, the fish can be poached in milk on top of the stove, or cooked in the oven at 180°C (350°F or Mark 4). Allow 10 minutes per 2.5 cm (1 inch) thickness of fish if cooked on the stove top, 15 minutes if cooked in the oven.

To serve 6 to 8

1 kg	smoked fish fillets	2 to 2½ lb
¼ litre	milk	8 fl oz
15 g	butter	½ oz
	pepper	
1 tbsp	flour worked with 15 g (½ oz) butter to make *beurre manié* (optional)	1 tbsp

In a covered pan, simmer the fish fillets in the milk until the flesh flakes easily when tested with a fork. Remove the fish to a warmed serving dish. Dot with the butter and season with pepper. Serve with the milk poured over the fish. Alternatively, stir the *beurre manié* into the milk, simmer until thickened, and pour over the fish.

GOVERNMENT OF CANADA, FISHERIES AND OCEANS
THE CANADIAN FISH AND SHELLFISH COOKBOOK SERIES

Kegeree

This Victorian breakfast dish—also spelt kedgeree—originated in British India. Any cold, cooked fish can be used, but smoked haddock is a traditional favourite in Britain.

To serve 1 or 2

125 g	cold cooked fish, bones and skin removed	4 oz
30 g	butter	1 oz
125 g	boiled rice	4 oz
1 tsp	prepared mustard	1 tsp
2	eggs, soft-boiled	2
	salt	
	cayenne pepper	

Melt the butter in a heavy saucepan. Add all the other ingredients and heat carefully over a low heat. Adjust the seasoning and serve very hot.

MRS. ISABELLA BEETON
THE BOOK OF HOUSEHOLD MANAGEMENT

Haddock Strachur

A rich and satisfying dish from Strachur in Argyllshire, Scotland. Fingers of buttered toast can be served with it.

To serve 6 to 8

1 kg	Finnan haddock	2 to 2½ lb
60 cl	double cream	1 pint
	freshly ground black pepper	

Poach the haddock in gently boiling water for 4 minutes. Drain and flake the fish, taking care to remove all the bones. Arrange the fish in a buttered fireproof dish; pour the cream over the fish until it is completely covered. Season with pepper; put under a hot grill until brown. Serve at once.

LIZZIE BOYD (EDITOR)
BRITISH COOKERY

Curried Haddock Fillets

Schelvisfillets met Kerrie

(Options: cod, redfish, wolf-fish, dogfish)

This recipe is one of many that show the influence of the East Indies on Dutch cookery. But the influence was only partial: the Dutch adapted rather than adopted. They created their own variations on Oriental themes and applied them to their own fish, as in this recipe.

To serve 4

1 kg	fresh haddock fillets, divided into 4 equal pieces	2 to 2½ lb
3 tbsp	soy sauce	3 tbsp
1 tbsp	lemon juice	1 tbsp
	salt	
5	peppercorns	5
1	bay leaf	1
75 g	butter	2½ oz
2	apples, peeled, cored and sliced	2
3	onions, sliced into rings	3
2 tbsp	flour	2 tbsp
1 tbsp	curry powder	1 tbsp
½ tsp	powdered dried thyme	½ tsp

Wash the fish fillets carefully and set them beside each other in a shallow dish. Sprinkle the soy sauce and lemon juice over them, cover the dish with aluminium foil or a lid and leave them for 30 minutes.

Heat about ½ litre (18 fl oz) water in a shallow saucepan. Add salt, the peppercorns and the bay leaf. Leave this mixture over a low heat for 10 minutes. Then place the fish fillets carefully in the water and poach them, with the water barely simmering, for 10 to 15 minutes.

Meanwhile, melt half the butter in a frying pan and cook the apple slices until golden-brown. Remove them to a plate. Add the onion rings to the butter remaining in the pan. Cook them until golden-brown, then transfer them to a plate. Keep the apple and onion rings warm.

Once the fish fillets are cooked, lift them carefully from their pan, set them beside each other in a warmed serving dish and keep them hot. Strain and reserve the cooking liquid in which the fish was cooked.

Melt the rest of the butter in a saucepan and add the flour and the curry powder, stirring well. As soon as the mixture is smooth, gradually stir in about 10 cl (4 fl oz) of the strained liquid. Add salt to taste and the thyme. Let the sauce continue to simmer for a further 4 to 5 minutes, then pour it over the fish fillets. Garnish the dish with the apple slices and onion rings before serving.

TON VAN ES
HET VOLKOMEN VISBOEK

Ham and Haddie

This dish is a favourite in Scotland. To convince her readers elsewhere that it is as good as it sounds, the author quotes a visitor to Scotland who described it as "altogether delectable" and declared that the combination of fried smoked ham and haddock was as perfect as the wedding of bacon and egg. She adds, however, for the benefit of those who prefer not to fry foods, that the dish can be successfully made by cooking the ham and haddie together, with a little water, in a cooking vessel with a tightly fitting lid.

To serve 4

600 g	pale, lightly smoked Finnan haddock, skinned (by passing it briefly over a flame until the skin buckles) and cut into neat pieces	1¼ lb
4	thin slices smoked ham	4
30 g	butter (optional)	1 oz
	pepper	

Fry the ham, which will provide its own fat for the purpose, then remove it and keep it hot while you fry the pieces of fish in the ham fat that is left in the pan. Add the butter if the ham fat is insufficient. Turn the fish once during the frying.

When the fish is done, after 5 to 10 minutes depending on the thickness of the pieces, season it with pepper. Serve the fish pieces wrapped up in the slices of ham.

F. MARIAN MCNEILL
THE SCOTS KITCHEN

Deep-Fried Whiting

Merlan Frit

(Options: cod, ling, burbot, weever)

For instructions on boning a whole fish, see pages 22 and 66. The fish should ideally be boned through the back, but if they are already cleaned when you buy them, you can bone them through the existing slit in the belly.

To serve 4

Four 250 g	whiting, boned and opened out	Four 8 oz
	salt and pepper	
10 cl	milk	4 fl oz
60 g	flour	2 oz
	oil for deep frying	
1	bunch parsley, main stems removed	1
	lemon wedges	

Season the fish with salt and pepper, dip them in the milk, then roll them in the flour until well coated.

Heat the oil until moderately hot, and fry the fish for 4 minutes. Turn up the heat and complete the cooking with 3 minutes at high heat. This graduated cooking will produce crisp, golden fish.

Drain the fish, and salt them lightly. As soon as the fish are removed from the hot oil, plunge the parsley in and remove it again as soon as the explosion of spluttering oil has ceased. Serve the whiting garnished with the deep-fried parsley and with the lemon wedges.

JULES GOUFFÉ
LE LIVRE DE CUISINE

Baked Whitings

(Options: small mackerel, pilchard, grey mullet, trout)

This receipt is a very convenient one, as it is prepared with little trouble. The fish should be opened only so much as will permit of their being emptied and perfectly cleansed. It is an advantage to take off the heads of the fish before they are dressed, and they may then be emptied without being opened.

The chili vinegar called for in this recipe can be made by macerating crushed chili pepper pods in vinegar for several weeks, then straining the vinegar. Alternatively, substitute wine vinegar, and increase the quantity of cayenne pepper.

To serve 4

4	whiting, cleaned, and the roe, if any, reserved	4
4 tbsp	port, sherry or dry wine	4 tbsp
1 to 2 tsp	chili vinegar	1 to 2 tsp
	salt	
	cayenne pepper	
	ground mace	
90 g	butter	3 oz
1 to 2 tsp	flour	1 to 2 tsp

Wash the fish and wipe them dry, then fold them in a soft cloth, and let them remain in it awhile. Replace the roes, and put the fish into a buttered baking dish of suitable size, with the wine, chili vinegar, a little salt, cayenne pepper and ground mace and 60 g (2 oz) butter, well blended with the flour. They must be turned round with the heads and tails towards each other, that they may lie compactly in the dish, and the backs should be placed downwards, that the sauce may surround the thickest part of the flesh.

Lay two buttered papers over, and press them down upon them; set the dish into a gentle oven, preheated to 170°C (325°F or Mark 3), for 20 minutes, or until cooked. Take off the papers and send the fish to the table in their sauce. When preferred so, they can be re-dished for the table, and the sauce poured over them.

ELIZA ACTON
MODERN COOKERY

Fish Hotpot

Fischlabskaus

(Options: whiting, cod, hake, plaice, lemon sole)

To serve 4

750 g	fish fillets	1½ lb
	salt	
1.25 kg	potatoes, boiled and mashed	2½ lb
90 g	butter	3 oz
1	large onion, chopped	1
	pepper	
2	anchovy fillets, pounded	2
2½ tsp	German mustard	2½ tsp
1	gherkin, thinly sliced	1

Poach the fillets in a little salted water for 7 or 8 minutes, or until tender but firm. Drain the fillets, flake them and mix them with the hot mashed potatoes. Meanwhile, melt the butter in a frying pan and cook the onion over a low heat until golden. Add the pepper, anchovy paste and mustard. Put the potato and fish mixture on to a warmed dish, spread with the onion sauce and garnish with the gherkin slices.

HANS KARL ADAM
GERMAN COOKERY

Whiting with Orange Sauce

(Options: small hake, sole, flounder, witch, megrim)

A recipe inspired by a similar one for scallops published in 1747 in Hannah Glasse's *Art of Cookery*.

To serve 6

6	whiting, filleted	6
3	Seville oranges, or 2 sweet oranges and 1 lemon	3
4 tbsp	double cream	4 tbsp
3	large egg yolks	3
10 to 15 cl	dry white wine	4 to 5 fl oz
	salt and black pepper	
	cayenne pepper	
125 g	butter	4 oz
	flour, seasoned with salt and pepper	
	chopped parsley	

Sprinkle the fish with the juice of half an orange (or half the lemon) and leave in a cool place while the sauce is being made. Beat together in a large pudding basin the cream, egg yolks, wine, and the juice of 1½ Seville oranges (cut the last orange down into wedges for the garnish). With sweet oranges, use the juice of 1 orange and of the second lemon half, and cut the second orange into wedges.

Set the basin over a pan of simmering water, or transfer the sauce to a heavy pan set directly over the heat, if you are used to cooking egg-thickened sauces. Stir until it thickens to a pouring-cream consistency or is a little thicker. Season with salt and the two peppers. Beat in 60 g (2 oz) of butter. Lower the heat so that the sauce keeps warm without more cooking.

Dip the whiting fillets in the flour and fry to golden-brown in the remaining butter. Arrange on a serving dish with the orange wedges tucked in between, and a little parsley scattered on top. Serve the sauce separately in a warm sauceboat.

The whiting are good with boiled parsnip rings tossed in butter, and natural brown rice.

JANE GRIGSON
FISH COOKERY

Hake in the Basque Style

Merluza a la Koskera

(Options: cod, haddock, angler-fish, conger eel)

To serve 3

About 750 g	hake, cut into 3 slices	About 1½ lb
4 to 6 tbsp	olive oil	4 to 6 tbsp
3	garlic cloves	3
1	small bay leaf	1
1 tbsp	flour	1 tbsp
2	sprigs parsley, chopped	2
10 to 25 cl	fish fumet (*page 174*) or water	4 to 8 fl oz
3 tbsp	peas, parboiled	3 tbsp
12	asparagus tips, parboiled	12
	salt (optional)	
3	eggs	3

Heat the oil with the garlic cloves in a fireproof earthenware casserole. Toss in the bay leaf, flour and parsley. Stir it all well and add the fish fumet or water. Add the slices of hake, the peas and the asparagus tips. Season with salt if necessary.

When the fish is cooked (after about 10 minutes, depending on the thickness of the slices) remove the bay leaf and break the eggs over the casserole. As soon as the eggs are cooked, the dish is ready to serve.

ANA MARIA CALERA
LA COCINA VASCA

Shrimp-Stuffed Hake in Shrimp Sauce

Filetes de Pescada Recheados con Crema de Camaroes

(Options: steaks or thick slices of fresh cod or sea bass)

Hake is the favourite fish of the Portuguese. The thick upper fillets (those of the back rather than the belly) of a large hake are recommended for this dish. If only small hake are available, use steaks cut right across the body.

To serve 6 to 8

1 kg	hake upper fillets, cut into steaks or medallions about 1 cm (½ inch) thick and 3 cm (1¼ inches) across	2 to 2½ lb
	salt and freshly ground pepper	
10 cl	white wine	4 fl oz
4 tbsp	olive oil	4 tbsp
2 to 3 tbsp	lemon juice	2 to 3 tbsp
75 g	dry breadcrumbs	2½ oz
2	eggs, lightly beaten	2
	oil for deep frying	
	Stuffing	
1 kg	shrimps or small prawns	2 to 2½ lb
30 g	butter	1 oz
2 tbsp	cornflour	2 tbsp
¼ litre	milk	8 fl oz
	Shrimp sauce	
	reserved shrimp heads, shells and cooking liquor	
4 tbsp	olive oil, or 60 g (2 oz) butter	4 tbsp
1	medium-sized onion finely chopped	1
1½ tbsp	flour	1½ tbsp
	salt and pepper	
2	egg yolks	2
2 tbsp	lemon juice	2 tbsp
1 tbsp	chopped parsley	1 tbsp

Place the pieces of fish in a dish, season and add the wine, olive oil and lemon juice. Leave to marinate for 1 to 2 hours.

Meanwhile, prepare the stuffing. Cook the shrimps for 5 minutes in about 60 cl (1 pint) of boiling salted water. Remove the shrimps, peel them, and reserve the heads and shells as well as cooking liquor. Heat the butter in a small saucepan and add the cornflour, stirring well. Stir in the milk and a little of the reserved liquor and continue stirring until the mixture reaches the boil. Chop half the peeled shrimp tails, add them to the pan and allow the mixture to cool.

Remove the fish pieces from the marinade, dry them with a cloth and cover them on one side only with the shrimp stuff-ing. Pat the stuffing into place, to help it to adhere. Coat on all sides with breadcrumbs, dip the stuffed fish in the beaten eggs and coat with crumbs again, patting them on firmly.

Meanwhile, make the sauce. Crush the reserved shrimp heads and shells in a mortar, and boil them for 10 to 15 minutes in the remaining shrimp cooking liquor. Strain and reserve the resulting broth. Heat the olive oil or butter in a saucepan, add the onion and cook until golden. Mash the onion, and add it, with the dissolved flour, to the broth. Season with salt and pepper; add the remaining shrimps, the egg yolks, lemon juice and chopped parsley.

Heat a sufficient quantity of oil to deep fry the fish. Lower the pieces into the pan, stuffing side up, and fry until they are evenly browned. Drain and place the fish pieces on a heated serving dish. Cover with the sauce and serve.

ANTÓNIO MARIA DE OLIVEIRA BELLO OLLEBOMA
CULINÁRIA PORTUGUESA

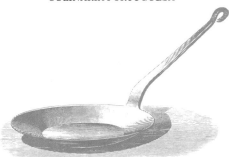

Galician Fish Pie

Pastel de Pescado

(Options: hake, haddock, sea bream, sar, bogue)

To serve 4 to 6

500 g	cod in thin fillets	1 lb
24	blanched almonds	24
3 tbsp	olive oil	3 tbsp
2	garlic cloves, chopped	2
4	onions, finely chopped	4
1	bay leaf	1
6	tomatoes, skinned, seeded and chopped	6
	salt	
30 g	butter	1 oz
6	potatoes, boiled, puréed and seasoned well with salt and pepper	6

In a frying pan, fry the almonds in the oil until lightly golden. Remove the almonds, drain them on paper towels and crush them in a mortar. Put the garlic, onions and bay leaf into the pan and cook slowly for about 15 minutes, or until the onions are tender. Add the tomatoes, season with salt and cook for 10 minutes. Reserve one-third of this mixture for use as sauce.

Add the almonds to the remainder and cook for 5 to 10 minutes longer. Take out the bay leaf.

Butter an ovenproof dish, line the bottom and sides with about two-thirds of the puréed potatoes, then fill it with alternating layers of the fried mixture and the fish fillets, starting with the fried mixture. Cover with the remaining potato and bake the pie in a hot oven, preheated to 200°C (400°F or Mark 6), for 40 minutes.

Serve in the same dish, accompanied by the sauce, or turn the pie out on to a warmed platter and coat with the sauce.

ANNA MACMIADHACHÁIN
SPANISH REGIONAL COOKERY

Fish Baked with Chard, as in Mallorca

Peix en es Forn

(Options: hake, cod, haddock, sar, garfish, scad, dogfish)

To serve 4

About 850 g	fish slices or fillets	About 1¾ lb
¼ litre	olive oil	8 fl oz
3	large potatoes, sliced	3
1	large onion, finely chopped	1
60 g	chopped parsley	2 oz
1 kg	chard, ribs removed, chopped	2 to 2½ lb
2	large tomatoes, skinned, seeded and chopped	2
	salt and pepper	
6 tbsp	white wine	6 tbsp

Oil the bottom of a large, shallow baking dish and cover it with the slices of potato. Add half the onion, parsley, chard and tomato. Season with salt and pepper. Lay the slices or fillets of fish on top, cover them with the remaining onion, parsley, chard and tomato. Season again, pour over the remaining olive oil and bake in an oven preheated to 200°C (400°F or Mark 6) for about 15 minutes. Then turn the oven to 170°C (325°F or Mark 3) and cook for a further 45 minutes. About 15 minutes before the cooking is completed, pour over the white wine.

ALAN DAVIDSON
MEDITERRANEAN SEAFOOD

Flat Fish

Paupiettes of Sole Paillard

Paupiettes de Soles Paillard

(Options: flounder, lemon sole, brill, John Dory)

This recipe is the creation of A. Deland, formerly head chef at the Restaurant Paillard. At the restaurant, the paupiettes were served on artichoke bottoms. To make the mushroom purée, put 300 g (10 oz) mushrooms through a food processor. Put them in a saucepan with 30 g (1 oz) butter, season with salt, pepper and a little lemon juice, and cook over a brisk heat until the mushroom liquid has evaporated. Chill before use.

To serve 4

8	sole fillets	8
	mushroom purée	
40 cl	mousseline (*page 174*)	¾ pint
	salt and pepper	
1	onion, finely sliced	1
100 g	mushrooms, finely sliced	3½ oz
1	bouquet garni	1
20 cl	fish fumet (*page 174*) or dry white wine	7 fl oz
2	egg yolks	2
20 cl	double cream	7 fl oz

Incorporate half the mushroom purée into the mousseline. Season the fillets, spread them thinly with the mousseline, and roll them up. Line a sauté pan with the finely sliced onion and mushrooms, put in the bouquet garni, and pack in the rolled fillets. If the pan is completely filled, the fillets will keep each other from unrolling.

Pour on the fumet or wine, cover the pan and cook in an oven preheated to 180°C (350°F or Mark 4) for 12 minutes. Drain the paupiettes, arrange them in a deep, buttered dish, cover and keep them warm.

Strain the cooking liquor into a saucepan, and add the remaining mushroom purée. Mix the egg yolks with the cream and add to the liquor. Bring just to the boil, whisking all the time, and adjust the seasoning. Coat the paupiettes with this sauce and serve immediately.

PROSPER MONTAGNÉ
LAROUSSE GASTRONOMIQUE

Paupiettes of Sole in Lettuce Leaves

(Options: lemon sole, flounder, brill, John Dory)

The fumet should be made with the fish carcass, flavouring vegetables, a piece of lemon peel, a sprig of tarragon, and 2 tablespoons of white wine, vermouth or wine vinegar.

	To serve 2 to 4	
4	fillets of sole, carcass reserved	4
60 g	peeled cooked prawns	2 oz
8	lettuce leaves	8
	salt and pepper	
3 tbsp	lemon juice	3 tbsp
	freshly grated nutmeg	
30 g	butter	1 oz
2	eggs	2
15 cl	fish fumet (*page 174*)	¼ pint

Choose good lettuce leaves, not the coarse outside ones, but large enough to roll up. Wash them and blanch them for 2 minutes in boiling salted water; drain them. Season the fillets of sole with salt, pepper, and a little lemon juice. In the centre of each arrange a few prawns, also seasoned; roll up the fillets. Arrange the lettuce leaves overlapping each other two by two, so that you have 4 leaves instead of 8. Put a rolled fillet in the centre of each, and roll the leaves round the fish. Squeeze these rolls in the hand, so that each forms a little parcel, which need not be tied. Grate a little nutmeg on to each *paupiette*. Melt the butter in a small shallow pan. Put the *paupiettes* in and cook very gently for 30 minutes, with the cover on the pan.

Beat the eggs in a bowl, add the strained fumet, the remaining lemon juice and a little salt. Remove the *paupiettes* to a warmed serving dish. Strain the egg and lemon mixture through a sieve into the butter remaining in the pan, and stir very fast until the sauce has thickened and frothed.

Pour the sauce over the *paupiettes* and serve at once.

ELIZABETH DAVID
SUMMER COOKING

Grilled Sole

Sole Grillée

(Options: lemon sole, flounder, plaice, megrim, dab)

	To serve 2	
Two 300 g	sole, skinned	Two 10 oz
	salt and pepper	
2 tbsp	lemon juice	2 tbsp
30 g	butter	1 oz
60 g	fresh breadcrumbs	2 oz

	Anchovy sauce	
2	anchovy fillets, soaked in water and drained	2
30 g	butter	1 oz
4 tbsp	dry white wine	4 tbsp
2 tbsp	lemon juice	2 tbsp

Season the sole with salt and pepper and the lemon juice. Melt the butter. Brush the fish with the melted butter then coat with the breadcrumbs. Grill the fish gently for about 10 minutes, turning them once.

Meanwhile, cook the anchovy fillets in the butter over low heat, stirring and crushing them to a purée. Add the wine and lemon juice and bring to the boil. Pour the anchovy sauce over the fish and serve immediately.

CHARLES DURAND
LE CUISINIER DURAND

Sole Fillets with Fines Herbes

Filets de Sole aux Fines Herbes

(Options: lemon sole, French sole, flounder)

	To serve 8	
Four 500 g	sole, filleted and soaked in cold water, carcasses and trimmings reserved	Four 1 lb
	salt and pepper	
300 g	unsalted butter	10 oz
1 tbsp each	chopped parsley and chervil	1 tbsp each
1 tsp	chopped tarragon	1 tsp
½ litre	fish fumet, made from sole carcasses and trimmings (*page 174*)	18 fl oz

Spread the fillets out, skin side up, on paper towels and place more towels over them, pressing well to sponge them dry. Slit the surface membrane of each fillet 3 or 4 times diagonally. Sprinkle with salt and pepper and place a thin sliver of butter half the total length of a fillet on the wider half of each. Fold over the narrower half of each fillet and press gently. Cut the remaining butter into small pieces and leave to soften.

Butter the bottom and sides of a copper sauté pan or a low, wide, fireproof earthenware or enamelled cast-iron casserole just large enough to hold the fillets without having to squeeze them in; sprinkle the bottom with half of the chopped herbs and place the folded fillets side by side on this bed. Pour in enough fumet barely to cover the fillets, sprinkle the surface lightly with salt and pepper (remembering that the fumet will be radically reduced, concentrating the saltiness) and the remaining chopped herbs. Press a piece of generously buttered greaseproof paper—cut to cover the top of the cooking utensil—over the fillets, buttered side down. Everything up to this point, assuming the fumet to be cold, may be done an hour or so ahead of time if desired.

Place the casserole, covered, over a medium to high heat (if earthenware is placed over a fireproof pad, the heat may be turned to maximum). As the liquid heats, check it regularly by lifting the edge of the buttered paper, and, the instant boiling point is reached, remove the fish from the heat and leave, tightly covered, to poach for 7 to 8 minutes. It is important that the fish should not boil.

Lift out the fillets, one by one, allowing them to drain well, and place them on a heated serving platter. Cover with a heated plate to keep them warm while finishing the sauce.

Transfer the liquid to a small saucepan. Reduce the sauce over a high heat, stirring constantly. The cooking liquid should be reduced to the consistency of a light syrup and removed immediately from the heat. One must sense the right moment. The liquid will pass first through a period of frothy "foaming up", then settle into a regular boil, which is soon transformed into a rapid staccato surface bubbling. Several seconds later it will arrive at the precise consistency desired. There should be only a few spoonfuls of liquid remaining. Once the liquid acquires a light syrupy consistency, remove the pan from the heat and, with a small whisk, whip in the softened butter in 3 batches, adding more butter as the preceding batch is absorbed.

Pour the sauce over the fillets and serve immediately. The sauce will be consistent and creamy in texture without feeling "thick". If wished, garnish with cucumbers.

RICHARD OLNEY
THE FRENCH MENU COOKBOOK

Soles Stewed in Cream

(Options: lemon sole, brill, flounder, megrim)

To serve 3 or 4		
3 or 4	medium-sized sole, cleaned	3 or 4
	salt	
30 to 60 cl	double cream	½ to 1 pint
	small blade mace, pounded	
	cayenne pepper	
2 tbsp	lemon juice	2 tbsp
2 tsp	grated lemon rind (optional)	2 tsp
1 tsp	arrowroot (optional)	1 tsp
1 tbsp	milk (optional)	1 tbsp

Put the soles into slightly salted boiling water, and simmer them for 2 minutes only; lift them out, and let them drain; lay them in a wide stewpan with as much cream as will nearly cover them; add a good seasoning of pounded mace, cayenne and salt; stew the fish gently for 6 to 10 minutes, or until the

flesh parts readily from the bones; dish them, stir the lemon juice into the sauce, pour it over the soles, and send them immediately to the table.

Some lemon rind may be boiled in the cream, if approved; arrowroot, mixed with milk, may be stirred into the sauce (should it require thickening) before the lemon juice is added.

ELIZABETH RAY (EDITOR)
THE BEST OF ELIZA ACTON

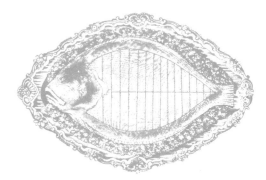

Sole Fillets in the Zandvoort Style

Zandvoortse Tongfilets

(Options: John Dory, lemon sole, small brill)

The Dutch fishing fleet takes something like 4 out of every 5 sole caught in the North Sea. Although many of these are exported, the sole is something of a Dutch speciality. Zandvoort lies south of the great Dutch fishing port of IJmuiden

To serve 4		
8	sole fillets	8
4	large tomatoes, halved crosswise, seeded and loose pulp removed	4
	salt and freshly ground pepper	
200 g	butter	7 oz
1	garlic clove, chopped	1
3 tbsp	chopped parsley	3 tbsp
1	lemon, sliced	1

Sprinkle the tomato halves with salt and pepper, then set them side by side in a buttered ovenproof dish. Lightly salt the fish fillets and roll them up. Fit one rolled fillet, upright, into each tomato half. Take about half the butter, divide it into 8 knobs and put one on top of each rolled fillet. Put the dish in an oven preheated to 200°C (400°F or Mark 6) and leave it for 15 minutes.

Meanwhile, melt the remaining butter in a pan. Fry the garlic in the butter until this sauce is lightly coloured. Add the parsley. Take the dish out of the oven and pour the sauce over the fish. Garnish the dish with lemon slices and serve with fluffy mashed potatoes.

TON VAN ES
HET VOLKOMEN VISBOEK

Gratin of Sole
Sole au Gratin
(Options: lemon sole, flounder, small brill, plaice, witch)

To serve 2

500 g	sole, cleaned	1 lb
60 g	butter	2 oz
2 tbsp	chopped parsley	2 tbsp
4 tbsp	chopped Welsh or spring onions, or shallots	4 tbsp
125 g	mushrooms, chopped	4 oz
	salt and white pepper	
30 g	dry white breadcrumbs	1 oz
10 cl	white wine, or 4 tbsp each brandy and strained, cooled fish fumet (page 174)	4 fl oz

Butter a gratin dish and sprinkle the base with half the parsley, onions or shallots, and mushrooms. Season with salt and white pepper and lay the fish on top. Cover with the rest of the chopped ingredients and top with the breadcrumbs. Add the wine or brandy and fumet, melt the remaining butter and sprinkle it over the dish.

Bake in an oven preheated to 220°C (425°F or Mark 7) for 15 minutes or until the fish is cooked and the top is crisp and golden. If necessary, at the end of the cooking, the dish may be passed under a hot grill to colour the top.

L. E. AUDOT
LA CUISINIÈRE DE LA CAMPAGNE ET DE LA VILLE

Turban of Sole Fillets
Filets de Sole en Torsade
(Options: flounder, lemon sole, brill, John Dory, salmon)

If desired, salmon can be combined with sole, or with any of the other suggested options, arranging the fillets in an alternating pattern (see page 86). The mousseline can be flavoured according to taste.

To serve 6 to 8

10	sole fillets	10
	salt and pepper	
750 g	mousseline (page 174)	1½ lb
30 g	butter, melted	1 oz
	velouté sauce (page 173)	

Butter a savarin, or ring, mould. Season the fillets and use them to line the mould by arranging them crosswise, slightly overlapping, with the ends hanging over the sides of the mould. Pack the mousseline into the mould, and tap the

mould to settle the contents. Fold the ends of the fillets over the mousseline and press them down to fix them in place. Put the mould in a larger pan, and pour hot water into the pan to come half way up the sides of the mould. Poach in an oven preheated to 170°C (325°F or Mark 3) for 35 to 40 minutes, or until the surface of the turban is springy to the touch.

Take the turban out of the oven, allow it to rest for a few minutes, then turn it out on to a warmed round dish. Brush with the melted butter, and serve with a velouté sauce.

PROSPER MONTAGNÉ
LAROUSSE GASTRONOMIQUE

Sole Stewed in Cider with Mussels
Sole en Matelote à la Normande
(Options: lemon sole, fillets of sea bream or John Dory)

This is not the elaborate restaurant dish called *sole à la normande*, but rather the primitive version from which, no doubt, the more luxurious concoction derived. Be sure to use a porcelain or enamel-lined dish for this recipe; tin or unlined cast-iron will turn the cider black.

To serve 2

500 g	sole, cleaned and skinned on both sides	1 lb
1	large onion, finely sliced	1
15 g	butter	½ oz
1.25 litres	small mussels, scrubbed	2 pints
10 cl	dry cider	4 fl oz
	salt and pepper	
	parsley butter, made by mashing 15 g (½ oz) butter with 1 tbsp chopped parsley	

Melt the onion in the butter, stewing it very gently until it is quite soft but still pale yellow. Meanwhile, put the cleaned mussels in a saucepan with the cider, set them over a high heat and extract them as soon as they open.

Put the onion mixture, well-seasoned, into a long, shallow fireproof dish. Put the sole on top. Through a muslin, pour in enough stock from the mussels barely to cover it. Cover the dish, and cook in a moderate oven, preheated to 180°C (350°F or Mark 4), for 15 minutes. Remove from the oven, put the shelled mussels round the fish, and the parsley butter on top of it. Return the dish to the oven for 5 minutes, just sufficient time to heat the mussels through. Serve in the same dish.

ELIZABETH DAVID
FRENCH PROVINCIAL COOKING

Poached Stuffed Sole with Truffles

La Sole Fourrée au Fumet de Meursault

(Options: French sole, lemon sole)

To justify the title, both the fish fumet and the velouté called for in this recipe should be made with Mersault, a white Burgundy wine, but any good white wine will serve. The technique of stuffing sole is demonstrated on page 67; and the technique of making a mousseline is shown on page 84.

To serve 4

Four 300 g	sole, skinned and cleaned	Four 10 oz
½ litre	fish fumet (*page 174*)	18 fl oz
	thin slices truffle	
¼ litre	velouté (*page 173*)	8 fl oz
10 cl	double cream	4 fl oz
1	egg yolk	1
1 tsp	lemon juice	1 tsp
15 g	butter	½ oz
	Mousseline stuffing	
300 g	sole fillets	10 oz
	salt and pepper	
125 g	mushrooms, finely chopped	4 oz
1	small truffle, finely chopped	1
15 g	butter	½ oz
1	egg white	1
¼ litre	double cream	8 fl oz

First make the mousseline stuffing. Season the chopped mushrooms and sauté them in the butter. When the mushrooms' liquid has evaporated, stir in the truffle and set aside to cool. Pound the sole fillets thoroughly in a mortar; pass the fish through a fine sieve and return it to the mortar. Pound in the egg white and season with salt and pepper. Turn the mixture into a bowl and refrigerate over crushed ice for 1 hour. With a spatula, work the cream into the mixture, a little at a time, refrigerating between each addition. Finally, mix the mushrooms and truffle into the chilled fish mixture.

Cut each of the sole along the length of the backbone and lift the fillets without detaching them completely. Fill the pockets with the prepared mousseline stuffing.

Arrange the fish in a large buttered sauté pan or ovenproof dish. Pour over the fumet, lay a buttered paper over the surface and cook in an oven preheated to 180°C (350°F or Mark 4) for 15 to 20 minutes, or until the mousseline is firm to the touch. Remove the fish and trim off the fins. Arrange the sole on a warmed serving dish and garnish with truffle slices.

Reduce the cooking liquor over a brisk heat and add it to the simmering velouté. Bind the sauce with the cream mixed with the egg yolk. Off the heat, whisk in the lemon juice and the butter. Pour the sauce over the fish and serve.

CURNONSKY
BONS PLATS, BONS VINS

Plaice with Normandy Sauce

Carrelet à la Sauce Normande

(Options: sole, small turbot, brill, flounder)

To serve 2

1	large plaice	1
100 g	butter	3½ oz
	salt and pepper	
30 cl	white wine	½ pint
2 or 3 tsp	flour	2 or 3 tsp
30	live mussels, scrubbed	30
10 or 12	mushrooms	10 or 12
2 tbsp	lemon juice	2 tbsp
4	egg yolks	4
4 tbsp	double cream	4 tbsp

Put the plaice in a generously buttered ovenproof dish. Season the fish, pour in 10 cl (4 fl oz) of the wine and put the dish in an oven preheated to 180°C (350°F or Mark 4) for about 20 minutes, or until the flesh of the fish is cooked.

Put 30 g (1 oz) of butter in a saucepan and, over a moderate heat, stir in the flour until the mixture becomes golden. Moisten this with butter and wine from the plaice, leaving behind in the dish only enough liquid to ensure that the fish does not dry up. Reduce the sauce mixture by half.

Put the mussels in a saucepan with 20 cl (7 fl oz) of the wine, cover and shake over a high heat until all the shells have opened. Poach the mushrooms for 2 to 3 minutes in a little water with the lemon juice, 15 g (½ oz) butter and a pinch of salt. Add the strained juice from the mussels and the mushrooms to the sauce; reduce it all a second time by half, then bind it with the egg yolks, mixed with the cream. Arrange the mussels and mushrooms around the plaice, and pour the sauce on top. Dot the dish here and there with the remaining butter, cut into small pieces; let the fish sit in the oven for 2 minutes, to allow the butter to melt, then serve.

ALAN AND JANE DAVIDSON
DUMAS ON FOOD

Grilled Fish Javanese-Style

Panggang Ikan Bawal Djawa

(Options: plaice, flounder, lemon sole)

To serve 2

500 g	flat fish, cleaned and skinned	1 lb
2 tbsp	soy sauce	2 tbsp
1 tbsp	brown sugar	1 tbsp
1	garlic clove, crushed	1
1 tbsp	water	1 tbsp
15 g	butter, melted	$\frac{1}{2}$ oz
5	fresh red chili peppers, finely sliced	5
1 tbsp	lemon juice	1 tbsp

Mix half the soy sauce and half the sugar with the garlic and water. Marinate the fish in this mixture for about 1 hour. Grill it on both sides over a very low heat, basting with the remaining marinade as it cooks. (You can do this under the oven grill, but a charcoal fire produces a more delicious result.) When the fish is tender, after about 15 to 20 minutes in all, remove it from the grill and lay it on a warmed plate. Pour the melted butter over it, then sprinkle with a final spice mixture made from the sliced chili peppers, remaining soy sauce and sugar, and the lemon juice.

ROSEMARY BRISSENDEN
SOUTH EAST ASIAN FOOD

Plaice with Bacon, Hamburg-Style

Scholle "Hamburger Art"

(Options: lemon sole, sole)

To serve 4

Two 600 g	plaice, cleaned, rinsed and patted dry	Two 1¼ lb
2 tbsp	lemon juice	2 tbsp
125 g	smoked streaky bacon, diced	4 oz
	salt	
	flour	
	lemon, cut into wedges	
6 to 8	sprigs parsley	6 to 8

Sprinkle the lemon juice over the fish and leave them for 10 minutes. Meanwhile, fry the diced bacon in a large frying pan. When the bacon is crisp, remove it and keep it warm, leaving the fat in the pan.

Sprinkle salt over the fish, and coat them with flour. Fry them in the bacon fat in the pan, allowing 3 to 4 minutes on each side, until they are golden-brown all over. Take great care that the heat is not too high and that the fish, with their light dusting of flour, do not burn.

Arrange the fish on a warmed platter with their more golden sides (the undersides, which were originally white) uppermost. Sprinkle the bacon over them, place the pieces of lemon around them, and garnish the dish with the parsley.

HEINZ KATZ
MARITIME LECKEREIEN
DAS FISCHKOCHBUCH VON DER WATERKANT

Fish Sauté Meunière

Poisson Meunière

(Options: plaice, sole, flounder, lemon sole, whiting)

For instructions on how to clarify butter, see page 72.

To serve 4

4	fish fillets, or whole small fish	4
10 cl	milk	4 fl oz
30 g	flour	1 oz
	salt and pepper	
	olive oil	
1 tbsp	lemon juice	1 tbsp
2 tbsp	chopped parsley	2 tbsp
4	lemon slices, peel removed	4
60 g	butter	2 oz

Dip the fish in milk, then in flour seasoned with salt and pepper. Put about 5 mm ($\frac{1}{4}$ inch) of oil in a frying pan and heat until very hot. Add the fish and cook until golden-brown on both sides. Remove to a warmed serving dish, sprinkle with a little pepper, a few drops of lemon juice and a little chopped parsley. Place the slices of lemon on top. Cook the butter in the same pan until it is nut-brown and pour it over the fish.

LOUIS DIAT
FRENCH COOKING FOR AMERICANS

Baked Fish with Horseradish

Ryba Zapiekana w Sosie Chrzanowym

(Options: plaice, lemon sole, flounder, haddock, redfish)

To serve 4

750 g	fish fillets, or one 750 g (1½ lb) fish, cleaned	1½ lb
	salt	
1 tsp	vinegar	1 tsp
30 g	butter, melted	1 oz

Horseradish sauce		
100 g	grated horseradish	3½ oz
1	medium-sized apple, peeled and shredded	1
15 to 20 cl	soured cream	6 fl oz
	salt	
	sugar	

Sprinkle the fish with salt and vinegar. Place it in a buttered baking dish and sprinkle with the melted butter. Bake in an oven preheated to 200°C (400°F or Mark 6) for 10 minutes. Meanwhile, mix the horseradish with the apple. Stir in the soured cream and season with salt and a pinch of sugar. Pour the horseradish sauce over the fish. Bake for another 15 minutes, and serve with boiled potatoes.

ALINA ZERÁNSKA
THE ART OF POLISH COOKING

Halibut Patties with Cream Sauce

Heilagfiskibuff með Rjómasósu

(Options: turbot, angler-fish, wolf-fish, sea bream)

To serve 4

750 g	halibut, skinned, boned and cut into 2.5 cm (1 inch) thick pieces	1½ lb
2	medium-sized onions, sliced	2
100 g	butter	3½ oz
1 tbsp	flour, seasoned with salt and pepper	1 tbsp
5 tbsp	double cream	5 tbsp

Flatten the halibut pieces slightly with the palm of your hand. Lightly brown the onions in half the butter in a frying pan, then transfer them to a warm plate. Add the remaining butter to the pan and heat it while coating the pieces of fish with the seasoned flour. Fry them in the butter, until they are well browned on both sides. This may take up to 10 minutes.

Arrange the fish pieces on a warmed serving platter and strew the onions over them. Keep them hot.

Add a little water to the juices in the frying pan and boil up together. Take the pan off the heat and stir in the cream. Then cook the sauce gently for a few minutes and strain it into a warmed sauceboat.

Serve the fish with boiled potatoes at one end of the dish, and pass the sauce separately. This is a very good hot dish to serve with cold dishes at a buffet meal.

HELGA SIGURÐARDÓTTIR
MATUR OG DRYKKUR

Fish Stew from Gotland

Gotländsk Fiskgryta

(Options: flounder, plaice, hake, cod, angel shark, redfish)

To serve 4 or 5

1 kg	fish, filleted	2 to 2½ lb
15 g	butter	½ oz
5 or 6	large potatoes, sliced	5 or 6
2	leeks, white parts only, sliced	2
1 tbsp	finely chopped chives	1 tbsp
1 tbsp	finely chopped parsley	1 tbsp
	salt and white pepper	

Butter the bottom of a fireproof casserole and make alternate layers of potatoes and leeks, sprinkling each layer with chives and parsley. Add salt and pepper, and enough water to cover. Cook, covered, over a low heat for 20 to 30 minutes, or until the potatoes are almost done. Lay the fish fillets on top and cover with buttered greaseproof paper. Cover the casserole and continue cooking for about 10 minutes, or until the fish are done. Season to taste with more salt, if required, and serve directly from the casserole.

OSKAR JAKOBSSON
GOOD FOOD IN SWEDEN

Halibut in Lemon Cream

(Options: sturgeon, John Dory, angler-fish)

To serve 4

1 kg	halibut fillet, cut into serving pieces and wiped with a damp cloth	2 to 2½ lb
	salt	
¼ litre	double cream	8 fl oz
1 tbsp	grated onion	1 tbsp
1 tsp	grated lemon rind	1 tsp
4 tsp	lemon juice	4 tsp
	freshly ground black pepper (optional)	
8	thin lemon slices	8

Sprinkle the fish pieces lightly with salt. Arrange them in a single layer in a shallow, buttered baking dish. Combine the cream, onion, lemon rind, lemon juice and ½ teaspoon salt and pour over the fish. Bake, uncovered, in a fairly hot oven, preheated to 200°C (400°F or Mark 6), for 20 minutes. Spoon the cream sauce over it as you serve the fish. Grind over some black pepper, if liked. Garnish with the lemon slices.

SHIRLEY SARVIS
CRAB AND ABALONE, WEST COAST WAYS WITH FISH AND SHELLFISH

Halibut with Leeks and Black Olives

(Options: swordfish, angler-fish, turbot)

To serve 4

750 g	halibut, divided into four steaks	1½ lb
2 tbsp	olive oil	2 tbsp
60 g	butter	2 oz
4	leeks, white and green parts, thinly sliced	4
8	large black olives, stoned and chopped	8
2 tbsp	white wine	2 tbsp
60 cl	water	1 pint
	salt and black pepper	
2 tbsp	chopped parsley	2 tbsp

Heat the oil and butter in a shallow, heavy pan that will accommodate the halibut steaks comfortably. Throw in the leeks and olives, and cook briskly until the leeks are soft; a considerable amount of liquid will come from the leeks. Add the wine and water, season and stir well. Now put in the fish (the steaks will not be completely covered) and bring all to simmering point. Simmer very gently for 10 minutes, basting continuously the parts that are not submerged. Then turn the steaks and repeat the operation for a further 10 minutes. Remove the steaks to a hot dish.

Boil up the contents of the pan for half a minute. Pour the sauce over the steaks, sprinkle with parsley and serve.

GEORGE LASSALLE
THE ADVENTUROUS FISH COOK

Brill in Cream and Shrimp Sauce

Barbue à la Havraise

(Options: turbot, flounder, large dab)

To serve 6 to 8

1 kg	brill, cleaned, scaled and trimmed	2 to 2½ lb
½ litre	vinegar court-bouillon (*page 174*)	18 fl oz
250 g	live shrimps	8 oz
150 g	butter	5 oz
	salt and pepper	
30 g	flour	1 oz
½ litre	double cream	18 fl oz

In a saucepan, bring the court-bouillon to the boil. Add the shrimps, boil them for 2 minutes, then drain and peel them. In the dark side of the brill, make an incision the length of the backbone. Grease a gratin dish with 60 g (2 oz) of the butter, sprinkle with salt and pepper, and put in the fish, white side up. Dot the fish with another 60 g (2 oz) of butter, salt it, and cover the gratin dish. Cook, basting from time to time, in an oven preheated to 170°C (325°F or Mark 3), for 30 minutes, or until the fish is done.

Meanwhile, gently heat the remaining butter in a saucepan and mix in the flour. Gradually stir in the cream, never allowing the sauce to come to the boil. When all the cream has been used, add the shrimps. Remove the fish to a warmed platter and stir the cooking juices into the sauce. Return the fish to the gratin dish and pour over the sauce. Turn the oven to 180°C (350°F or Mark 4) and put the dish, uncovered, in the oven for 8 to 10 minutes. Serve the fish hot on warmed plates.

LA GASTRONOMIE

Steamed Fish

Jing Yü

(Options: flounder, sole, lemon sole, dab, ballan wrasse)

"Golden needles" (gum jum) *are dried tiger lily buds. These, together with dried Chinese dates* (hoong joe) *and mushrooms, are obtainable from Chinese food shops.*

To serve 2

1	medium-sized fish, cleaned	1
½ tsp	salt	½ tsp
¼ tsp	pepper	¼ tsp
½ tsp	sugar	½ tsp
2 tsp	cornflour	2 tsp
2 tbsp	soy sauce	2 tbsp
2 tbsp	oil	2 tbsp
2 each	dried Chinese mushrooms and dried Chinese dates, soaked in warm water for 30 minutes, or until soft, and drained	2 each
12	golden needles, soaked in warm water for 15 minutes, or until soft	12
2	slices ginger root, cut into fine slivers	2
1	spring onion, chopped	1
1	thin slice smoked ham, cut into *julienne* strips	1

Mix together the salt, pepper, sugar, cornflour, soy sauce and oil. Place the fish in a dish and rub it all over with half of the seasoned mixture.

Slice the mushrooms and dates finely. Cut the golden needles in half. Combine the remaining seasoned mixture with the mushrooms, dates, golden needles, ginger root, spring onion and ham. Spread this mixture over the surface of the fish. Place in a steamer and steam for about 20 minutes.

DOREEN YEN HUNG FENG
THE JOY OF CHINESE COOKING

Baked Turbot

(Options: brill, angel shark)

To serve 3

500 g	turbot, cleaned	1 lb
¼ litre	yogurt, lightly beaten	8 fl oz
1 tbsp	lemon juice	1 tbsp
2 tbsp	white wine	2 tbsp
1	blade mace, pounded	1
1	egg yolk, lightly beaten	1
	salt and pepper	
60 g	breadcrumbs, lightly sautéed in butter	2 oz
2 tbsp	finely chopped parsley	2 tbsp

Place the fish in a buttered baking dish. Mix together the yogurt, lemon juice, wine, mace and egg yolk and pour it over the fish. Add the seasoning. Cover with the breadcrumbs and bake in an oven preheated to 180°C (350°F or Mark 4) for 45 to 50 minutes. Serve hot, garnished with parsley.

IRFAN ORGA
COOKING WITH YOGURT

Turbot Fillets with Leeks and Cream Sauce

Suprême de Turbot aux Poireaux

(Options: brill, small halibut, large flounder)

This recipe is from Madame Sylvie Beauvalot, of La Bretagne restaurant, Saint-Omer, Brittany.

To serve 4

Four 200 g	turbot fillets, unskinned	Four 7 oz
90 g	butter	3 oz
2	shallots, finely sliced	2
	salt and pepper	
About ¼ litre	fish fumet (*page 174*)	About 8 fl oz
4	leeks, white parts only, finely sliced	4
15 cl	double cream	¼ pint
4	thin slices truffle (optional)	4

Place the turbot fillets skin-side down, side by side in a buttered sauté pan. Add the shallots, salt and pepper, and fish fumet just to cover the fillets. Cover with buttered grease-proof paper, and cook in an oven preheated to 180°C (350°F or Mark 4) for about 10 minutes.

Meanwhile, put the leeks into a fireproof casserole with salt, pepper, 15 g (½ oz) of the butter and a couple of table-spoons of water and cook, covered, for about 5 minutes. Keep the leeks warm until the dish is ready to serve.

When the fish fillets are cooked, remove them and keep

them hot. Over a high heat, reduce the cooking liquid to a syrupy consistency. Add the cream and reduce again until the sauce coats a spoon. Off the heat, whisk in 60 g (2 oz) of butter, previously softened or diced.

Remove the skin from the turbot fillets, and arrange them, surrounded by the leeks, on a warmed serving dish. Coat with the sauce, put a slice of truffle on each fillet, and serve.

LA REYNIÈRE
200 RECETTES DES MEILLEURES CUISINIÈRES DE FRANCE

Mackerel, Bonito, Tuna and Swordfish

Grilled Mackerel with Cumin

Maquereaux Grillés au Cumin

(Option: small bonito)

The arrissa called for in this recipe is a spicy paste made from red chili peppers and garlic, seasoned with coriander, cara-way and salt. Widely used in Tunisian cooking, it is obtain-able from Oriental delicatessens. If unavailable, substitute cayenne or paprika. The technique for scoring each side of a fish is demonstrated on page 80.

To serve 4

1 kg	medium-sized mackerel, washed and cleaned, heads removed	2 to 2½ lb
½ tsp	arrissa, mixed with 3 tbsp water	½ tsp
3 tbsp	oil	3 tbsp
2	garlic cloves, crushed	2
2 tsp	ground cumin	2 tsp
	salt	
1	lemon, quartered	1

Make 2 diagonal cuts in each side of each fish. Put the *arrissa* into a large shallow bowl with the oil, garlic, cumin and salt. Mix together well, and put the mackerel into the bowl to marinate for 15 minutes, turning over the fish from time to time. Then grill the fish for about 7 to 8 minutes on each side, over charcoal or under a preheated grill. Arrange them on a large dish and serve very hot, with the lemon.

EDMOND ZEITOUN
250 RECETTES CLASSIQUES DE CUISINE TUNISIENNE

Mackerel in Port with Leeks
Maquereaux aux Poireaux
To serve 8

8	mackerel, cleaned and washed, heads and tails removed and reserved, each fish cut into 3 pieces	8
40 g	butter	1½ oz
1	carrot, sliced	1
1	large onion, roughly chopped	1
1	bouquet garni	1
	salt and pepper	
20 cl	port	7 fl oz
35 cl	water	12 fl oz
5	leeks, white part only, sliced crosswise	5
1 tbsp	flour	1 tbsp

Melt 15 g (½ oz) of the butter in a large saucepan and sauté the heads and tails of the mackerel for 5 minutes. Add the carrot, onion, bouquet garni, salt and pepper, port and water. Cover and cook over a medium heat for 15 minutes. Strain the stock, return it to the cleaned pan, and leave to simmer over a low heat. Meanwhile, in another pan, sauté the leeks in 15 g (½ oz) of the butter for 2 to 3 minutes. Add the leeks and the pieces of mackerel to the simmering stock, and let them simmer very gently, covered, for 10 minutes. With a slotted spoon, remove the fish and leeks to a warmed serving dish. Blend the remaining butter with the flour and stir this *beurre manié* into the stock. Cook for a minute or two until lightly thickened, pour this sauce over the fish, and serve.

ROBERT J. COURTINE
MON BOUQUET DE RECETTES

Hot Masala Mackerel
(Options: pilchard, herring)
To serve 6

6	mackerel, cleaned, halved crosswise and drained	6
1 tsp	ground turmeric	1 tsp
	salt	
8 tbsp	oil	8 tbsp

Masala		
12	dried red chili peppers, seeded	12
8	garlic cloves	8
1 tsp	cumin seeds	1 tsp
¼ tsp	mustard seeds	¼ tsp
2	medium-sized onions	2
1 tbsp	sugar	1 tbsp
4	peppercorns	4
2.5 cm	stick cinnamon, or 1 tsp ground cinnamon	1 inch
1 cm	ginger root	½ inch

Sprinkle the fish with the turmeric and a little salt. Heat the oil in a pan and fry the mackerel pieces until golden-brown on both sides. Remove the fish and set it aside.

Remove the pan from the heat. Grind the masala ingredients to a smooth paste in a mortar or blender then mix the paste into the oil remaining in the pan. Add about 15 to 20 cl (about 6 fl oz) water and mix well. Now place the fish in this mixture. Return the pan to a fairly low heat, and simmer for about 10 minutes, or until the fish is cooked. Serve hot.

PREMILA LAL
SEA-FOOD DISHES

Mackerel with Fennel and Gooseberries
Maquereaux au Fenouil et Groseilles dans la Saison

For best results, the fish should be grilled over embers, using a fish grill: line one side of the grill with fennel stalks, place the fish in the grill, arrange the rest of the fennel stalks on top and close the grill. The technique of boning through the back is demonstrated on page 66.

To serve 4

Four 250 g	mackerel, washed, cleaned and boned through the back	Four 8 oz
	salt and pepper	
30 g	butter, melted	1 oz
8	wild fennel stalks	8
60 g	butter	2 oz
1 tbsp	chopped fennel leaves	1 tbsp
	grated nutmeg	
1 tsp	flour	1 tsp
1 tbsp	vinegar	1 tbsp
15 cl	water	¼ pint
125 g	white or green gooseberries	4 oz

Lay the mackerel in a dish, season them with salt and pepper, pour on the melted butter, and turn the fish to coat them on both sides. Put four of the fennel stalks on a hot barbecue grill and lay a fish on each one. When the fish are cooked on one side, after 5 to 7 minutes, put four more fennel stalks on the grill and turn the fish over, on to the fresh fennel, and grill for a further 5 to 7 minutes.

Meanwhile, melt the butter in a saucepan. Add the chopped fennel leaves and season with salt, pepper and nutmeg. Stir in the flour, then add the vinegar and water. When the sauce has thickened, add the gooseberries and simmer for 10 minutes. Taste for seasoning.

When the fish are done, arrange them on a warmed serving dish side by side, open up the slits in the back, and pour the sauce into the slits and over the fish.

VINCENT DE LA CHAPELLE
LE CUISINIER MODERNE

Mackerel Baked with Tomatoes and Potatoes

Maquereaux La Varenne

(Options: herring, pilchards)

To serve 8

8	small mackerel, cleaned and washed	8
1 tsp	thyme	1 tsp
1	bay leaf, finely crumbled	1
	salt and pepper	
60 g	butter	2 oz
2	potatoes, diced, rinsed and dried in a towel	2
2	tomatoes, skinned, seeded and diced	2
2 tbsp	chopped parsley	2 tbsp
2 tsp	lemon juice	2 tsp
	Duxelles	
3 tbsp	olive oil	3 tbsp
1	small onion, chopped	1
1	shallot, chopped	1
150 g	mushrooms, finely diced	5 oz
	salt and pepper	
10 cl	dry white wine	4 fl oz

To make the *duxelles*, heat the oil and sauté the onion and shallot over a low heat until softened. Add the mushrooms, raise the heat, and season with salt and pepper. Cook for 5 minutes, stirring. Moisten with the wine. Boil rapidly, stirring, until nearly all the liquid has evaporated. Spread out the *duxelles* in a large, oval fireproof dish.

Mix together the thyme, bay leaf, and salt and pepper. Rub the fish, inside and out, with this seasoning mixture. Lay the fish on top of the *duxelles*.

Heat half of the butter, and sauté the potatoes for 10

minutes, or until they are almost tender. Add the tomatoes and cook for 2 minutes more. Cover the fish with the potatoes and tomatoes, and dot with the remaining butter, cut into small bits. Heat the dish on the stove for two or three minutes then transfer it to an oven preheated to 200°C (400°F or Mark 6). Bake for 12 to 14 minutes. Sprinkle with the parsley and the lemon juice, and serve in the cooking dish.

PROSPER MONTAGNÉ
MON MENU

Bonito with the Sauce Used for Partridge

Bonito en Salsa Perdiz

(Options: large mackerel, skipjack, swordfish)

The bonito is a very popular fish in the north of Spain. Among the numerous recipes which are to be found along Spain's Atlantic coast, this is one which calls for the use of a little chocolate. Spaniards are the only Europeans who regularly make use of chocolate in fish dishes, perhaps because chocolate was first introduced to Europe in Spain.

To serve 4

600 g	bonito steak	1¼ lb
1 tbsp	olive oil	1 tbsp
50 g	green bacon, chopped	2 oz
10 cl	white wine	4 fl oz
3	onions, quartered	3
2	garlic cloves, chopped	2
1 tbsp	fine dry breadcrumbs	1 tbsp
½ to 1 tbsp	grated cooking chocolate	½ to 1 tbsp
¼ litre	meat stock	8 fl oz
4	bread slices, fried	4

Put the piece of bonito, either whole or cut in half, in a fireproof earthenware cooking pot with the olive oil. Add the bacon, white wine, onions and garlic. Cook over a medium heat for 5 minutes, then turn the fish and cook for 5 minutes more, until the fish is golden all over. Cover the pot and cook over a low heat for 2 hours.

Transfer the fish to a warmed earthenware casserole and add the breadcrumbs, chocolate and stock to the remaining contents of the pot. Mix well together, then strain the sauce through a fine sieve over the fish. Serve the fish garnished with the slices of fried bread.

ANA MARIA CALERA
LA COCINA VASCA

Bonito with Peas

Palamita con Piselli

(Options: large mackerel, tuna)

To serve 4

1 kg	bonito, fins, tail and head removed, cleaned, washed, dried and cut into thick slices	2 to 2½ lb
10 cl	olive oil	4 fl oz
3	garlic cloves, chopped	3
4 tbsp	chopped parsley	4 tbsp
400 g	tomatoes, skinned, seeded and coarsely chopped, or drained, canned tomatoes	14 oz
	salt and pepper	
1 kg	peas, shelled, parboiled for 5 minutes in salted water with 1 garlic clove and 1 sprig parsley, and drained	2 to 2½ lb

Heat the olive oil in a large skillet and lightly sauté the garlic and 3 tablespoons of the parsley. Before the garlic is golden, add the tomatoes. Season with salt and pepper and after 5 minutes add the fish slices. Cook, uncovered, for 10 minutes, then add the drained, parboiled peas. Simmer, covered, over a slow heat for another 10 minutes. Sprinkle with the remaining parsley and serve.

PAOLO PETRONI
IL LIBRO DELLA VERA CUCINA MARINARA

Tuna with Chartreuse

Thon à la Chartreuse

(Options: large bonito, skipjack, swordfish)

To serve 4

750 g	tuna steak, soaked in water and vinegar for 15 minutes	1½ lb
12	large lettuce leaves	12
2	medium-sized onions, sliced	2
500 g	tomatoes, skinned, seeded and coarsely chopped	1 lb
4	lemon slices	4
	salt and pepper	
4 tbsp	olive oil	4 tbsp
10 cl	water	4 fl oz
10 cl	white wine	4 fl oz
3 tbsp	Chartreuse	3 tbsp

Line the base of a round gratin dish with 4 of the lettuce leaves, then put in a layer made up of half the onion, half the tomato and 2 lemon slices. Season with salt and pepper. Put the tuna on top and cover with a layer made up of the rest of the onion, tomato and lemon, followed by a layer of the remaining lettuce leaves. (This final layer of lettuce has to be thicker than the first, because the top leaves will burn during the cooking and will have to be removed.) Season again, and add the oil, water, wine and Chartreuse.

Cook in a very cool oven, 150°C (300°F or Mark 2), for 2 hours, basting from time to time. Serve in the same dish, remembering to remove the burnt lettuce leaves from the top.

C. CHANOT-BULLIER
VIEILLES RECETTES DE CUISINE PROVENÇALE

Tuna Chartreuse-Style

Thon à la Chartreuse

(Options: swordfish, porbeagle shark, sturgeon, large bonito)

Chartreuse is a term widely used to describe a braised dish in which the main ingredient is surrounded by leaves—a method traditionally used by the Carthusian monks. The technique of larding a tuna steak with anchovies is shown on page 60.

To serve 4

750 g	tuna steak, about 3 cm (1¼ inches) thick	1½ lb
3 tbsp	lemon juice	3 tbsp
16	anchovy fillets, soaked, drained and halved	16
4 tbsp	olive oil	4 tbsp
1	medium-sized onion, sliced	1
4	medium-sized carrots, finely sliced	4
4	lettuce hearts, blanched	4
100 g	sorrel, shredded	3½ oz
	salt and pepper	
15 to 20 cl	white wine	6 fl oz

Blanch the tuna steak in boiling salted water to which the lemon juice has been added. Remove and drain the fish, then lard it with the anchovy fillets.

Put the oil, onion and carrots into a saucepan. Lay the tuna steak on top and cover the casserole; place it over a low heat and let the fish sweat. Turn the fish over once, arrange the blanched lettuce hearts around it and the sorrel on top of it. Cover the pan again and let the tuna sweat for a few more minutes; then season it with salt and pepper.

When the onion and carrots have begun to brown, and the liquid in the pan is absorbed, pour in the white wine and leave the dish to simmer, covered, for a further 30 minutes. During this time, turn the lettuce hearts over a few times, without disturbing the fish.

To serve, place the sorrel in a heap at one end of a warmed dish, and place the onion and carrots at the other end. Place the tuna steak in the middle and arrange the lettuce hearts around it. Finally, pour the cooking juices over the steak.

J. B. REBOUL
LA CUISINE PROVENÇALE

Tuna Braised with Spinach or Chard

Thon Braisé aux Épinards ou aux Blettes

(Options: bonito, swordfish, sturgeon)

To serve 4 to 6

750 g	fresh tuna steak, skinned	1½ lb
1 kg	spinach or chard leaves, trimmed, washed, parboiled for 2 to 3 minutes and well drained	2 to 2½ lb
10 cl	olive oil	4 fl oz
500 g	tomatoes, skinned, seeded and quartered	1 lb
2	medium-sized onions, chopped	2
6 to 8	garlic cloves	6 to 8
50 g	anchovy fillets, soaked in water, drained and finely chopped	2 oz
1	bouquet garni of thyme, bay leaf and 1 stick celery	1
	salt and pepper	
50 g	butter	2 oz

Immerse the tuna in boiling water for 5 minutes to draw out excess fat. Drain the tuna, put it into a casserole just large enough for the purpose, and add the olive oil, tomatoes, onions, garlic, anchovy and bouquet garni. Season with salt and pepper, but be sparing with the salt because the anchovies will contribute some saltiness. Cook for a minute or two over a medium heat, then turn the tuna steak over and continue cooking, turning frequently, until the steak is coloured on both sides. Add water to cover, bring to the boil, then lower the heat, put the lid half on the casserole and simmer gently for 45 to 50 minutes, or until the tuna is tender. By the end of the cooking, the liquid should have been reduced by half. Remove the bouquet garni.

Meanwhile, sauté the parboiled spinach or chard in the butter and season with salt and pepper. Spread the cooked greens on a warmed serving platter, place the tuna on this bed of greens, and pour the contents of the casserole over the fish.

MOHAMED KOUKI
POISSONS MÉDITERRANÉENS

Fish Teriyaki

(Options: tuna, bonito, mackerel, halibut, eel)

Teriyaki refers to the process of marinating foods in a mixture of soy sauce, *mirin* (sweet rice wine) and *sake* (stronger rice wine), and then grilling them, preferably over charcoal.

	To serve 6	
6	fish fillets or steaks, about 1 kg (2 to 2½ lb) in all	6
6 tbsp	soy sauce	6 tbsp
6 tbsp each	*mirin* and *sake*	6 tbsp each
1	garlic clove, finely chopped (optional)	1

Mix the soy sauce, *mirin* and *sake* together in a small saucepan and bring to the boil. Add the garlic, if using. Remove the pan from the stove and marinate the fish fillets in the soy sauce mixture for 15 to 20 minutes.

Preheat the grill, and cook the pieces at a moderate heat for 5 to 10 minutes on each side, brushing three or four times with the marinade. When done the fish should be coated with a rich brown glaze. Serve immediately.

PETER AND JOAN MARTIN
JAPANESE COOKING

Baked Swordfish

Kılıç Fırında

(Options: porbeagle shark, halibut)

To serve 2 to 4

2	swordfish steaks, 2.5 cm (1 inch) thick	2
	salt and pepper	
4 tbsp	olive oil	4 tbsp
2 bunches	spring onions, including green tops, chopped	2 bunches
3 tbsp	chopped parsley	3 tbsp
3 tbsp	chopped dill	3 tbsp
4 tbsp	tomato juice	4 tbsp
4 tbsp	lemon juice	4 tbsp
6	green olives, stoned (optional)	6

Preheat the oven to 180°C (350°F or Mark 4). Place the steaks on an oiled baking dish. Sprinkle with salt and pepper and pour over the oil. Mix the spring onions, parsley and dill, and spread over the fish. Pour over the tomato and lemon juices. Decorate the top of the steaks with the green olives. Bake for 25 minutes, or until the fish is cooked. Serve hot.

NESET EREN
THE ART OF TURKISH COOKING

Swordfish Pie

Impanata di Pesce Spada

(Options: angler-fish, bonito, porbeagle shark, halibut)

The waters around Sicily are rich fishing grounds for the swordfish. Sicilians have more recipes for this fish than any other people in Europe, and this is one of the best.

To serve 4 to 6

400 g	swordfish steak, skinned, cut into 2.5 cm (1 inch) cubes	14 oz
7 to 8 tbsp	olive oil	7 to 8 tbsp
1	medium-sized onion, finely sliced	1
10 cl	puréed tomato	4 fl oz
1	stick celery, thinly sliced	1
50 g	green olives, stoned and chopped	2 oz
1 tbsp	capers, rinsed and drained	1 tbsp
	salt and pepper	
1	egg	1
4	medium-sized courgettes, trimmed and cut into *julienne* strips	4
50 g	flour	2 oz
15 g	butter	½ oz
3 to 4 tbsp	dry breadcrumbs	3 to 4 tbsp
1	egg yolk	1
	Pastry	
300 g	plain flour	10 oz
2 tbsp	finely grated orange peel	2 tbsp
	salt	
125 g	castor sugar	4 oz
3	egg yolks, lightly beaten	3
50 g	lard, cut into small pieces	2 oz
125 g	butter, cut into small pieces and slightly softened	4 oz

First make the pastry. Put the flour on a pastry board together with the grated orange peel, a pinch of salt and the sugar. Mix these ingredients and make a well in the centre. Pour the egg yolks into the well and add the lard and butter. Knead everything together, but only enough to amalgamate the ingredients. Then form the dough into a ball, wrap it in greaseproof paper and leave it in the refrigerator for an hour.

Heat 4 tablespoons of the olive oil in a fireproof casserole, preferably an earthenware one, and add the onion. Cook it over a very low heat, stirring frequently, until the onion is just lightly coloured.

When the onion is ready, add to it the puréed tomato, the celery, olives, capers and fish. Sprinkle with salt and pepper, mix altogether, cover the casserole and simmer over a very low heat for about 30 minutes, stirring frequently. At the end of the cooking, the sauce should be considerably reduced.

Break the egg into a soup plate, season it and beat it lightly with a fork. Coat the strips of courgette with flour, then dip them in the beaten egg, turning them carefully so that they are well coated.

Heat 3 to 4 tablespoons of olive oil in a frying pan. When the oil is hot, add the courgettes and let them brown over a medium heat, turning them from time to time. When they are done, after about 3 to 4 minutes, drain them on paper towels.

Butter a fairly deep, 23 cm (9 inch) diameter mould (preferably a spring mould). Sprinkle the bottom of the tin with the breadcrumbs, then shake out any loose crumbs. Divide the pastry dough into three parts. Roll out one part into a disc just large enough to cover the bottom of the tin. Put the pastry disc into the tin and prick it all over with a fork. Spread half the fried courgettes evenly over this base, then pour over half the fish mixture. Roll out a second piece of dough the same size as the first and place it in the tin followed by the remaining courgettes, then the rest of the fish mixture. Take care that all these layers are uniform. Finally, roll out the third piece of dough into a disc slightly larger than the first two. Place it on top of the pie, pressing it firmly against the inside wall of the mould to ensure a proper seal. Cut two or three slits in the pastry lid. Lightly beat the egg yolk, and use a pastry brush to brush it over the top of the pie.

Cook the pie in a moderate oven, preheated to 180°C (350°F or Mark 4), for about 45 minutes. Remove it when done, let it rest for a few minutes, then slide a knife blade round the edge. Undo the clasp of the tin and transfer the pie to a serving dish.

A. GOSETTI DELLA SALDA
LA CUCINA ITALIANA

Swordfish Casserole

Teglia di Pesce al Forno

(Options: tuna, turbot, angler-fish, dogfish)

To serve 6

750 g	swordfish, cut into medium-thick steaks	1½ lb
	salt and pepper	
15 cl	olive oil	¼ pint
1 kg	potatoes, thinly sliced	2 to 2½ lb
1	large onion, sliced	1
1	garlic clove, finely chopped	1
4	sprigs parsley, finely chopped	4
½	fresh chili pepper, finely chopped	½

Sprinkle the fish steaks with salt and pepper on both sides. Brush a large, moderately deep baking dish with some of the oil, and cover the bottom with half of the potato and onion slices. Sprinkle with salt and pepper, and add all the fish steaks in a single layer. Sprinkle them with more oil, the garlic and parsley, and scatter the chili pepper over the top. Cover with the remaining potato and onion slices, sprinkle with a little more salt and pepper, and sprinkle over the rest of the oil. Bake in a moderate oven, preheated to 180°C (350°F or Mark 4), for at least 1 hour, or until the potatoes are soft.

ADA BONI
ITALIAN REGIONAL COOKING

Barbecued Swordfish Rolls

Involtini di Pesce Spada

(Options: porbeagle shark, angel shark, dolphin fish)

The pecorino *called for in this recipe is a sharp, sheep's milk cheese, obtainable from delicatessens. If unavailable, substitute sharp* provolone *cheese, diced.*

To serve 4

400 g	swordfish, cut into 12 thin slices	14 oz
50 g	swordfish flesh, poached and chopped	2 oz
125 g	fresh breadcrumbs	4 oz
30 g	grated *pecorino*	1 oz
1 tbsp	capers, chopped	1 tbsp
10	green olives, stoned and chopped	10
3 or 4	sprigs parsley, chopped	3 or 4
1 tbsp	puréed tomato	1 tbsp
	salt	
	cayenne pepper	
2 to 3 tbsp	olive oil	2 to 3 tbsp
16	bay leaves	16
1	large onion, quartered and separated into 16 pieces	1

Pound the fish slices to widen them as much as possible without breaking them. In a bowl mix together the cooked swordfish, breadcrumbs, cheese, capers, olives and parsley. Add the puréed tomato, season with salt and cayenne pepper and moisten with oil. Stir thoroughly. Spread the stuffing on the fish slices, roll up the slices and thread the rolls on to skewers (allowing 3 rolls per skewer), alternating the rolls with bay leaves and onion wedges. Barbecue over a charcoal fire, basting the rolls once or twice with a few drops of olive oil, for about 10 minutes or until the flesh is firm to the touch.

PINO CORRENTI
IL LIBRO D'ORO DELLA CUCINA E DEI VINI DI SICILIA

Sharks, Skates and Rays

Shark Baked with Tomato and Citrus Sauce, Vietnamese-Style

Ngamantha Khayanchinthi si Piyan

(Options: porbeagle shark, dogfish, skate, ray)

To serve 3

500 g	shark meat, cut into 6 serving pieces	1 lb
1 tsp	salt	1 tsp
About 4 tbsp	oil	About 4 tbsp
2 to 4	garlic cloves, crushed	2 to 4
8	sprigs coriander	8
6 tbsp	puréed tomato	6 tbsp
2 tbsp	citrus juice (lime, lemon or bitter orange)	2 tbsp
1 tsp	freshly pulverized dried hot red chili pepper	1 tsp
About 10 cl	water	About 4 fl oz

Rub the salt well into the pieces of fish. Oil a suitable oven dish (large enough to take the pieces of fish side by side, but no larger), and put in the fish.

Heat the remaining oil in a pan, and gently fry the garlic until it turns golden. Then add the coriander, followed a few minutes later by the puréed tomato and citrus juice. Keep stirring the mixture. It will soon give off an irresistible aroma, the sort of smell which creates total confidence in the cook. At this point, pour it over the fish, sprinkle on the chili pepper, and add the water.

Cook in an oven preheated to 220°C (425°F or Mark 7) for 25 to 30 minutes. The exact cooking time will depend on the thickness of the pieces of shark, but you can tell when the dish is ready by looking to see that oil has collected on top of the pieces and by probing the meat with a fork.

ALAN DAVIDSON
SEAFOOD OF SOUTH-EAST ASIA

Dogfish Croquettes

Palombo da Augustarello a Estaccio

(Options: cod, pike-perch, angler-fish)

This recipe from Lazio, in Italy, is a highly effective way of transforming the humble dogfish into an unmistakably Mediterranean delicacy.

	To serve 6	
12	slices dogfish, each about 1 cm (½ inch) thick and weighing about 75 g (2½ oz)	12
2	eggs, beaten	2
	salt	
3	garlic cloves, chopped	3
3½ tbsp	chopped parsley	3½ tbsp
40 g	Parmesan cheese, grated	1½ oz
2 tbsp	dry breadcrumbs	2 tbsp
10 cl	olive oil	4 fl oz
	pepper	
3	lemons, halved	3

Wash, skin and pat dry the slices of fish. Immerse them in the lightly salted beaten egg for 45 minutes, turning the slices over in the dish several times.

Remove the fish slices, and drain off any excess egg. Pound together to a paste the garlic, 1½ tablespoons of the parsley, the cheese and breadcrumbs. Spread the paste on the fish slices, pressing to make it adhere.

Have the oil very hot in a wide frying pan. Fry the slices of fish for about 5 minutes on each side, until golden and crisp. Lift them out, drain them and season with salt and pepper to taste. Arrange them, slightly overlapping, on a warmed serving platter. Garnish with lemon halves and the remaining chopped parsley and serve at once.

LUIGI CARNACINA AND LUIGI VERONELLI
LA BUONA VERA CUCINA ITALIANA

Skate or Ray with Black Butter

Raie au Beurre Noir

The wings are the best part of the skate or ray. Their flavour and texture are improved if, after washing, they are left for a couple of days in salted water in the refrigerator. Once cooked and skinned, the wings can be returned to their cooking liquor until ready to use. If refrigerated, the liquor will jell and the wings can be stored for another couple of days.

	To serve 4	
4	skate or ray wings, washed	4
1	medium-sized onion, grated	1
1	sprig parsley	1
1	small bay leaf	1
2	sprigs thyme	2
	salt	
5 tbsp	wine vinegar	5 tbsp
	pepper	
2 tbsp	chopped parsley	2 tbsp
2 tbsp	capers	2 tbsp
1 tbsp	lemon juice	1 tbsp
60 g	butter	2 oz

Put the wings in a saucepan, cover with about 1 litre (1¾ pints) water and add the onion, parsley, bay leaf, thyme, ½ tablespoon of salt and 4 tablespoons of the vinegar. Bring to the boil and simmer, covered, for 20 to 25 minutes. Drain the wings and place them on a towel. Remove the skin from both sides and take off the edges, which should slip off with the skin.

Place the wings in a warmed serving dish and sprinkle with salt and pepper, the chopped parsley, capers, the remaining vinegar and the lemon juice. Keep the wings hot. Melt the butter and continue cooking it until very brown, then pour it over the fish. Serve very hot.

LOUIS DIAT
FRENCH COOKING FOR AMERICANS

Skate or Ray with Capers

Rog met Kappertjes

	To serve 4	
750 g	skate or ray wings	1½ lb
2 tbsp	wine vinegar	2 tbsp
	salt	
	freshly ground white pepper	
3 to 4 tbsp	capers	3 to 4 tbsp
75 g	butter	2½ oz

Cut the wings into 4 or 8 pieces, as convenient. Put enough water to cover them into an enamelled or stainless steel saucepan, add 1 tablespoon of the vinegar and some salt, and bring the water to the boil. Lower the heat, add the pieces of fish and poach them over a very gentle heat for about 15 minutes, until done. Remove and drain the fish and transfer to a warmed serving dish. If you wish, take off the skin and cut away the cartilage that runs along the inner side of each wing.

Pepper the pieces of fish and strew capers over them. Heat the butter in a pan until it is a light golden-brown, then pour it over the fish and capers. Heat the remaining vinegar in the same pan and sprinkle it over the fish.

WINA BORN
HET GROOT VISBOEK

Ray or Skate with Cheese

Raie au Fromage

To serve 4

Four 250 g	ray or skate wings, skinned	Four 8 oz
15 g	butter	½ oz
1 tsp	flour	1 tsp
¼ litre	milk	8 fl oz
2	cloves	2
2	Welsh or spring onions, chopped	2
1	garlic clove, crushed	1
1	bay leaf	1
2	sprigs thyme	2
	salt and pepper	
12	small onions	12
150 g	Gruyère cheese, grated	5 oz
75 g	bread croûtons	2½ oz

Melt the butter in a large saucepan, blend in the flour, and stir in the milk. Add the cloves, spring onions, garlic, bay leaf, thyme, salt and pepper. Place the fish in the pan, bring to the boil, cover and cook for 8 to 10 minutes over a low heat. Remove and drain the fish. Sieve the cooking liquid and return it to the cleaned pan. Add the small onions, cover, and cook for 10 minutes. Remove the onions, and reduce the liquid over a high heat until it has thickened into a sauce.

Cover the bottom of a buttered gratin dish with half the grated cheese. Put the fish and the onions in the dish, and arrange the croûtons around the edge. Pour over the sauce,

and cover with the remaining cheese. Put the dish in an oven preheated to 220°C (425°F or Mark 7) for 10 minutes, or until the top has browned.

CHARLES MONSELET
LETTRES GOURMANDES

Fricasséed Skate

The earliest version of this recipe that I have found is by John Farley (*The London Art of Cookery*, 1787). His instructions, whether or not they were the first to be published, have been copied word for word by numerous later authors, usually without either attribution or comment. I wonder whether any of them tried the recipe. I had to test it three times before I evolved a version that was both compatible with what Farley wrote and also successful. In fact this amplified version, given below, is more than successful; it is superb.

To serve 4 to 6

1.25 kg	skate wings	2½ lb
¾ litre	water	1¼ pints
½ tsp	ground mace	½ tsp
	grated nutmeg	
1	bouquet garni	1
	salt	
50 g	butter	2 oz
4 tbsp	flour	4 tbsp
¼ litre	single cream	8 fl oz
20 cl	white wine	7 fl oz

If what you have is a section of a large wing of skate, dress it so that you have clean pieces, free of cartilage, each about 2.5 cm (1 inch) across and 5 cm (2 inches) long. (Do not worry about the exact size or shape. A wing of skate being what it is, you are bound to finish up with some triangles and rhomboids.) A small wing can just be cut along the lines of the fibres, from the thick to the thin side, into strips 2.5 cm (1 inch) wide. The flesh will slip off the cartilage easily enough after cooking.

Place the pieces of skate in a stewpan and add the water. Also add the mace and a good pinch of nutmeg, the bouquet garni and salt. Bring all this to the boil, cover and leave to simmer for 15 minutes. Then discard the bouquet garni, remove the skate and keep it hot. (Any remaining cartilage may be removed at this stage.) You will find that you have about 15 to 20 cl (6 fl oz) cooking liquid left in the pan. In a saucepan, melt butter, add the flour, stir, then add the cooking liquid and a very little salt. Add the cream and the white wine. Bring the mixture back to the boil, reduce the heat and let it simmer gently and thicken for 3 to 4 minutes. Heat the pieces of skate in the sauce and serve hot.

ALAN DAVIDSON
NORTH ATLANTIC SEAFOOD

A Mixed Catch

Baked Red Sea Bream Spanish-Style

Besugo Asado con Piriñaca

(Options: other sea bream)

To serve 4

1 kg	red sea bream, cleaned	2 to 2½ lb
3	tomatoes, sliced	3
½	small cucumber, sliced	½
1	medium-sized onion, finely chopped	1
3	garlic cloves, finely chopped	3
1	bay leaf, finely chopped	1
2 tsp	chopped parsley	2 tsp
1	sweet green pepper, cored, seeded and finely chopped	1
	salt	
1 to 2 tbsp	lemon juice	1 to 2 tbsp
2 tbsp	olive oil	2 tbsp

The bream is placed whole on a greased ovenproof dish. The slices of tomato and cucumber are placed on the fish. The rest of the ingredients are mixed together and sprinkled on the top. The fish is then baked in an oven preheated to 190°C (375°F or Mark 5) for about 45 minutes.

ELIZABETH CASS
SPANISH COOKING

Lemon Fish

Psari Lemonato

(Options: sea bream, bogue, grey mullet, haddock)

The technique of scoring fish is demonstrated on page 80.

To serve 5

1 kg	fish, cleaned	2 to 2½ lb
4 to 6 tbsp	lemon juice	4 to 6 tbsp
	salt and pepper	
500 g	potatoes, thinly sliced	1 lb
10 cl	olive oil	4 fl oz
2 tsp	dried oregano	2 tsp

Slash the fish on each side in 2 or 3 places. Sprinkle the fish inside and out with some of the lemon juice and season with salt and pepper. Place the fish in an oiled shallow baking dish.

Arrange the sliced potatoes around the fish and pour the remaining lemon juice over the potatoes and fish. Season the potatoes and pour the olive oil over the contents of the dish. Sprinkle with the oregano and cover the dish with a lid or foil.

Cook in a moderate oven, preheated to 180°C (350°F or Mark 4), for 40 minutes. Remove the cover and continue to cook for a further 20 minutes, or until the fish and potatoes are cooked. Serve immediately with a boiled leafy green vegetable such as spinach.

As a variation, 2 tablespoons of capers mixed with a little olive oil may be added during the last 10 minutes of cooking.

TESS MALLOS
GREEK COOKBOOK

Baked Sea Bream with Green Sauce

Pargo Asado con Salsa Esmeralda

(Options: any of the sea bream family or sea bass)

To serve 6

2.5 to 3 kg	sea bream, gutted and scaled, head and tail left on	5 to 6 lb
2 tsp	salt	2 tsp
¼ tsp	freshly ground pepper	¼ tsp
4	garlic cloves, crushed	4
¼ tsp each	oregano and ground cumin	¼ tsp each
6 tbsp	lime juice	6 tbsp
15 g	butter	½ oz
1 kg	potatoes, thickly sliced	2 to 2½ lb
¼ litre	olive oil	8 fl oz
4 tbsp	chopped parsley	4 tbsp
2	sweet red peppers, grilled and peeled, seeded and cut into strips	2

Green sauce

3	garlic cloves, crushed	3
2 tbsp	chopped capers	2 tbsp
4	hard-boiled eggs, yolks only, mashed	4
1 tsp	salt	1 tsp
¼ tsp	white pepper	¼ tsp
2 tbsp	chopped parsley	2 tbsp
60 g	almonds, toasted and ground	2 oz
15 cl	olive oil	¼ pint
5 tbsp	white vinegar	5 tbsp

Mix together the salt, pepper, garlic, oregano, cumin and lime juice, and rub the mixture into the fish, inside and out. Set the fish aside to marinate for 30 minutes.

Butter an ovenproof dish large enough to hold the fish comfortably. Arrange the potatoes on the bottom of the dish; place the fish on top, pouring the marinade over the fish. Pour the oil over the fish and potatoes. Cook in an oven preheated to 200°C (400°F or Mark 6) for 45 minutes to 1 hour. Lower the temperature to 180°C (350°F or Mark 4) after 30 minutes and cover with aluminium foil if the fish is colouring too much.

Meanwhile, make the sauce. In a mortar, mash together the garlic, capers, egg yolks, salt, pepper, parsley and almonds. Beat in the oil, little by little, and at the last minute add the vinegar. Decorate the fish with the parsley and peppers, and serve with the green sauce.

ELISABETH LAMBERT ORTIZ
CARIBBEAN COOKING

Gilt-Head Bream with Noodles

Mes Daurades aux Nouilles

(Options: dentex, sea bass, sea bream)

This recipe is from Marinette Vacheron, of the restaurant Le Râtelier in Lyon.

To serve 6

3	gilt-head bream, each weighing 850 g (1¾ lb), filleted and skinned	3
	salt and pepper	
15 cl	dry vermouth	¼ pint
30 cl	double cream	½ pint
200 g	sorrel, stems removed, washed and finely shredded	7 oz
500 g	freshly made noodles	1 lb
60 g	butter	2 oz

Arrange the fish fillets, without salt, pepper, butter or anything, in a large gratin dish, taking care that the fillets do not overlap. Put them into a fairly hot oven, preheated to 200°C (400°F or Mark 6), for 8 to 10 minutes. Remove from the oven, and keep the fish hot. Season lightly with salt and pepper.

Meanwhile, in a saucepan reduce the vermouth to a syrup over a moderate heat. Add the cream and reduce it, too, until the mixture coats the back of a wooden spoon. Season with salt and pepper. Add the sorrel, and bring quickly to the boil. Arrange the fish fillets on a warmed serving dish, coat them with the sauce, and serve.

Freshly made noodles, cooked *al dente* and tossed in butter, make a very agreeable accompaniment.

MADELEINE PETER
GRANDES DAMES DE LA CUISINE

Fish Baked in Vine Leaves

Psari Fournou me Ambelofila

(Options: sea bream, red mullet, gurnard, ballan wrasse)

To serve 5

5	medium-sized fish, cleaned but heads left on	5
2 to 3 tbsp	olive oil	2 to 3 tbsp
2 to 3 tbsp	lemon juice	2 to 3 tbsp
1 tbsp each	chopped parsley, thyme and fennel leaves	1 tbsp each
	salt and freshly ground pepper	
3 or 4	anchovy fillets, soaked in water, drained and mashed	3 or 4
30 g	butter	1 oz
12 to 15	large vine leaves	12 to 15
1	lemon, sliced	1
1 tbsp	fennel leaves	1 tbsp

In a glass or earthenware bowl, beat together the oil, lemon juice, parsley, thyme and fennel and a pinch each of salt and pepper. Put the fish in the mixture, turning to coat well, and leave to marinate for 1 to 2 hours in the refrigerator.

Remove the fish from the marinade and drain. Beat the anchovies and butter together and spread the mixture on to the fish with a knife. Wrap each fish in 2 or 3 vine leaves and place it, seam-side down, in an ovenproof dish. Bake in an oven preheated to 180°C (350°F or Mark 4) for 30 minutes. Serve hot, garnished with lemon slices and fennel leaves.

VILMA LIACOURAS CHANTILES
THE FOOD OF GREECE

Gilt-Head Bream in Chablis

Daurade Djénane

(Options: sea bream, red sea bream)

To serve 4 to 6

1 kg	gilt-head bream, cleaned	2 to 2½ lb
¾ litre	Chablis or other dry white wine	1¼ pints
	salt and pepper	
1	clove	1
2	fresh sage leaves	2
1	bay leaf	1
125 g	mushrooms	4 oz
75 g	black olives	2½ oz
2	large tomatoes, each cut into 6 slices	2
2	lemon slices	2

Place the fish in an oval, ovenproof earthenware dish. Pour over the wine and add salt and pepper, the clove, sage and bay leaves, mushrooms and olives. Arrange the tomato and lemon slices on the fish. Cook uncovered in a moderate oven, preheated to 180°C (350°F or Mark 4), basting every 10 minutes, for about 45 minutes. Serve straight from the dish.

GASTON DERYS
L'ART D'ÊTRE GOURMAND

Gilt-Head Bream Grilled with Aromatic Oils

Lou Bésugou Rimat a la Nissarda

(Options: sea bass, dolphin fish, large red mullet)

The aromatic oils called for in this recipe should be made with olive oil. Put several dried red chili peppers into one small bottle of oil, a large sprig of thyme into another, and sprigs of dried fennel into a third. Let the oils steep for 2 weeks.

To serve 4

1 kg	gilt-head bream, cleaned and scaled	2 to 2½ lb
1 tsp each	aromatic oils: chili peppers, thyme and fennel	1 tsp each
2 tbsp	olive oil	2 tbsp
	salt	
2 to 3 tbsp	lemon juice or 1 tsp aromatic oil (optional)	2 to 3 tbsp

Make several shallow, diagonal incisions in each side of the fish. Heat a grill rack over a charcoal grill in which the embers are glowing but already covered with white ash. (Preheating the rack will prevent the fish from sticking.)
Mix the aromatic oils with the olive oil. Add a little salt

and, using a brush, daub the fish with the mixture. Grill for about 15 minutes on each side, or until done.
Lift the fish on to a warmed platter and, if desired, sprinkle with lemon juice or oil. Serve immediately.

JACQUES MÉDECIN
LA CUISINE DU COMTÉ DE NICE

Baked Sea Bass, Corsican-Style

Ragnola au Four

(Options: gilt-head bream, grouper)

Ragnola is the Corsican name for sea bass. The author explains that this recipe is also suited to the gilt-head bream (palmata in Corsica) or the ordinary sea bream (occhione). It calls for two typically Corsican ingredients: brocciu *and* gulagna. *The former is a fresh, dry cheese similar to* ricotta *or* brousse; *the latter is smoked pork jowl and is not easy to find, but very thin slices of smoked bacon can be used instead.*

To serve 6

1	sea bass, cleaned and scaled	1
60 g	soft breadcrumbs	2 oz
10 cl	milk	4 fl oz
½ tsp	thyme	½ tsp
1	garlic clove, pounded	1
½	medium-sized onion, finely chopped	½
200 g	fresh sheep's cheese (*brocciu* or *ricotta*)	7 oz
8	thin slices *gulagna*, or thin rashers smoked bacon	8
About ½ litre	veal stock	About 18 fl oz

Lightly oil an ovenproof dish of the right size to accommodate the fish (cut off the tail if necessary).
Gently cook the breadcrumbs in the milk, with the thyme, garlic and onion, for 5 minutes. Drain off the excess liquid and combine with the cheese. Stuff the fish with the mixture.
Make several shallow incisions in each side of the fish. Cut 2 slices of *gulagna*, or bacon rashers, into thin strips and insert these into the incisions. Place the fish in the prepared dish and cover it completely with the remaining *gulagna* or bacon. Pour the veal stock over all. (The exact quantity of the stock will depend on the size of the dish in relation to the fish. The fish should be half immersed in the stock.)
Put the dish in an oven preheated to 180°C (350°F or Mark 4) and bake it for 50 to 60 minutes, or until the flesh of the fish parts easily from the bone.

SIMONE COSTANTINI
GASTRONOMIE CORSE ET SES RECETTES

Herb-Stuffed Bass in Lettuce Casing

Bar aux Herbes en Chemise

(Options: gilt-head bream, grey mullet, sea trout)

To serve 4

750 g	sea bass, scaled, cleaned, gills torn out, boned	1½ lb
2	large round lettuces	2
	salt	
30 to 60 g	butter	1 to 2 oz
2 tbsp	shallots, finely chopped	2 tbsp
	pepper	
2 tbsp	dry vermouth	2 tbsp
10 cl	dry white wine	4 fl oz
10 cl	double cream	4 fl oz
	Stuffing	
250 g	spinach, parboiled, squeezed dry and finely chopped	8 oz
60 g	day-old bread, crusts removed, finely crumbled	2 oz
30 g	butter, softened	1 oz
About 60 g	finely shredded young sorrel leaves	About 2 oz
About 60 g	finely chopped parsley	About 2 oz
1 tsp	finely chopped fresh tarragon	1 tsp
	salt and pepper	
1	egg, beaten	1

To make the stuffing, mix the spinach, bread and butter together well, mashing with a fork, before adding the other ingredients and stirring well. Stuff the fish, pressing the fillets and stuffing firmly together so as to re-form the fish in the original shape. Place it on its side on the table top.

Put about 20 of the largest and most perfectly formed outer lettuce leaves in a saucepan, add salt, pour over boiling water, simmer for a minute or so, and drain, pouring carefully into a sieve or colander so as not to damage the leaves or bunch them up into a mass. Run a bit of cold water over the leaves to cool them and delicately, one by one, lift them out and spread them on a towel to drain.

Have ready an elongated buttered gratin dish, the bottom of which has been scattered with the shallots. Salt and pepper the fish's surface. Wrap the fish from head to tail (muzzle and tail tip remaining exposed): arrange overlapping leaves of lettuce the length of the belly section, the rib ends gently tucked beneath the fish and the fragile leaf extremities pressed to the surface. Repeat the process along the length of the back, tucking rib tips under and pressing the leaves well into place. Turn the fish over and place it in the prepared dish;

salt and pepper the newly exposed surface and repeat the performance with the lettuce so that, when finished, the fish is firmly wrapped, mummy-like.

Dribble the dry vermouth over the surface of the fish, pour the white wine into the bottom of the gratin dish, adding the bones that were removed from the fish, line the fish's surface with dabs of butter, press over lightly a sheet of aluminium foil or buttered greaseproof paper and bake for about 30 minutes in a hot oven, preheated to 220°C (425°F or Mark 7), basting regularly during the last 15 minutes. Detach the muzzle and tail tip from the sides of the dish if they touch it, and transfer the fish, using spatulas, to a heated serving dish. Discard the bones. Pour the juices into a small saucepan, reduce to a light syrup, add the cream, and—stirring—reduce the liquid at a high boil by approximately half or until the liquid takes on the consistency of a light sauce. If you like, whisk in 30 g (1 oz) of butter away from the heat. Pour the sauce over the fish and cut into cross-sections for serving.

RICHARD OLNEY
SIMPLE FRENCH FOOD

Baked Fish in Hot Sauce

Samaki Harra

(Options: sea bass, grouper, large grey mullet, bonito)

To serve 6 to 8

2 to 2.5 kg	fish, cleaned	4 to 5 lb
	salt	
6	sprigs fresh coriander	6
15	garlic cloves, crushed	15
	pepper	
¼ litre	olive oil	8 fl oz
125 g	walnuts, ground	4 oz
8 tbsp	lemon juice	8 tbsp
	cayenne pepper	

Rub the fish well inside and outside with salt. Pound the coriander with the garlic, season with pepper, and rub the inside of the fish with this mixture. Tie it with string if necessary to close the opening. Put the fish on a piece of aluminium foil, pour on the oil, and wrap the foil around the fish. Place it in a baking tin and bake in an oven preheated to 180°C (350°F or Mark 4) for about 40 minutes or until tender.

Meanwhile, blend the walnuts, lemon juice and a pinch of cayenne pepper to a smooth sauce. Put the fish on a warmed serving platter, and serve the sauce separately in a sauceboat.

AIDA KARAOGLAN
A GOURMET'S DELIGHT

Fish Croquettes
Balik Koftesi

(Options: sea bass, grey mullet, gurnard, redfish, cod)

To serve 4

350 g	fish, cleaned and washed	12 oz
1	small onion, quartered	1
2	sprigs parsley	2
1	small carrot	1
2	slices lemon	2
1	bay leaf	1
5	peppercorns	5
	salt	
30 g	white bread, crusts removed, soaked in water and squeezed dry	1 oz
2	eggs	2
2	spring onions, including the green tops, chopped	2
2 tbsp each	chopped dill and chopped parsley	2 tbsp each
15 g	blackcurrants	½ oz
15 g	shelled pine-nuts	½ oz
½ tsp	ground allspice	½ tsp
	pepper	
90 g	flour	3 oz
¼ litre	oil	8 fl oz

Put 35 cl (12 fl oz) water into a saucepan with the onion, parsley, carrot, lemon slices, bay leaf, peppercorns and salt. Bring to the boil. Add the fish, cover, and simmer for 10 to 15 minutes or until the fish is tender. Remove the fish and cool. Then remove all the skin and bones from the fish.

Place the fish in a bowl. Add the bread, eggs, spring onions,

dill, parsley, blackcurrants, pine-nuts, allspice, and salt and pepper to taste. Mash all the ingredients with a fork, working the mixture into a fairly smooth paste. From the paste form croquettes about 6 cm (2½ inches) long and 2.5 cm (1 inch) in diameter and roll them in the flour.

Heat the oil in a heavy sauté pan and fry the croquettes until golden-brown on all sides. Shake the pan often to prevent burning. Serve hot or cold with a lettuce salad.

NESET EREN
THE ART OF TURKISH COOKING

Roman Fish Omelette
Patina Zomoteganon

(Options: sea bass, grey mullet, sea bream, ballan wrasse)

The liquamen *called for in this ancient Roman recipe is a salty fish sauce: alternatives are pounded anchovies or one of the oriental fermented fish sauces. Use white or red wine according to taste—or even a mixture of dry white wine and port.*

To serve 4

750 g	fish fillets	1½ lb
4 tbsp	olive oil	4 tbsp
1 tbsp	*liquamen*	1 tbsp
¼ litre	wine	8 fl oz
1	bouquet garni of leek and fresh coriander leaves	1
2	sprigs lovage	2
1 tsp	dried oregano	1 tsp
	pepper	
4	eggs, lightly beaten	4

Place the fish in a shallow pan. Add the oil, *liquamen*, wine and bouquet of leek and coriander. Cover and poach over a low heat for 10 to 12 minutes.

Meanwhile, pound the lovage and oregano with some pepper. When the fish is cooked, arrange the fillets in a shallow oven dish. Add the leek and coriander to the pounded herbs. Pound all together. Transfer the mixture to a bowl and strain over the fish stock. Stir in the eggs until blended, then pour the mixture through a sieve on to the fish fillets. Cook in an oven preheated to 150°C (300°F or Mark 2) for 20 minutes, or until the egg custard is set. Sprinkle with pepper and serve.

BARBARA FLOWER AND ELISABETH ROSENBAUM
THE ROMAN COOKERY BOOK, A CRITICAL TRANSLATION OF THE ART OF
COOKING BY APICIUS

Fish Fillets in Sesame Sauce

Tajen Samak bi Tahini

(Options: sea bass, sea bream, trout, haddock)

The tahini *called for in this Arab recipe is a sesame paste. It is obtainable from delicatessens and oriental food stores.*

To serve 6

1.5 kg	fish fillets, rubbed with lemon juice, sprinkled with salt and refrigerated for a few hours	3 lb
15 cl	olive oil	¼ pint
200 g	onions, sliced	7 oz
35 cl	*tahini*	12 fl oz
10 cl	lemon juice	4 fl oz
2	garlic cloves, crushed	2
1½ tsp	salt	1½ tsp

Remove the fish fillets from the refrigerator 30 minutes before cooking time. Wash and dry the fillets. Rub them with olive oil and bake them in an oven, preheated to 200°C (400°F or Mark 6), for 10 minutes. Baste them with a little more olive oil and place them under a hot grill for a minute or two.

Lower the heat of the oven to 180°C (350°F or Mark 4). Sauté the onions in the remaining olive oil and spread them over the fish in the baking dish. Blend the *tahini*, lemon juice, garlic and salt thoroughly, adding water until the sauce is of a creamy consistency. Bring to the boil and pour the sauce over the fish. Return the baking dish to the oven and bake for about 20 minutes or until the sauce thickens. Serve with rice.

AIDA KARAOGLAN
A GOURMET'S DELIGHT

Cornish Conger Eel in Cider

(Options: any firm white fish, such as coley, dogfish, halibut)

This fish stew from Cornwall finds its counterpart in the one prepared by the fishermen of Normandy.

To serve 6 to 8

1.5 kg	conger eel, cut into 2 or 3 pieces	3 lb
60 g	butter	2 oz
250 g	onion, chopped	8 oz
30 g	flour	1 oz
1.25 litres	cider	2 pints
	salt and pepper	

Melt the butter in a fireproof casserole and fry the onions until golden. Add the eel pieces and brown lightly. Stir in the flour and cook until brown. Gradually stir in the cider, season

with salt and pepper and cover the casserole. Bake in a moderate oven, preheated to 180°C (350°F or Mark 4), for 1 hour. Serve the fish in the sauce.

LIZZIE BOYD (EDITOR)
BRITISH COOKERY

Chilean Conger Eel in Casserole

Congrio en Fuente a la Chilena

(Options: dogfish, angler-fish, halibut)

The chef at the Hotel Crillon in Santiago, who supplied this recipe, says conger eel is the best-liked fish dish in all Chile. These marine monsters, sometimes as long as 2.5 metres (8 feet), are certainly fine in flavour and very meaty. Even if you don't care for freshwater eels, you should go for fat congers.

To serve 6

1 kg	conger eel, cut into serving portions	2 to 2½ lb
3 tbsp	olive or vegetable oil	3 tbsp
	salt and pepper	
15 g	butter	½ oz
15 g	lard	½ oz
2	medium-sized onions, chopped	2
2	garlic cloves, crushed	2
½ tsp	dried marjoram	½ tsp
¼ tsp	ground cumin	¼ tsp
4	tomatoes, skinned and thinly sliced	4
4	medium-sized potatoes, sliced	4
2	ears sweetcorn, kernels scraped off, cobs discarded	2
250 g	peas or lima beans, boiled (optional)	8 oz
	croûtons, fried in butter	
6	sprigs parsley	6

Heat the oil in a frying pan. Season the eel with salt and pepper, brown lightly in the oil, then remove from the pan. Heat the butter and lard in a saucepan; add the onions, garlic, marjoram and cumin. Fry gently until the onions are soft, then add the tomatoes, potatoes and sweetcorn kernels. Stir and cover. Cook over a low heat for about 20 minutes, or until the potatoes are done, then season to taste. At this point, the cooked peas or lima beans may be added for a fuller dish.

Place half of this vegetable mixture in a casserole. Lay the fish over it and cover with the remaining vegetable mixture. Cover, put in an oven, preheated to 150°C (300°F or Mark 2), and cook for 40 minutes, or until the fish is done. Garnish the dish with the bread croûtons and sprigs of parsley. Serve hot.

CORA, ROSE AND BOB BROWN
THE SOUTH AMERICAN COOK BOOK

Conger Eel Stew from Bragança
Congro Ensopado a Moda de Bragança

To serve 4

750 g	conger eel (centre cut), cleaned and cut into 4 slices	1½ lb
10 cl	olive oil	4 fl oz
1	medium-sized onion, chopped	1
	pepper	
1	bay leaf	1
	salt	
1 tbsp	vinegar	1 tbsp
10 cl	water	4 fl oz
4	thick slices day-old bread	4
3	egg yolks	3
1 tbsp	chopped parsley	1 tbsp

Heat the oil in a saucepan, and add the onion, pepper and bay leaf. Cook until the onion is golden, then put the slices of fish on top, adding salt to taste and the vinegar and water. Simmer, covered, for 10 to 15 minutes, until the fish is done, then remove from the heat.

Place the slices of bread on a serving dish and put the slices of cooked fish on top of them. Beat the egg yolks with the parsley and pour this mixture into the liquid in which the fish was cooked. Mix well and heat gently until the sauce has thickened. Pour this sauce over the fish and serve at once.

MARIA ODETTE CORTES VALENTE
COZINHA REGIONAL PORTUGUESA

Fried Fish with Groundnut Sauce

(Options: small gurnard, grey mullet, whiting)

To serve 4

4	small fish, cleaned	4
	salt	
10 cl	oil	4 fl oz
2	onions, chopped	2
1 tsp	curry powder	1 tsp
2	tomatoes, skinned, seeded and chopped	2
75 g	groundnuts, roasted and pounded	2½ oz

Sprinkle the fish with salt. Heat the oil and fry the fish slowly until light brown on both sides. Remove the fish and discard all but 2 tablespoons of the oil from the pan. Add the onions and curry powder to the pan and fry until brown. Then add the tomatoes and fry lightly, for 3 to 4 minutes. Mix the pounded groundnuts with about 35 cl (12 fl oz) water and add this to the onions and tomatoes. Cook slowly for about 5 minutes. Place the fried fish in the sauce and heat through slowly. Season with salt to taste and serve hot.

JENNY VAN DER MEER AND BEATRICE R. MANSUR
TANZANIAN FOOD WITH TRADITIONAL AND NEW RECIPES

Fish with Herbs, Flambé
Riba-Flambé

(Options: grey mullet, sea bream, dentex, hake, mackerel)

This Bulgarian dish is very easy to prepare, and is a particularly suitable way of treating grey mullet.

To serve 2

About 750g	fish, scaled and cleaned	About 1½ lb
	salt and pepper	
About 2 tbsp	oil	About 2 tbsp
1 tbsp each	finely chopped dill and parsley	1 tbsp each
4 tbsp	brandy, warmed	4 tbsp

Season the fish with salt and pepper, and rub it all over with oil. Grill the fish over a charcoal grill, or under a stove grill, using a moderate heat, for about 15 minutes on each side.

Arrange the grilled fish neatly in a fireproof dish of a shape that fits it, and sprinkle the chopped dill and parsley over it. Pour the warmed brandy over the fish and light it. The herbs will burn and give the fish a special aroma, while the flaming dish will create an air of festivity.

PENKA CHOLCHEVA
KNIGA ZA VSEKI DEN I VSEKI DOM

Peruvian Picante

(Options: grey mullet, gurnard, plaice, mackerel)

To serve 4

1 kg	whole fish, cleaned and cut into 2.5 cm (1 inch) pieces, or several small fish, cleaned	2 to 2½ lb
	coarse sea salt	
1	garlic clove, crushed	1
1	sweet yellow or green pepper, cored, seeded and chopped	1
10 cl	bitter orange juice, or 4 tbsp sweet orange juice and 3 tbsp lemon juice	4 fl oz

Cover the fish thickly on all sides with sea salt and let stand for 1 hour or more. Put the garlic, sweet pepper and orange juice into a saucepan. Pour in enough water just to cover the fish when they are added, and bring to the boiling point. Wash the salt from the pieces of fish and add the fish to the pan. Bring rapidly back to the boiling point. Cover tightly and simmer for 10 to 15 minutes, or until the fish is done.

CORA, ROSE AND BOB BROWN
THE SOUTH AMERICAN COOK BOOK

————————◆————————

Poached Red Mullet with a Rustic Sauce

Rougets Pochés à la Nage

The author of this recipe, M. Raymond Thuilier of L'Oustau de Baumanière in Provence, suggests that the rustic sauce should be prepared several days in advance. The liver of the red mullet is a delicacy; do not remove it when you clean the fish.

To serve 4

Four 250 g	red mullet, cleaned and washed	Four 8 oz
1 litre	live mussels, scrubbed	1¾ pints
	Court-bouillon	
½ litre	dry white wine	18 fl oz
1 litre	water	1¾ pints
2 tbsp	vinegar	2 tbsp
	salt and freshly ground pepper	
1	large bouquet garni of thyme, bay leaf, fennel and rosemary	1
4 each	orange and lemon slices	4 each
1 tbsp	torn-up basil leaves	1 tbsp
	Rustic sauce	
30 g	basil leaves	1 oz
¼ litre	olive oil	8 fl oz
1	garlic clove, crushed	1
1	tomato, skinned, seeded and chopped	1
1 tbsp	chopped fennel leaves	1 tbsp
1 tsp	finely chopped rosemary leaves	1 tsp
½ tsp	paprika	½ tsp
½ tsp	coriander seeds, crushed	½ tsp
	salt and freshly ground pepper	
	Garnish	
1 tbsp	shredded basil leaves	1 tbsp
	orange and lemon slices	

To make the sauce, crush the basil leaves in the oil in a mortar. Blend in the remaining ingredients, cover, and set aside to steep for several days.

For the court-bouillon, put all the ingredients into a large enamelled or stainless steel pan, add a few of the mussels, and simmer, covered, for 30 minutes.

Remove a ladle of the court-bouillon to another large pan, add the remaining mussels, cover and cook over a high heat until the mussels have opened, about 2 to 3 minutes.

Meanwhile, plunge the red mullet into the simmering court-bouillon and poach them for 5 to 6 minutes, without letting the liquid boil. The fish must remain firm and unbroken. When they are just cooked, lift them out and arrange them on a warmed serving dish. Coat the mullet with the rustic sauce, sprinkle with basil, and garnish with orange and lemon slices. Surround with the opened mussels in their shells, and serve immediately.

LES PRINCES DE LA GASTRONOMIE

————————◆————————

Grilled Red Mullet with Green Sauce

Rougets Grillés Sauce Verte

(Options: small grey mullet, small sea bream)

Grey mullet or sea bream, unlike red mullet, should be gutted if used for this dish.

To serve 6

6	red mullet, gills removed	6
	Marinade	
3 tbsp	olive oil	3 tbsp
	salt and pepper	
1	onion, finely chopped	1
1 each	bay leaf and sprig thyme	1 each
	Green sauce	
4 tbsp	olive oil	4 tbsp
1 tbsp	wine vinegar	1 tbsp
1 tbsp each	finely chopped chives, parsley and chervil	1 tbsp each
1 tsp	finely chopped tarragon	1 tsp
1 tbsp each	finely chopped gherkins and capers	1 tbsp each
	salt and pepper	

Marinate the fish in a dish containing the oil, salt, pepper, chopped onion, bay leaf and thyme. After 30 minutes to 1 hour, remove the fish, and grill them for 5 to 10 minutes on each side—depending on the size of the fish—basting them with the marinade liquid.

To make the sauce, put the oil and vinegar in a serving dish; add the chives, parsley, chervil, tarragon, gherkins and capers. Mix together well, and season with salt and pepper. Lay the grilled mullet on this green sauce and serve.

ALOIDE BONTOU
TRAITÉ DE CUISINE BOURGEOISE BORDELAISE

Red Mullet with Tomato Sauce

Triglie alla Livornese

(Options: small sea bream, small grey mullet, whiting)

To serve 6

12	small red mullet, cleaned	12
4 tbsp	olive oil	4 tbsp
1	garlic clove, thinly sliced	1
3 tbsp	coarsely chopped parsley	3 tbsp
	salt and pepper	
700 g	tomatoes, skinned, seeded and chopped	1½ lb

Put the oil in a skillet with the garlic, parsley, a pinch each of salt and pepper, and the tomatoes. Simmer for about 10 minutes to cook the tomatoes, then increase the heat to reduce the sauce and cook for a further 10 to 15 minutes. Add the red mullet and cook briefly (8 to 10 minutes) until they are done.

FLAVIO COLUTTA
CUCINA E VINI DELLA TOSCANA

Maltese Dolphin Fish Pie

Torta Tal-Lampuki

(Options: hake, bonito, halibut, dogfish)

To serve 4 to 6

750 g	dolphin fish, head and tail removed, cut into thick slices	1½ lb
	sifted flour	
10 cl	olive oil	4 fl oz
175 g	onion, chopped	6 oz
250 g	tomato, skinned, seeded and chopped	8 oz
125 g	parboiled peas	4 oz
250 g	cauliflower, broken into florets	8 oz
1 tsp	dried mixed herbs (thyme, oregano, marjoram, savory)	1 tsp
175 g	black olives, stoned and sliced	6 oz
2 tsp	grated lemon rind	2 tsp
500 g	shortcrust pastry (*page 175*)	1 lb
	salt and pepper	
2	eggs, beaten	2
1	egg yolk, beaten with 1 tbsp water	1

Dip the fish slices in the sifted flour. Heat 4 tablespoons of the oil in a frying pan and fry the fish gently on both sides. Remove the fish, let it cool, then discard all the bones.

Using the remaining oil, fry the onions, then add the

tomatoes. Reduce, then add the peas, cauliflower, herbs, olives, lemon rind and fish. Cover and simmer for 5 minutes. Meanwhile, grease a 1 litre (2 pint) pie dish and line it with two-thirds of the pastry. Season the mixture with salt and pepper, add the beaten eggs, and pour the mixture into the pie dish. Cover with pastry, brush with the beaten yolk, and cut slits in the pastry lid. Bake in a fairly hot oven, preheated to 190°C (375°F or Mark 5), for 40 minutes, or until golden.

ANTON B. DOUGALL
KĊINA MALTIJA: MALTESE CUISINE

Angler-Fish with White Wine and Shallots

Tranches de Lotte au Four

(Options: sole, whiting)

To serve 8

2 kg	angler-fish tail, cleaned and cut into thick slices	4 lb
8	shallots, finely chopped	8
250 g	mushrooms, finely chopped	8 oz
	salt and pepper	
8	sprigs parsley	8
250 g	butter, cut into large pieces	8 oz
20 cl	white wine	7 fl oz
100 g	fresh breadcrumbs	3½ oz

Cover the bottom of an ovenproof casserole with half the shallots and mushrooms. Arrange the slices of fish on top and season with salt and pepper. Cover with the remaining shallots and mushrooms, the parsley, butter and the white wine. Sprinkle on the breadcrumbs.

Bake in an oven preheated to 230°C (450°F or Mark 8) for about 15 minutes, or until the top is golden-brown and slightly crisp and the sauce reduced to a syrupy consistency.

CURNONSKY
CUISINE ET VINS DE FRANCE

Angler-Fish with Ratatouille

Gigot de Mer à la Palavasienne

(Options: angel shark, centre cut of conger eel)

This recipe is from Languedoc, on the south coast of France. Angler-fish is invariably sold in tail portions only. The appearance of the head is thought to be too alarming for the customer's sensibilities.

To serve 4

1 kg	tail-end of angler-fish	2 to 2½ lb
4	garlic cloves, cut in slivers	4
	salt and pepper	

Ratatouille		
3	onions, chopped	3
3	garlic cloves, chopped	3
4 tbsp	olive oil	4 tbsp
3	sweet peppers, cut into strips	3
250 g each	aubergines and courgettes, sliced	8 oz each
500 g	tomatoes, skinned, seeded and chopped	1 lb

Make slits in the flesh of the fish, and insert slivers of garlic into them. Season with salt and pepper.

Make the ratatouille by cooking the onions and garlic in the olive oil. As they soften, add the sweet peppers. As the peppers soften in turn, add the aubergines and courgettes, and, after 10 minutes, the tomatoes. Simmer steadily for 45 minutes, uncovered. When you have a well-flavoured, unwatery stew, put it into an ovenproof dish and lay the fish on top. Bake in a moderate to fairly hot oven, preheated to 180° to 190°C (350° to 375°F or Mark 4 or 5) for 30 to 45 minutes, turning the fish over from time to time.

JANE GRIGSON
FISH COOKERY

Angler-Fish Stew

Waterzooi van Staartvis

(Options: turbot, angel shark, pike, pike-perch, eel)

Waterzooi is most often made with freshwater fish or chicken. On the Flemish coast, however, it is prepared with sea fish, as in this recipe from the Old Fisher Restaurant at Knokke-Heist.

To serve 4

1 kg	tail-end of angler-fish, cut into pieces, 2 to 2½ lb each weighing about 50 g (2 oz)	
30 g	butter	1 oz
4	shallots, finely chopped	4
15 cl	dry white wine	¼ pint
40 cl	fish fumet (*page 174*)	¾ pint
8	carrots, cut into *julienne* strips and blanched	8
1	heart celery, cut into *julienne* strips and blanched	1
3 or 4	leeks, cut into *julienne* strips and blanched	3 or 4
	salt and pepper	
20 cl	double cream	7 fl oz
2 to 3 tbsp	finely chopped parsley	2 to 3 tbsp

Melt the butter in a heavy saucepan and sweat the shallots in it briefly. Add the pieces of fish and cook them for a couple of minutes, turning them once or twice with a spoon. Pour in the white wine and the fish fumet, add the vegetables, season with salt and pepper, and bring the contents of the pan to the boil. Stir in the cream and simmer over a moderate heat for 10 minutes. Finally, garnish with the parsley and serve the stew in soup plates with boiled potatoes as an accompaniment.

FONS VERMEERSCH
OP ZOEK NAAR SPIJS EN DRANK

Fish Balls

Albóndigas de Pescado

This recipe is by Carmen Bustamente, a cookery writer from near Santander on the northern coast of Spain.

(Options: any firm-fleshed white fish)

To serve 4 to 6

500 g	cooked fish, bones removed	1 lb
1	small onion, very finely chopped	1
40 g	fresh breadcrumbs	1½ oz
2	eggs, lightly beaten	2
2 tbsp	olive oil	2 tbsp
2 tbsp	chopped parsley	2 tbsp
1 to 2 tsp	oregano	1 to 2 tsp
	salt and pepper	
About 125 g	flour	About 4 oz
4 to 5 tbsp	lemon juice	4 to 5 tbsp
	olive oil for frying	
	Sauce	
About 40 cl	fish fumet (*page 174*)	About ¾ pint
	salt	
1 tbsp	chopped parsley	1 tbsp
1	small onion, finely chopped	1
30 g	almonds, toasted and ground	1 oz

Pound the fish flesh in a mortar. In a bowl, combine the fish, onion, breadcrumbs, eggs, olive oil, parsley, oregano and season with salt and pepper. Mix together thoroughly, then form the mixture into balls about the size of small eggs. Roll the fish balls in flour, dip them in lemon juice, then roll them again in flour. In a frying pan, heat olive oil to a depth of about 5mm (¼ inch) and fry the fish balls until golden-brown all over. Drain the fish balls and place them in a shallow casserole.

Add the fish fumet, salt, parsley and onion. Simmer, covered, for about 10 minutes, add the almonds and simmer uncovered for a further 5 minutes to thicken the sauce. Serve straight from the casserole.

PETITS PROPOS CULINAIRES

Crustaceans

Lobster Thermidor

(Option: spiny lobster)

This recipe is from Wheeler's restaurant in Old Compton Street, London. The technique of cutting a lobster in half is demonstrated on page 54.

	To serve 2	
750 g	live lobster, poached in boiling water or court-bouillon, halved, meat extracted and shell reserved	1½ lb
60 g	butter	2 oz
30 g	shallots, chopped	1 oz
1 tbsp	flour	1 tbsp
1 tbsp	dry sherry	1 tbsp
1 tbsp	dry white wine	1 tbsp
10 cl	fish fumet (*page 174*)	4 fl oz
60 g	Parmesan cheese, grated	2 oz
1 tbsp	chopped parsley	1 tbsp
1 tbsp	double cream	1 tbsp
1 tsp	dry English mustard	1 tsp
	salt and pepper	

Cut the lobster meat into pieces about 2.5 cm (1 inch) square. Melt 40 g (1½ oz) of the butter in a large frying pan and lightly fry the chopped shallots, but do not brown them. Stir in the flour then add the sherry, white wine, lobster meat and fumet, and simmer for 3 to 4 minutes stirring all the time. Add about half the grated cheese, the parsley and the cream. Take the pan off the heat, add the dry mustard to the lobster mixture and mix well. Spoon the lobster pieces into the reserved lobster shells.

To the sauce left in the pan add the remaining butter and the rest of the cheese. Mix, then coat the lobster pieces with the sauce and glaze under a hot grill.

MACDONALD HASTINGS AND CAROLE WALSH
WHEELER'S FISH COOKERY BOOK

My Great-Grandmother's Lobster Newburg

(Options: spiny lobster, prawns, crab meat)

For instructions on cutting up a lobster, see page 26.

	To serve 6 to 8	
2 kg	lobster, boiled, shelled and cut into small, delicate pieces	4 lb
60 g	butter	2 oz
2 tsp	salt	2 tsp
¼ tsp	cayenne pepper	¼ tsp
¼ tsp	grated nutmeg	¼ tsp
¼ litre	double cream	8 fl oz
4	egg yolks	4
2 tbsp	brandy	2 tbsp
2 tbsp	sherry	2 tbsp

Heat the butter in a frying pan and add the lobster. Cook slowly for 5 minutes. Add the salt, cayenne pepper and nutmeg. Lightly beat the cream with the egg yolks and add the mixture to the pan, stirring constantly. Finally, add the brandy and sherry as the mass begins to thicken.

Serve in vol-au-vent cases or on toast.

THE JUNIOR LEAGUE OF CHARLESTON
CHARLESTON RECEIPTS

Boiled Lobsters with Savoury Butter Sauce

Homards à la Nage et Beurre Blanc

(Option: spiny lobster)

This recipe is from the restaurant Lucas Carton, in Paris.

	To serve 4	
Four 500 to 600 g	live lobsters	Four 1 to 1¼ lb
	Court-bouillon	
2 each	carrots, and onions, sliced	2
4	shallots, sliced	4
1	small garlic clove	1
1	sprig thyme	1
½	bay leaf	½
60 g	parsley sprigs	2 oz
	salt and pepper	
40 cl	white wine	¾ pint
About 20 cl	water	About 7 fl oz
¼	bulb fennel, finely sliced	¼

Savoury butter sauce		
2 tbsp	finely chopped shallots	2 tbsp
15 cl	vinegar	$\frac{1}{4}$ pint
30 cl	white wine	$\frac{1}{2}$ pint
	salt and pepper	
100 g	very cold butter, diced	$3\frac{1}{2}$ oz

Mix all the court-bouillon ingredients in a large pan and boil for 5 minutes, adding more water if necessary. Plunge the lobsters into the pan and simmer, covered, for 15 minutes.

Meanwhile, make the savoury butter sauce. Put the chopped shallots into a stainless steel or enamelled pan with the vinegar and half the wine. Season with salt and pepper and reduce until the liquid is thick and syrupy. Add the remaining wine, and return to the boil. Vigorously whisk in the butter until the sauce is thick and creamy. It is important to remove the pan from the heat before the last piece of butter is absorbed into the sauce.

Drain the lobsters and arrange them in a warmed serving dish. Serve the sauce separately in a warmed sauceboat.

LES PRINCES DE LA GASTRONOMIE

Fisherman's Spiny Lobster

Langouste Pêcheur

(Option: lobster)

For instructions on cutting up a live lobster, see page 54.

To serve 2

1 kg	live female spiny lobster, cut into pieces, coral and tomalley reserved	2 to $2\frac{1}{2}$ lb
4 tbsp	olive oil	4 tbsp
1	large onion, finely chopped	1
2	large tomatoes, skinned, seeded and chopped	2
10 cl	water	4 fl oz
	salt and pepper	
	Mayonnaise	
	reserved coral and tomalley	
1	egg yolk	1
$\frac{1}{4}$ litre	olive oil	8 fl oz

Heat the oil in a sauté pan, add the onion and tomatoes and cook slowly until the onion is golden. Add the lobster pieces, mix well into the sauce, and cook for a few minutes more, then add the water and season with salt and pepper. Cover and simmer very gently for about 10 minutes.

Meanwhile, pound the coral and tomalley in a mortar, then add the yolk and beat vigorously with the pestle, gradually

adding the oil until the mixture thickens into a mayonnaise.

When the lobster is cooked, remove the pan from the heat. Mix some of the hot sauce into the mayonnaise, then pour the mayonnaise into the pan. Mix well. Serve the lobster pieces with their sauce on a hot serving dish.

EUGÈNE BLANCARD
METS ET PRODUITS DE PROVENCE

Spiny Lobster with Tomato and Wine Sauce

Langouste à l'Américaine

(Option: lobster)

For instructions on cutting up a live lobster, see page 54.

To serve 10

Three 800 to 900 g	live spiny lobsters, cut up, coral reserved	Three $1\frac{3}{4}$ to 2 lb
$\frac{1}{4}$ litre	olive oil	8 fl oz
	salt and pepper	
200 g	butter	7 oz
100 g	shallots, finely chopped	$3\frac{1}{2}$ oz
1	garlic clove, crushed	1
6 tbsp	cognac	6 tbsp
$\frac{1}{2}$ litre	dry white wine	18 fl oz
1 kg	tomatoes, skinned, seeded, and roughly chopped	2 to $2\frac{1}{2}$ lb
	cayenne pepper	
$\frac{1}{2}$ tsp each	chopped chervil and tarragon	$\frac{1}{2}$ tsp each
2 tbsp	chopped parsley	2 tbsp

Heat the oil in a very large sauté pan, season the lobster pieces and toss them into the pan. Stir over a high heat until they are very red, about 5 minutes.

Drain off the oil, leaving the lobster in the sauté pan, and add 50 g (2 oz) of the butter. Add the shallots and garlic. Simmer for a few minutes over a gentle heat, then heat the cognac in a small pan, ignite it, and, when the flames die, add the cognac to the sauté pan, along with the white wine, the tomatoes and a pinch of cayenne pepper. Mix everything over a high heat. When the mixture comes to the boil, lower the heat, cover the pan and cook for 20 minutes.

Crush the coral in a bowl, add the rest of the butter and knead together. Take the lobster pieces from the pan and arrange them in a warmed, deep serving dish.

Reduce the sauce over a high heat to about 30 to 40 cl ($\frac{1}{2}$ to $\frac{3}{4}$ pint). Lower the heat, add the kneaded coral and butter, and stir thoroughly. Add the chervil and tarragon, and heat the sauce, without allowing it to boil. Pour the sauce over the lobster. Sprinkle with the parsley and serve immediately.

ODETTE KAHN
LA PETITE ET LA GRANDE CUISINE

Indonesian Prawn Rissoles

Garnalengehakt

To serve 4

500 g	peeled prawns, finely chopped	1 lb
5	potatoes, boiled and mashed	5
1	small leek, finely chopped	1
	salt and pepper	
	grated nutmeg	
2 tbsp	milk	2 tbsp
1	egg, lightly beaten	1
40 g	dry breadcrumbs	1½ oz
60 g	butter	2 oz
10 cl	fish fumet (*page 174*)	4 fl oz

Mix the prawns with the mashed potatoes, leek, salt, pepper, nutmeg, milk and egg. Form flat rounds of the mixture and roll them lightly in the breadcrumbs. In a large frying pan, fry these rissoles in 40 g (1½ oz) of the butter until they are golden-brown. Remove them from the pan. Add the remaining butter and the fish fumet to the pan and reduce the liquid a little. Return the rissoles to the pan and simmer for a few minutes until heated through.

EMMA W. K. STEINMETZ
ONZE RIJSTTAFEL

Tempura

To serve 4

24	large fresh prawns	24
60 g each	string beans, peeled aubergines and courgettes, washed, dried thoroughly and cut into strips the same size as the prawns	2 oz each
	oil for deep frying	
	Batter	
1	egg	1
¼ litre	water	8 fl oz
150 g	rice flour or plain flour	5 oz

	Sauce	
4 tbsp	soy sauce	4 tbsp
10 cl	fish fumet (*page 174*)	4 fl oz
2 tsp	sugar	2 tsp
	Condiments	
	white radish, peeled and grated	
2 tbsp	horseradish, freshly grated	2 tbsp
1 tbsp	ginger root, freshly grated	1 tbsp

Shell the prawns, leaving the tail fins attached to the flesh. Remove the black veins. Slit the undersection of each prawn to prevent excessive curling. Wash and dry them thoroughly.

Prepare the batter by beating the egg and water together, then adding the flour and mixing lightly. Two or three stirs should do, even though some lumps may remain. The secret of a good batter is to avoid overmixing. An overmixed batter will result in heavy and excessively crusty *tempura*.

Have a deep pan at least three-quarters full of cooking oil and heat until very hot. To test the oil for proper temperature, make a small ball of flour and water and drop it into the hot oil. The temperature is just right if the ball floats to the surface immediately. Dip the prawns and vegetables one at a time into the batter and drop them into the hot oil. Large bubbles will form. When these bubbles become small, the *tempura* is done. Drain and serve hot.

Meanwhile, mix the sauce ingredients in a small saucepan and warm over a low heat. Serve the sauce in individual bowls together with separate condiment dishes of white radish, horseradish and ginger root. Each diner stirs as much of each of the condiments as he chooses into his bowl of sauce. Dip the hot *tempura* into the sauce-condiment mixture and eat.

TATSUJI TADA
JAPANESE RECIPES.

Prawn Gratin

Gratin de Queues de Crevettes

(Option: crayfish)

To serve 2

250 g	prawns, peeled	8 oz
75 g	butter	2½ oz
	pepper	
3 tbsp	cognac	3 tbsp
¼ litre	double cream	8 fl oz
3 or 4	green, outside lettuce leaves, finely shredded	3 or 4

Lightly cook the prawns in a covered pan in 40g (1½ oz) of the butter, adding a little pepper but no salt. After 5 to 6 minutes add the cognac and let it reduce, then add the double cream. Let the cream simmer for a few seconds, then remove the pan from the direct heat, but keep it hot.

Meanwhile, put the shredded lettuce in another pan with the remaining butter, cover, and cook over a low heat for a few minutes. Add the lettuce to the prawns, stirring carefully to ensure they are well mixed. Adjust the seasoning. Put the mixture in a gratin dish, place it in a hot oven, preheated to 220°C (425°F or Mark 7), for 10 minutes or until the surface is bubbling and lightly browned. Serve very hot.

FERNAND POINT
MA GASTRONOMIE

Prawns in Coconut

Udang Masak Lemak

To make the santan, or coconut cream, called for in this recipe, shell and grate a fresh coconut. Pour 15 to 20 cl (6 fl oz) boiling water over the grated flesh, and let stand for 20 minutes. Strain through a fine sieve, pressing to extract all the liquid.

	To serve 2	
10	medium-sized prawns, peeled and washed	10
2 tsp	coconut oil	2 tsp
1	large onion, finely sliced	1
$\frac{1}{4}$ tsp	ground turmeric	$\frac{1}{4}$ tsp
15 to 20 cl	*santan*	6 fl oz

Heat the oil in a saucepan, add the onion and the turmeric, and fry over a medium heat for 1 minute. Add the prawns and the *santan* and simmer for 8 to 10 minutes, without allowing

the mixture to boil, until the prawns are cooked and the sauce has thickened. Serve the prawns and sauce in heated bowls with a separate dish of boiled rice.

LILIAN LANE
MALAYAN COOKERY RECIPES

Dublin Bay Prawns on Skewers

Spiedini di Scampi

(Option: large prawns)

For this recipe the prawn tails should be cooked in their shells which are removed at table. If you shell the prawn tails before cooking, reduce the cooking time to about 8 to 10 minutes.

	To serve 6	
24	large Dublin Bay prawn tails	24
18	fresh bay leaves	18
	salt and freshly ground pepper	
About 3 tbsp	olive oil	About 3 tbsp
90 g	butter	3 oz
2	garlic cloves, crushed	2
6 tbsp	brandy	6 tbsp
	Worcestershire sauce	
6	anchovy fillets, soaked in water and drained	6
1 tbsp	French mustard	1 tbsp
1 tsp	lemon juice	1 tsp

With the point of a sharp knife, slit the underneath part of the shell of each prawn tail on both sides. Thread 4 prawn tails on to each of 6 skewers, alternating the prawn tails with the bay leaves. Season with salt and pepper. Oil a baking tin and arrange the skewered prawn tails in it. Sprinkle with the remaining oil and cook in an oven, preheated to 180°C (350°F or Mark 4), for about 15 minutes, basting occasionally.

In a small pan, melt 30 g (1 oz) of the butter and sauté the garlic until golden. Discard the garlic, add the brandy and a few drops of Worcestershire sauce, and reduce to about half the volume over a brisk heat. Pound the remaining butter with the anchovies and add to the brandy sauce, together with the mustard and lemon juice. Pour this sauce on to a warmed serving dish, arrange the prawn tails on it, and serve very hot.

LUIGI CARNACINA AND LUIGI VERONELLI
LA BUONA VERA CUCINA ITALIANA

Shrimp Croquettes
Garnalenkroketten

(Option: prawns, peeled and coarsely chopped)

To serve 4

400 g	peeled shrimps	14 oz
30 g	butter	1 oz
1	onion, chopped	1
100 g	potato, boiled and mashed	3½ oz
	salt and freshly ground pepper	
	grated nutmeg	
1 tbsp	chopped parsley	1 tbsp
2 to 3 tbsp	milk	2 to 3 tbsp
60 g	fresh breadcrumbs	2 oz
1	large egg, beaten with 2 tbsp water	1
	oil for deep frying	

Melt the butter in a pan and cook the onion until transparent. Transfer the onion to a bowl and mix with the potato, the shrimps, salt, pepper, nutmeg and parsley. Add sufficient milk to bind the mixture, and leave it to cool. Shape the mixture into cork-shaped croquettes and roll these first in the breadcrumbs, then in the beaten egg, and again in the breadcrumbs. Deep fry the croquettes in hot oil until they are evenly brown, about 3 to 4 minutes.

TON VAN ES
HET VOLKOMEN VISBOEK

Shrimps Pommern-Style
Krabben auf Pommersche Art

(Options: prawns or Dublin Bay prawns, split)

To serve 4

400 g	peeled shrimps	14 oz
500 g	potatoes, sliced	1 lb
	salt and pepper	
	paprika	
100 g	butter	3½ oz
1 tbsp	chopped dill	1 tbsp

Dry the potato slices and sprinkle them with salt, pepper and paprika. Mix well. Grease an ovenproof dish with 15 g (½ oz) of the butter. Put in one layer of potato slices. Make a second layer with shrimps and sprinkle with dill. Continue in this way until all ingredients are used, finishing with a layer of potatoes. Cover the surface with thin shavings of the remain-

ing butter. Bake in a hot oven, preheated to 220°C (425°F or Mark 7), for 30 minutes or until the potatoes are tender. Serve with a green salad.

FRITZ BECKER
DAS KOCHBUCH AUS MECKLENBURG, POMMERN UND OSTPREUSSEN

Crab Korma

A korma is a North Indian curry that was originally made with meat. The technique of dissecting crab is demonstrated on page 28. The dried coconut, cumin seeds and whole turmeric called for are available from oriental food stores.

To serve 8 to 12

4	large cooked crabs, cut into pieces	4
¼ litre	curd cheese or yogurt	8 fl oz
2 tbsp	vegetable oil	2 tbsp
4	medium-sized onions, sliced	4
3	cloves	3
3	peppercorns	3
4	green chili peppers, seeded and chopped	4
1	stick cinnamon, 2.5 cm (1 inch) long	1
3	cardamoms, pods removed	3
3 tbsp	lemon juice	3 tbsp
8	sprigs coriander, chopped	8
	salt	
	Masala	
90 g	dried coconut	3 oz
10	garlic cloves	10
1	piece fresh ginger root, 2.5 cm (1 inch) long	1
1 tsp	cumin seeds	1 tsp
1	stick cinnamon, 2.5 cm (1 inch) long	1
1	piece turmeric, 1 cm (½ inch) long, or ½ tsp ground turmeric	1
4	dried red chili peppers	4
2 tbsp	coriander seeds	2 tbsp
1 tbsp	poppy seeds	1 tbsp

Grind the *masala* ingredients to a fine paste, mix with the curd cheese or yogurt and set aside.

Heat the oil in a frying pan and fry the onions until golden-brown. Remove them from the pan and keep aside. Fry the cloves, peppercorns, chili peppers, cinnamon and cardamoms in the same oil for a few minutes, then add the *masala* mixture and the crab pieces and fry well. When the *masala* begins to stick to the pan, add a little water and let the mixture simmer for a few minutes. Then add the fried onions and a little more water to make a gravy. Simmer for a couple of minutes and remove the pan from the heat. Add the lemon juice and the chopped coriander, stir and season to taste with salt. Let the korma stand for 2 minutes before serving hot.

PREMILA LAL
SEA-FOOD DISHES

Crabs in the Toulon Manner

Crabes à la Toulonnaise

If cooked crabs are used for this recipe, the preliminary poaching in court-bouillon should be omitted. For instructions on extracting crab meat from the shell, see page 28.

To serve 4

2	large live crabs, preferably female	2
1 litre	wine court-bouillon (*page 174*)	1¾ pints
1	garlic clove	1
1	sprig fennel	1
1 tsp	lemon juice	1 tsp
1 kg	live mussels, scrubbed	2 to 2½ lb
4 to 5 tbsp	water	4 to 5 tbsp
	salt and pepper	
50 g	butter	2 oz
1 tbsp	flour	1 tbsp
30 cl	milk	½ pint
2 tbsp	toasted breadcrumbs	2 tbsp
1 tbsp	olive oil	1 tbsp

In a large pot, cook the crabs in the court-bouillon for 30 minutes. Take the pot off the heat. When the crabs have cooled, remove everything from the shells. Discard the gills and gravel sac. Wash the empty shells and keep them. Set aside the meat from the claws and legs. In a mortar, pound the crab coral (if any), liver and meat with the garlic and the fennel. Moisten with lemon juice.

Put the mussels in a sauté pan with the water and some salt and pepper. Shake them, covered, over a high heat until they have opened—about 3 to 4 minutes. Strain and reserve the cooking liquid. Remove the mussels from their shells and chop them roughly. Set them aside.

Melt the butter in a large saucepan, add the flour and cook until this roux is very lightly coloured. Stir in the milk and the reserved mussel liquid. Continue stirring until the boil is reached. Then add the pounded crab-meat mixture, the mussels and the meat from the claws and legs. Adjust the seasoning, if necessary, and allow to simmer for a few minutes; then stuff the empty crab shells with the mixture.

Sprinkle the breadcrumbs and olive oil over the top and brown for about 10 minutes in a hot oven, preheated to 220°C (425°F or Mark 7), or brown the dish under a preheated grill.

IRÈNE BORELLI
LA CUISINE PROVENÇALE

Crab Meat Casserole

This dish should be prepared in a shallow earthenware or glass casserole that can be heated on the stove.

To serve 4 to 6

500 g	crab meat	1 lb
60 g	butter	2 oz
4	large mushrooms, thinly sliced	4
2 tsp	grated mild-flavoured onion	2 tsp
2	tomatoes, skinned and thickly sliced	2
	salt	
	cayenne pepper	
¼ litre	double cream	8 fl oz
2 tsp	finely chopped parsley	2 tsp
1 tsp	finely cut chives	1 tsp
3 tbsp	brandy	3 tbsp
100 g	rice, boiled	3½ oz

Melt the butter in a fireproof casserole; add the mushrooms and cook for 5 minutes over a low heat. Add the onion and tomatoes and cook for another 5 minutes. Then add the crab meat, leaving it in as large lumps as possible. Season with salt and cayenne pepper and heat through; then add the cream, stirring gently. Boil for no longer than 1 minute, then add the parsley, chives and brandy. Serve at once from the casserole into soup plates, each containing a spoonful of cooked rice.

THE JUNIOR LEAGUE OF CHARLESTON
CHARLESTON RECEIPTS

Polly Hamblet's Devilled Crab

(Option: peeled, chopped prawns)

To serve 4

500 g	crab meat	1 lb
100 g	cracker crumbs, crushed	3½ oz
125 g	celery, finely diced	4 oz
150 g	onion, chopped	5 oz
125 g	butter, melted	4 oz
4 tbsp	milk	4 tbsp
1 tsp	dry mustard	1 tsp
½ tsp	salt	½ tsp
	cayenne pepper	
2 tbsp	chopped parsley	2 tbsp
1 tbsp	chopped sweet green pepper	1 tbsp

Combine the crab meat with the crumbs, celery and onion and moisten with melted butter and milk. Season with the mustard, salt, cayenne, parsley and sweet green pepper. Mix thoroughly, pile into shells or a casserole, and bake in the oven, preheated to 180°C (350°F or Mark 4), for about 30 minutes. Serve immediately.

JAMES BEARD
FISH COOKERY

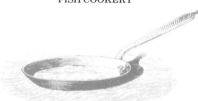

Poached Crayfish

Écrevisses

To serve 5

25	live crayfish, washed	25
1	onion, thickly sliced	1
8	sprigs parsley	8
	salt and pepper	
10 cl	red wine	4 fl oz

Put the crayfish into a 3 litre (5 pint) saucepan. Add all the other ingredients, reserving 1 sprig of parsley. Cover the pan and cook over a high heat, tossing 3 times during the cooking time, for about 10 minutes. The crayfish are cooked when they are red all over.

To serve, remove the onion and parsley, arrange the crayfish in a mound on a deep, warmed platter and pour over the cooking liquor. Put a sprig of parsley on top of the pile.

JULES GOUFFÉ
LE LIVRE DE CUISINE

Gratin of Braised Crayfish Tails

This recipe is by a noted amateur of foods who uses the pen-name Tante Ursule. The first part of the recipe uses the technique of braising à la Bordelaise, shown on page 56.

To serve 4

1 kg	live crayfish, washed	2 to 2½ lb
90 g	butter	3 oz
1	large onion, finely chopped	1
2	carrots, chopped	2
1	stick celery, chopped (optional)	1
1	bay leaf, crumbled	1
1 tsp	crumbled thyme or mixed herbs (thyme, oregano, savory, marjoram)	1 tsp
	salt	
4 tbsp	cognac	4 tbsp
40 cl	dry white wine	¾ pint
	cayenne pepper	
40 g	flour	1½ oz
1.25 litres	fish fumet (*page 174*)	2 pints
15 cl	double cream	¼ pint

Melt 30 g (1 oz) of the butter in a large sauté pan, add the chopped vegetables and the crumbled herbs, and season with salt. Cook over a low heat, stirring from time to time, for 10 minutes, or until the vegetables are softened but not coloured. Turn up the heat, add the crayfish, pour on the cognac and set it alight. Extinguish the flames by pouring on the wine. Season with cayenne, cover and simmer for 8 to 10 minutes. Leave to cool. When the crayfish are cool enough to handle, pull each of them in half, shell the tails and put them aside.

Melt the remaining butter in a heavy saucepan, stir in the flour, and add the fumet to make a fish velouté. Simmer and skim the sauce for at least 1 hour; it should reduce by about two-thirds. In a mortar, pound all the crayfish debris—heads, claws, tail shells—to a paste, a small portion at a time. Add this paste, with the vegetables and juices from the sauté pan, to the velouté. Bring to the boil and simmer for 5 to 10 minutes. Pass the sauce first through a food mill, discarding the shells that remain behind, and then through a fine sieve, discarding the fine debris. You should have a thick purée. Stir the cream into the sauce.

Arrange the crayfish tails tightly in a single layer in a gratin dish, and pour over the sauce. Put in a very hot oven, preheated to 230°C (450°F or Mark 8), for 10 minutes, or until the sauce is bubbling gaily. If the surface has not yet formed an irregular burnished gratin, pass the dish beneath the grill for a few moments before serving. Exquisite.

PETITS PROPOS CULINAIRES

Squid, Cuttlefish and Octopus

Provençal Stuffed Squid

Les Tóuteno Farcies

The technique of cleaning squid is demonstrated on page 24.

To serve 4

1 kg	squid, cleaned, tentacles cut off, chopped and reserved	2 to 2½ lb
2 tbsp	olive oil	2 tbsp
10 cl	brandy	4 fl oz
1	garlic clove, crushed	1
2 tbsp	chopped parsley	2 tbsp
4	anchovy fillets, soaked, drained and chopped	4
2 tbsp	chopped capers	2 tbsp
1 tbsp	flour	1 tbsp
30 cl	white wine	½ pint

Stuffing

	reserved chopped squid tentacles	
1	onion, chopped	1
4 tbsp	olive oil	4 tbsp
3	tomatoes, skinned, seeded and chopped	3
100 g	day-old bread, crusts removed, soaked in milk and squeezed	3½ oz
1	garlic clove, crushed	1
2 tbsp	finely chopped parsley	2 tbsp
2 or 3	egg yolks	2 or 3

To make the stuffing, sauté the onion briefly in the oil. Add the chopped tentacles and sauté for 5 to 10 minutes. Off the heat, add the tomatoes, soaked bread, garlic, parsley and egg yolks, and mix thoroughly. Stuff the squid with this mixture, leaving some room for the stuffing to swell during cooking. Sew up the squid.

Heat the olive oil in a fireproof casserole and sauté the stuffed squid for a minute or two. Pour on the brandy, set it alight and, when the flames die down, add the garlic, parsley, anchovies and capers. Sprinkle with the flour, stirring, and moisten with the wine. Bring to the boil, then cover and cook for 1 hour over a low heat or in an oven preheated to 170°C (325°F or Mark 3).

RENÉ JOUVEAU
LA CUISINE PROVENÇALE

Squid in Their Own Ink

Calamares en su Tinta

(Option: cuttlefish)

The technique of preparing squid and cuttlefish is demonstrated on page 24.

To serve 4

1 kg	tiny squid	2 to 2½ lb
3 to 4 tbsp	olive oil	3 to 4 tbsp
2	onions, chopped	2
2	tomatoes, skinned, seeded and chopped	2
2	garlic cloves, finely chopped	2
1 tbsp	chopped parsley	1 tbsp
2 tbsp	fresh breadcrumbs	2 tbsp
4 tbsp	brandy	4 tbsp
	salt	

Wash the squid well, removing the stomach and the backbone from each of them, cut off the tentacles, and reserve the bags of ink in a cup. Push the tentacles into the bodies of each squid.

Heat the oil in a large frying pan, and gently cook the onions and tomatoes. When the onions begin to soften, add the squid and cook until they become opaque, about 15 minutes. Remove the squid and put them into a shallow, fireproof earthenware dish. Make a sauce in the frying pan by adding the garlic, parsley, breadcrumbs, brandy, a few tablespoons of water, and salt. Cook for a few minutes and add the ink from the bags. Pour this sauce over the squid.

Cover and cook gently either on top of the stove or in an oven preheated to 170°C (325°F or Mark 3) for 1 hour or until the squid are tender. Serve in the same dish, with triangles of fried bread croûtons and white rice.

ANNA MACMIADHACHÁIN
SPANISH REGIONAL COOKERY

Squid Stewed in their Own Ink

Calamares en su Tinta

(Options: cuttlefish, small octopus)

The technique of cleaning and preparing squid, cuttlefish and octopus is demonstrated on page 24.

To serve 6

1 kg	small fresh squid, cleaned, ink sacs reserved	2 to 2½ lb
30 cl	dry red wine	½ pint
3 tbsp	olive oil	3 tbsp
1	garlic clove, crushed lightly	1
3	medium-sized onions, chopped	3
90 g	blanched almonds	3 oz
15 cl	fish fumet or water	¼ pint
	salt and pepper	

Pour the ink from the ink sacs into a bowl, mix with 3 tablespoons of the wine and keep for later use. Chop the squid heads and tentacles into small pieces, and slice the bodies into rings. Cover all the squid flesh with the remaining wine and leave to stand for a couple of hours.

Heat the oil; fry the garlic in it until brown and then discard. Fry the onion until soft, remove it and set aside.

Drain the squid flesh, but keep the liquor in which it was steeped. Fry the squid in the oil for 2 to 3 minutes, stirring constantly. Add the onion, the ink mixed with wine, the liquor in which the squid flesh was steeped, the almonds, the fish fumet or water, and salt and pepper to taste. Cover and simmer for 1 hour on a low heat. Serve with plain boiled rice.

MARINA PEREYRA DE AZNAR AND NINA FROUD
THE HOME BOOK OF SPANISH COOKERY

Stuffed Squid Greek-Style

Kalamarakia Yemista

The technique of cleaning squid is demonstrated on page 24.

To serve 4 or 5

1 kg	medium-sized squid, cleaned	2 to 2½ lb
	salt	
6 tbsp	olive oil	6 tbsp
10 cl	white wine	4 fl oz
35 cl	tomato juice, heated	12 fl oz

Stuffing

1	large onion, finely chopped	1
6 tbsp	olive oil	6 tbsp
90 g	rice	3 oz
4 tbsp	pine-nuts	4 tbsp
4 tbsp	currants	4 tbsp
2 tbsp	chopped parsley	2 tbsp
	salt and pepper	

Rub the squid with salt and rinse well in running water.

To make the stuffing, cook the onion in the oil until soft. Add the rice, pine-nuts, currants, parsley, salt and some pepper. Partially fill the squid with the stuffing, leaving room for the rice to swell. Sew up the openings. Heat the oil in a large frying pan and over a high heat sauté the stuffed bodies and the tentacles. Arrange these in a fireproof casserole. Add the wine, the hot tomato juice and salt to taste. Cover the casserole and cook over a very low heat, or bake in an oven preheated to 180°C (350°F or Mark 4) for about 1½ hours, or until the squid are tender and the sauce is thick. Serve hot or cold.

CHRISSA PARADISSIS
THE BEST OF GREEK COOKERY

Grilled Squid from Setúbal

Lulas Grelhadas à Setubalense

This recipe is from a Portuguese fishing town near Lisbon. The technique of preparing squid is demonstrated on page 24.

To serve 4

700 g	small squid	1½ lb
1	sprig parsley, chopped	1
	salt and pepper	
15 g	butter, softened	½ oz
2 tbsp	olive oil	2 tbsp

Clean the squid, removing the cartilage from the hoods and discarding the ink sacs. Cut off the squid tentacles and chop them up. Mix them with the parsley, salt, pepper and butter. Stuff the bodies of the squid with this mixture and close the open end of each squid with a wooden toothpick. Season with salt and pepper, brush them with olive oil and grill them, turning once, for 10 to 15 minutes in all.

Serve the squid with boiled potatoes sprinkled with melted butter, lemon juice and chopped parsley.

MARIA ODETTE CORTES VALENTE
COZINHA REGIONAL PORTUGUESA

Stuffed Squid

Calmars ou Tautennes Farcies

The technique of preparing squid is demonstrated on page 24.

To serve 4

1 kg	squid cleaned, tentacles finely chopped and reserved	2 to 2½ lb
5 to 6 tbsp	dried breadcrumbs	5 to 6 tbsp
2 tbsp	olive oil	2 tbsp
	Sauce	
1	medium-sized onion, chopped	1
2 tbsp	olive oil	2 tbsp
1	bay leaf	1
1	garlic clove, crushed	1
1 tbsp	flour	1 tbsp
15 cl	white wine	¼ pint
15 cl	hot water	¼ pint
	salt and pepper	
	Stuffing	
	reserved squid tentacles	
1	medium-sized onion, finely chopped	1
About 4 tbsp	olive oil	About 4 tbsp
2 or 3	large tomatoes, skinned, seeded and chopped	2 or 3
	salt and pepper	
100 g	bread, crusts removed, soaked in milk and squeezed	3½ oz
2	garlic cloves, finely chopped	2
2 tbsp	finely chopped parsley	2 tbsp
2 tbsp	hot water	2 tbsp
2 or 3	egg yolks	2 or 3

To prepare the sauce, lightly sauté the onion in the olive oil. Add the bay leaf, garlic and flour. Stir well, add the wine and hot water and season with salt and pepper. Bring to the boil, cover and simmer for about 15 minutes.

To make the stuffing, sauté the onion in the oil, add the chopped tentacles, then the tomatoes. Season with salt and pepper and cook, stirring, until the tomatoes' liquid is reduced. Add the bread, garlic and parsley, and mix thoroughly. Moisten with the hot water, mix in the egg yolks and remove from the heat. You should have a fairly thick and well-flavoured stuffing mixture.

Spread the squid pouches out on a cloth. Fill the pouches three-quarters full with the stuffing, then sew up the openings. Place the stuffed pouches side by side in an oiled sauté pan, and pour over the sauce. Sprinkle with the breadcrumbs, then with the remaining oil, and bake in an oven, preheated to 180°C (350°F or Mark 4), for about 50 minutes, or until a gratin crust has formed. Serve the squid on a warmed serving dish with the sauce around.

J. B. REBOUL
LA CUISINIÈRE PROVENÇALE

Cuttlefish and Squid Stew

Seppie e Calamari in Zimino

Zimino *is a Genoese stew of fish. The original recipe suggests that* moscardini—*tiny octopus, common in the Mediterranean—can be prepared in the same way. The technique of preparing squid and cuttlefish is demonstrated on page 24.*

To serve 4

1.5 kg	cuttlefish or squid, or both	3 lb
500 g	chard or spinach leaves, ribs removed, chopped	1 lb
	salt and pepper ·	
500 g	tomatoes, skinned, seeded and chopped	1 lb
	Sofrito	
1	onion, finely chopped	1
1 tbsp each	finely chopped parsley, wild fennel leaves and celery leaves	1 tbsp each
1	garlic clove, finely chopped	1
3 to 4 tbsp	olive oil	3 to 4 tbsp

Make the *sofrito* by frying the onion, parsley, fennel and celery leaves, and the garlic in the oil in a fireproof casserole. When it has cooked a minute or two, add the chard or spinach. Let the mixture simmer for a few minutes in the covered casserole, and then add the cuttlefish or squid, salt, pepper and tomatoes, and continue cooking until the fish are tender, which will take between 30 and 45 minutes.

Some people prefer the dish without tomatoes and, if this is the case, the quantity of parsley, celery leaves and other green stuff can be increased.

GUELFO CAVANNA
DONI DI NETTUNO

Cuttlefish Stewed with Green Olives

Seiches à la Mode de l'Estaque

For instructions on how to prepare cuttlefish, see page 25

To serve 4

1 kg	cuttlefish, cleaned and cut into small pieces	2 to 2½ lb
750 g	tomatoes, skinned, seeded and chopped	1½ lb
3	garlic cloves, crushed	3
1	bouquet of fennel and bay leaf	1
3 tbsp	olive oil	3 tbsp
	salt and pepper	
15 to 20 cl	white wine	6 fl oz
75 g	green olives, stoned	2½ oz

Put the cuttlefish into a fireproof, earthenware casserole with the chopped tomatoes, garlic, bouquet of fennel and bay leaf, olive oil, salt and pepper. Bring to the boil, then add the white wine and the olives.

When the sauce has returned to the boil, cover the casserole and simmer slowly for about 1 hour. Remove the herb bouquet before serving.

C. CHANOT-BULLIER
VIEILLES RECETTES DE CUISINE PROVENÇALE

Octopus with Potatoes and Peas

Pulpo con Patatas y Guisantes

The technique of preparing octopus is described on page 24.

To serve 4

1 kg	octopus, cleaned and skinned	2 to 2½ lb
	salt	
15 cl	olive oil	¼ pint
1	large onion, chopped	1
3 or 4	garlic cloves, chopped	3 or 4
250 g	tomatoes, skinned, seeded and chopped	8 oz
¼ tsp	chili pepper	¼ tsp
500 g	potatoes, peeled and cut into chunks or thick slices	1 lb
250 g	cooked peas	8 oz

Put the octopus in a large saucepan without adding any water. Sprinkle with salt, cover, and let the octopus cook in the juices which exude from it over a low heat for about 45 minutes. Three or four times during the cooking, lift the octopus out, using a fork, and dip it into a pan of boiling water; then run the octopus under cold water and return it to the saucepan to continue cooking.

Heat the olive oil in a fireproof casserole and gently fry in it the onion, garlic, tomatoes and chili pepper for 10 minutes, or until the onion is soft and the tomatoes have reduced. Add the potatoes and cook for about 5 minutes. Then add the octopus and enough of its cooking liquid to cover the contents of the casserole. Add salt as necessary, and let the dish cook gently, uncovered, for about 30 minutes, or until the potatoes are tender and the sauce is largely reduced. Finally, add the cooked peas to the casserole and heat through. Serve the octopus and vegetables straight from the casserole.

LEONORA RAMIREZ
EL PESCADO EN MI COCINA

Galician Octopus Pie

(Options: squid, angler-fish, lobster)

This version of a famous Galician dish, the like of which I have not met elsewhere in the world, is that given to me by Señora Pilar Bustamante, whose home in Galicia is at La Coruña. Before I give her instructions, let me make clear that the resulting "pie" is as wide and flat and thin as a pizza.

To serve 4

500g	octopus, cleaned	1 lb
2	bay leaves	2
	salt	
2	large onions, chopped	2
3 tbsp	olive oil	3 tbsp
4	large tomatoes, skinned, seeded and chopped	4
1	sweet red pepper, seeded and chopped	1
	Pastry	
2	eggs	2
½ tsp	salt	½ tsp
10 cl	milk	4 fl oz
10 cl	olive oil	4 fl oz
1 tbsp	rendered pork fat or melted lard	1 tbsp
350 g	flour	12 oz

To make the pastry, mix together in a large bowl the eggs, salt, milk, oil and melted fat. Then add the flour, little by little, so as to form a soft dough (*masa blanda*). You will know when it is right because the dough will no longer stick to your fingers, although it will still be quite moist. Knead the dough very briefly, roll it out and let it rest while you cook the octopus and prepare the rest of the pie filling.

Fill a fireproof casserole with boiling water and drop the bay leaves into it. Take hold of one tentacle and lower the octopus 3 or 4 times successively into the water, which must continue to boil hard, until the octopus curls. Once it has curled, leave the octopus in the water and simmer for about half an hour. Towards the end of cooking, add a little salt. Remove the octopus, let it cool, then cut it into small pieces.

Meanwhile, fry the onions very gently in the oil, covered, taking care that they do not brown. Add the tomatoes and let them cook, too. Then add the red pepper and the pieces of octopus, and continue cooking for 10 to 15 minutes more. Let the mixture cool before using it.

Divide the pastry dough into two. Take a wide and shallow baking tin—for example, a round one of 30 cm (12 inches) diameter or a rectangular one 25 by 32 cm (10 by 13 inches). Lightly oil the tin. Roll out half the dough so that it will cover the bottom of the tin. Place the rolled dough in the tin so that the dough comes up the sides and overlaps the edges. Spread the filling over this. Roll out the rest of the dough to make the top of the pie, and put this in place, rolling the edges over and crimping them to make a tight seal all the way round. Cook the pie in a moderate oven, preheated to 180°C (350°F or Mark 4), for about 30 minutes, until it is a light golden-brown.

ALAN DAVIDSON
NORTH ATLANTIC SEAFOOD

Octopus and Fennel in Wine, Cretan-Style

Oktapodi Maratho Krasato

The technique of cleaning octopus is described on page 24.

To serve 4

600 to 700g	octopus, cleaned	1¼ to 1½ lb
5 to 6 tbsp	olive oil	5 to 6 tbsp
1	medium-sized onion or 5 spring onions, chopped	1
¼ litre	dry red wine	8 fl oz
1	bunch wild fennel leaves and tender sprigs, chopped	1
3 or 4	tomatoes, skinned, seeded and chopped	3 or 4
	salt and freshly ground pepper	

Using a sharp knife, cut the octopus into rounds, the thickness of a little finger. Heat the oil in a casserole, add the onion and cook over a low heat until translucent and soft. Add the octopus slices to the onion, pour in the wine, and simmer, covered, for 15 minutes. Put the fennel and tomatoes on top of

the octopus, season with salt and pepper to taste, and give the casserole a shake to mix. Cover and simmer until the octopus is fork-tender (45 to 50 minutes or longer, depending on the size and age of the octopus). Serve warm or cold.

VILMA LIACOURAS CHANTILES
THE FOOD OF GREECE

Stewed Octopus

Poulpe à la Marseillaise

The technique of cleaning octopus is described on page 24.

To serve 4

1 kg	octopus, cleaned and cut into small pieces	2 to 2½ lb
4 to 6 tbsp	olive oil	4 to 6 tbsp
	salt and pepper	
1	leek, chopped	1
1	onion, chopped	1
1	bouquet of thyme, fennel, bay leaf and celery	1
4	medium-sized tomatoes, skinned, seeded and chopped	4
¼ tsp	powdered saffron	¼ tsp
1	garlic clove, crushed	1
175 g	rice, rinsed and drained	6 oz

Heat the oil in a fireproof casserole. Toss in the pieces of octopus, and sauté over a brisk heat, adding salt and pepper. When the pieces are golden, add the leek, onion and bouquet garni. As soon as the leek starts to turn golden, add the tomatoes, saffron and the garlic.

Add enough water to cover the contents of the casserole by about 1 cm (½ inch). Cover and cook over low heat for 1 hour, adding water from time to time to keep the level of the liquid constant. About 20 minutes before serving, add the rice. Serve straight from the casserole, or in a heated serving dish.

H. HEYRAUD
LA CUISINE À NICE

Shellfish

Oyster Pie

Tourte d'Huîtres Fraîches

The technique of opening oysters is demonstrated on page 30.

To serve 6

500 g	shelled oysters	1 lb
125 g	butter	4 oz
2 tbsp	chopped parsley	2 tbsp
4	Welsh or spring onions, chopped	4
125 g	button mushrooms, thinly sliced or coarsely chopped	4 oz
	salt and pepper	
4	hard-boiled egg yolks	4
2	large artichoke bottoms, quartered and parboiled for 15 minutes	2
60 g	morels	2 oz
125 g	asparagus tips, parboiled	4 oz
	shortcrust or rough puff pastry (*page 175*)	
1 tbsp	flour	1 tbsp
15 cl	unripe grape juice, or white wine mixed with 2 tbsp lemon juice	¼ pint
	grated nutmeg	
2	egg yolks, beaten with 1 tbsp unripe grape juice	2

Plunge the oysters into boiling water and drain them. Melt half the butter in a sauté pan and add the parsley, Welsh onions and mushrooms. Sauté for a minute or two, then add the oysters, season well with salt and pepper, and sauté for another minute. Cool in a bowl.

Melt the remaining butter in the pan, and sauté the hard-boiled egg yolks, artichoke bottoms, morels and asparagus tips, turning them for a minute or two to coat them well with the butter. Add them to the oysters in the bowl and set the sauté pan aside to cool.

Line a deep 1 litre (2 pint) pie dish with two-thirds of the pastry and fill with the cooled mixture. Cover the pie with the remaining pastry, cutting a hole in the middle. Crimp the edges to seal well. Bake in an oven preheated to 180°C (350°F or Mark 4) for 30 minutes or until the pastry is well browned.

Meanwhile, stir the flour into the juices in the sauté pan, and stir over a medium heat until lightly browned. Stir in the grape juice or the wine and lemon juice, and continue to cook until the sauce has thickened. Season the sauce with nutmeg, remove from the heat and stir in the beaten egg yolks and grape juice. Pour the mixture through a funnel into the pie, shaking the pie dish slightly to mix the sauce with the filling. Return to the oven for 5 minutes and serve hot.

LA VARENNE
LE CUISINIER FRANÇOIS

Oysters Rockefeller

(Options: mussels, scallops)

A famous dish said to have been invented at Antoine's, the celebrated New Orleans restaurant, at the end of the last century. Some inspired customer allegedly remarked that the oysters stuffed in this way were "as rich as Rockefeller".

The technique of opening oysters is demonstrated on page 30.

To serve 4 to 6

48	oysters, scrubbed and opened, deeper shells reserved	48
500 g	coarse salt	1 lb
125 g	butter	4 oz
8	rashers bacon, crisply cooked, drained and crushed	8
300 g	spinach, finely chopped	10 oz
3 tbsp	chopped parsley	3 tbsp
3 tbsp	chopped celery leaves	3 tbsp
3 tbsp	chopped spring onions	3 tbsp
6 tbsp	dry breadcrumbs	6 tbsp
½ tsp	salt	½ tsp
	Tabasco sauce, or pepper and paprika	
1 tsp	pastis	1 tsp

For this dish the oysters are usually arranged in their deeper shells, on a bed of coarse salt, in 4 or 6 shallow pans according to whether you are serving 4 or 6 people.

Melt the butter. Add the bacon crumbs and spinach, and the rest of the ingredients except the pastis. Cook for 5 to 10 minutes over a low heat, stirring the mixture until you have a lightly cooked stuffing. Taste and adjust the seasonings. Divide the stuffing between the oysters. Place under a hot grill or in an oven preheated to 220°C (425°F or Mark 7) until the oysters are bubbling and lightly browned. Just before serving, put a few drops of pastis on each oyster with an eye-dropper. Serve in the pans of salt.

JANE GRIGSON
FISH COOKERY

Stuffed Oysters, Williamsburg

This is an old colonial recipe, in use not only on Long Island but also along the Maryland and Virginia tidewater districts 200 years ago.

The technique of preparing oysters is shown on page 30. If walnut ketchup is not available, substitute vinegar in which walnuts have been pickled. Alternatively, use wine vinegar.

	To serve 4	
24	oysters, shelled, drained of their liquor and chopped; deeper shells cleaned and reserved	24
2	slices bread, crusts removed, crumbled	2
1	small onion, finely chopped	1
1 tbsp	chopped parsley	1 tbsp
2 tbsp	finely chopped celery	2 tbsp
1 tsp	walnut ketchup	1 tsp
30 g	butter	1 oz
2 or 3 tbsp	lemon juice	2 or 3 tbsp
2 tsp	grated lemon rind	2 tsp
	salt and pepper	
	cayenne pepper	
2	eggs, beaten	2
60 g	breadcrumbs, lightly fried in butter	2 oz
1	lemon, sliced	1

Put the oysters into a pan and add the crumbled bread, onion, parsley, celery, walnut ketchup, butter, lemon juice and rind, salt, pepper and a pinch of cayenne pepper. Cook for 15 minutes over a low heat, stirring constantly. Then add the beaten eggs, mixing them in thoroughly. Fill the reserved oyster shells with this mixture. Sprinkle with the breadcrumbs and brown in a hot oven, preheated to 220°C (425°F or Mark 7), for about 10 minutes. Garnish with the lemon slices.

J. GEORGE FREDERICK AND JEAN JOYCE
LONG ISLAND SEAFOOD COOK BOOK

Cockle Pie

Pastai Gocos

(Option: small clams)

For this recipe from South Pembrokeshire, the cockles should be soaked overnight in salt water to which a little oatmeal has been added. (The oatmeal helps to clean the cockles.)

	To serve 3 or 4	
1.25 litres	cockles, soaked overnight and drained	2 pints
	salt and pepper	
40 cl	white sauce (*page 172*)	$\frac{3}{4}$ pint
	shortcrust pastry (*page 175*), or 6 tbsp grated Cheddar cheese	

Boil the cockles in clean water until the shells open. Take the cockles out of their shells and put them into a 90 cl (1½ pint) pie dish. Season with salt and pepper and pour the white sauce over them. Cover with shortcrust pastry, and cut a few slits in the pastry, or sprinkle over a thick layer of grated cheese. Bake in a fairly hot oven, preheated to 190°C (375°F or Mark 5), until golden-brown—about 40 minutes for pastry, 20 minutes for cheese topping.

S. MINWEL TIBBOTT
WELSH FARE

Scallops in White Wine

Coquilles Saint-Jacques "Maître Paul"

For instructions on how to clean and open scallops, see page 31. This recipe will serve 10 to 12 people as an hors d'oeuvre.

	To serve 6	
24	scallops, shells removed, corals reserved, white muscles cut into 2 or 3 slices	24
100 g	butter	3½ oz
	salt and pepper	
3	shallots, very finely chopped	3
2 tbsp	chopped parsley	2 tbsp
10 cl	white wine	4 fl oz

Put the scallops, with their corals, into a heavy-based saucepan. Add the remaining ingredients. Simmer, covered, over a moderate heat for 3 to 5 minutes or until the scallops are cooked. Remove the scallops, turn up the heat, and reduce the sauce for 5 to 10 minutes or until it is smooth, syrupy and the colour of ivory. Return the scallops to the pan and heat through. This recipe is, in my opinion, the one which best brings out the delicate flavour of scallops.

CURNONSKY
CUISINE ET VINS DE FRANCE

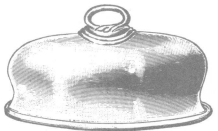

Scallops with Mushrooms

Coquilles Saint-Jacques à la Ménagère

The technique of opening scallops is demonstrated on page 31. Scrub the insides of the concave shells and reserve them for serving scallops or other fish dishes. The technique of preparing court-bouillon is demonstrated on page 34.

	To serve 6	
12	live scallops, opened and cleaned	12
300 g	butter	10 oz
250 g	button mushrooms, thinly sliced	8 oz
2 tbsp	flour	2 tbsp
2	egg yolks	2
3 to 4 tbsp	fine breadcrumbs	3 to 4 tbsp
	Court-bouillon	
¼ litre	water	8 fl oz
10 cl	dry white wine	4 fl oz
1	sprig thyme	1
½	bay leaf	½
1	medium-sized onion, finely chopped	1
	salt and pepper	

Prepare the court-bouillon. Then poach the cleaned scallop muscles and corals in this court-bouillon for 4 minutes. Strain the scallops and corals and reserve the cooking liquid. Set the corals aside and cut the scallop muscles into slices about 5 mm (¼ inch) thick.

Heat 50 g (2 oz) of the butter in a frying pan, toss in the mushrooms and cook them rapidly, then add the scallop slices, mix well and remove the pan from the heat. Keep the mixture hot, covered.

In a sauté pan, melt 100 g (3½ oz) of the butter. Add the flour and cook gently, stirring, for 10 minutes to make a roux. Remove the pan from the heat and cool the roux. Stir 2 tablespoons of the court-bouillon into the egg yolks; heat the remainder and add it to the roux, stirring until you have obtained a smooth sauce. Bring the sauce to the boil, stirring with a whisk, and cook for 1 minute.

Off the heat, thicken the sauce with the egg yolks. Continue to whisk the sauce while heating. Remove the pan from the heat when the mixture approaches boiling point: do not let the sauce boil, or the egg yolks will cook and form small lumps.

Whisk in 100 g (3½ oz) of the butter and check the seasoning.

Plunge 6 of the concave scallop shells into boiling water, drain them and wipe them dry. Place 1 tablespoon of the sauce into each shell. Then add to each shell the meat of about 2 sliced scallops, some mushrooms and, finally, 2 pieces of coral. Cover with the sauce and sprinkle over some fine breadcrumbs. Melt the remaining butter and sprinkle it over the breadcrumbs. Brown the scallops in a very hot oven, preheated to 240°C (475°F or Mark 9), for 5 to 6 minutes.

Serve the scallops on a platter on top of a folded napkin.

PAUL BOCUSE
THE NEW CUISINE

Scallops with Saffron

Coquilles Saint-Jacques au Safran

This is a recipe from Maxim's, Paris. To make the rice pilau that is suggested as an accompaniment to this dish, sauté raw rice in a little oil or butter in a saucepan; add twice as much boiling water as the volume of rice used. Cover and cook gently until all the liquid is absorbed.

The technique of removing scallops from their shells is demonstrated on page 31.

	To serve 4	
4 kg	scallops, shells removed, flesh and coral cleaned	9 lb
75 g	butter	2½ oz
1	shallot, chopped	1
¼ tsp	ground saffron	¼ tsp
	salt and pepper	
1 tsp	cognac	1 tsp
1 tsp	vermouth	1 tsp
2	large tomatoes, skinned, seeded and roughly chopped	2
100 g	mushrooms, finely sliced	3½ oz
40 cl	double cream	¾ pint

Heat the butter in a sauté pan and add the shallot. As soon as the shallot turns transparent, add the scallops' flesh and coral and the saffron and season with salt. Stew for 2 minutes, add the cognac and vermouth, then the tomatoes, mushrooms and cream. Stew for 8 minutes.

Remove the scallops, arrange them in a warmed serving dish. Reduce the sauce until it thickens slightly, and taste for salt and pepper. Coat the scallops with the sauce. Serve them hot, with a rice pilau.

LES PRINCES DE LA GASTRONOMIE

Maine Coast Clam Fritters

(Option: any edible clam)

To serve 4

500 g	freshly shelled clam meat, very finely chopped	1 lb
2	large eggs, beaten	2
125 g	flour	4 oz
¼ litre	milk	8 fl oz
½ tsp	salt	½ tsp
¼ tsp	pepper	¼ tsp
	oil or fat for deep frying	

Make the batter by beating the eggs and adding the flour gradually. Add the milk slowly, then the salt and pepper. Add the chopped clams and stir all together. Heat the fat to about 190°C (375°F) or until it colours a 2.5 cm (1 inch) cube of bread golden-brown. Drop the clam mixture by spoonfuls into the fat. When the fritters are brown, turn them and brown on the reverse side. Serve piping hot.

A MAINE COOKBOOK

Clam Pie

(Option: cockles)

To serve 4

1.5 kg	clams	3 lb
½ litre	white wine	18 fl oz
1	carrot, finely sliced	1
1	onion, finely sliced	1
1	bay leaf	1
1 tsp	freshly ground black pepper	1 tsp
90 g	butter	3 oz
2 tbsp	flour	2 tbsp
500 g	mushrooms	1 lb
	salt	
3 tbsp	sherry or Madeira	3 tbsp
	shortcrust or rough puff pastry (page 175)	
1	egg yolk, beaten with 2 tbsp water	1

Steam the clams in the white wine with the carrot, onion, bay leaf and pepper, until the clam shells have all opened. Remove the clams from their shells; strain the cooking broth.

Melt half the butter, stir in the flour, and add the strained clam broth to make a velouté sauce. Simmer for at least 10 minutes, preferably longer, stirring occasionally, and season to taste. Sauté the mushrooms in the remaining butter;

season to taste. Combine the mushrooms, clams and velouté sauce, and add the sherry or Madeira. Cool thoroughly.

Pour the mixture into a deep 1 litre (2 pint) baking dish and top with the pastry, rolled out to a thickness of about 5 mm (¼ inch) thick. Cut a small hole in the centre of the pastry. Decorate with leaves cut from the remaining pastry, brush with the egg yolk mixed with water, and bake in an oven, preheated to 230°C (450°F or Mark 8), for 15 minutes. Reduce the heat to 180°C (350°F or Mark 4) and bake for about 20 minutes longer, until nicely browned.

JAMES BEARD
JAMES BEARD'S NEW FISH COOKERY

Conch Fritters

(Option: whelk)

The conch is a marine snail, the warm-water equivalent of the whelk. It occurs along the east coast of the United States and the Gulf of Mexico. The conch has an excellent flavour but its meat, like that of the abalone, is tough and needs tenderizing treatment. It is usually pounded or minced and made into fritters or chowder.

To serve 4 to 6

12	live conches	12
3	eggs, yolks separated from whites	3
100 g	onion, very finely chopped	3½ oz
1	large tomato, skinned, seeded and chopped	1
2 tbsp	very finely chopped parsley	2 tbsp
1	garlic clove, very finely chopped	1
1 tsp	salt	1 tsp
½ tsp	black pepper	½ tsp
70 g	fine cracker crumbs	2½ oz
1 tbsp	cream (if needed)	1 tbsp

In a large pot, cover the live conches with cold water, bring to the boil and simmer covered for about 15 minutes. Drain the conches and remove the meat from the shells using a trussing needle or small skewer. Rinse the meat and put it through a food chopper. Beat the egg yolks slightly. Combine the conch meat, egg yolks, onion, tomato, parsley, garlic, salt and pepper and crumbs. Blend thoroughly. If the mixture is too stiff to drop from a spoon, blend in the cream. Beat the egg whites until stiff and fold them into the conch mixture.

Heat a well-greased, heavy frying pan or griddle to sizzling. Drop the mixture, a tablespoonful at a time, into the hot pan. Cook until evenly browned on one side, turn and brown the other side. Serve with a salad.

FRANCES MACILQUHAM
FISH COOKERY OF NORTH AMERICA

Mussels Bordeaux-Style

Moules à la Bordelaise

To serve 4

3.5 litres	live mussels, scrubbed	6 pints
10 cl	white wine	4 fl oz
30 g	butter	1 oz
2	shallots, chopped	2
500 g	tomatoes, skinned, seeded and chopped	1 lb
	salt and pepper	
1	garlic clove, chopped	1
3 tbsp	chopped parsley	3 tbsp
30 g	fresh breadcrumbs, soaked in milk and strained	1 oz
1 tsp	grated lemon peel	1 tsp

Put the mussels and the wine in a large pan, cover and let the mussels open over a high heat. Strain the mussels and remove the empty half-shells. Reserve some of the cooking liquor.

In a small pan melt the butter, and in this sauté the shallots over a low heat; add the tomatoes, seasoning, garlic, parsley and the breadcrumbs. Raise the heat slightly and stir the sauce until the tomatoes are cooked, then add a little of the strained juice from the mussels, and the grated lemon peel. Put the cooked mussels into a fireproof gratin dish, pour the sauce over them and simmer for 3 to 4 minutes, until the mussels are hot.

ELIZABETH DAVID
FRENCH COUNTRY COOKING

Mussels Steamed in Wine

Moules à la Marinière

To serve 8

4 litres	live mussels, scrubbed	7 pints
1	onion, chopped	1
2	shallots, chopped	2
150 g	parsley, finely chopped	5 oz
	freshly ground pepper	
150 g	butter	5 oz
40 cl	dry white wine	¾ pint
3 tbsp	lemon juice	3 tbsp

Put the mussels into a saucepan with the onion, shallots, parsley, pepper, 100 g (3½ oz) of the butter and the white wine. Cover and cook the mussels for a few minutes over a high heat, shaking the pan several times to ensure even cooking.

When all the mussels have opened, transfer them to a heated serving dish and keep them warm.

Strain the cooking liquid into a smaller saucepan. Over a high heat, reduce the liquid to one-third its original quantity. Remove from the heat and whisk in the remaining butter, cut into chunks, until the sauce has thickened and become foamy. Whisk in the lemon juice and pour the sauce over the mussels. Serve very hot.

ACADÉMIE CULINAIRE DE FRANCE
CUISINE FRANÇAISE

Creamed Mussels

Mouclade

To serve 8

2.5 litres	live mussels, scrubbed	4 pints
15 cl	dry white wine	¼ pint
2	shallots, chopped	2
	salt and pepper	
	Sauce	
50 g	butter	2 oz
30 g	flour	1 oz
	salt and pepper	
1	garlic clove, chopped	1
1	egg yolk	1
1 tbsp	lemon juice	1 tbsp
10 cl	cream	4 fl oz
1 tsp	curry powder	1 tsp
	chopped parsley	

Put the mussels in a saucepan with the white wine, shallots, salt and pepper. Cover and place over a high heat, shaking the saucepan occasionally, until all the mussels have opened. Remove the mussels. Strain the cooking liquor through a muslin-lined sieve and set aside. Discard one half shell from each mussel and keep the mussels hot in the remaining half shells, arranged on a warmed platter.

To make the sauce, melt the butter in a saucepan and, using a wooden spoon, stir in the flour. Just as the mixture begins to turn golden, add the strained mussel-cooking liquor and stir well. Season with salt and pepper and add the garlic. Simmer for 10 minutes over a low heat, stirring all the time. Put the egg yolk into a bowl; add the lemon juice, cream and curry powder, then slowly pour in the sauce, stirring.

Coat the mussels with the sauce and sprinkle with parsley.

ODETTE KAHN
LA PETITE ET LA GRANDE CUISINE

Mussels in Basil Sauce

Moules au Pistou

To serve 2

500 g	live mussels, scrubbed	1 lb
1 tbsp	olive oil	1 tbsp
3	garlic cloves, crushed	3
4	large tomatoes, skinned, seeded and roughly chopped	4
4 to 5 tbsp	double cream	4 to 5 tbsp
	salt, pepper and cayenne pepper	
$\frac{1}{8}$ tsp	sugar	$\frac{1}{8}$ tsp
1 tbsp	kirsch	1 tbsp
1	large bouquet basil, leaves only, finely shredded just before use	1
1 tbsp	finely chopped parsley	1 tbsp

Heat the oil in a sauté pan with the garlic, tomatoes, cream, salt and pepper, a pinch of cayenne and the sugar. Reduce the mixture by about one-third. Toss in the mussels and sauté them until the shells open. Remove each one from the pan as soon as it has opened. Discard the shells, and keep the mussels warm in a covered dish. Reduce the liquid again, to evaporate the juice from the mussels. Add the kirsch, adjust the seasoning and add half the basil. Return the mussels to the pan for a few seconds. Pour the contents of the pan into a hot dish, sprinkle over the parsley and remaining basil and serve.

JEAN AND PAUL MINCHELLI
CRUSTACÉS, POISSONS ET COQUILLAGES

Mussels Stuffed with Spinach

Moules aux Épinards

For the technique of opening mussels with a knife see page 92.

To serve 4

1 kg	large live mussels, scrubbed	2 to 2$\frac{1}{2}$ lb
500 g	small live mussels, scrubbed	1 lb
1 kg	spinach, blanched and finely chopped	2 to 2$\frac{1}{2}$ lb
90 g	fresh breadcrumbs, soaked in milk and squeezed	3 oz
	salt and pepper	
4 tbsp	olive oil	4 tbsp
2	onions, chopped	2
4	large tomatoes, skinned, seeded and chopped	4

Put the small mussels into a pan containing a little simmering water. When the shells have opened, remove the mussels from the pan, shell them, and discard the shells. Mix the small mussels with about two-thirds of the spinach. Add the breadcrumbs, and season with salt and pepper. One by one, open the large mussels with a knife, making sure that the flesh remains attached to both halves of the shell, and stuff them with this mixture. Tie each mussel securely with string.

Heat the oil in a large pan and sauté the onions and tomatoes until the onions are soft. Mix in the remaining spinach, season, and add the mussels. Cook gently, covered, for 15 minutes. Remove the mussels to a warmed serving dish, snip off the string, pour over the sauce, and serve.

C. CHANOT-BULLIER
VIEILLES RECETTES DE CUISINE PROVENÇALE

Mussels in Green Sauce

Moules au Vert

(Options: cockles, small clams)

To serve 6

3 kg	live mussels, scrubbed	6 to 7 lb
40 g	butter	1$\frac{1}{2}$ oz
1	onion, thinly sliced	1
40 g	parsley, finely chopped	1$\frac{1}{2}$ oz
$\frac{1}{2}$	celery stick, thinly sliced	$\frac{1}{2}$
	salt and pepper	
15 to 20 cl	dry white wine	6 fl oz
50 g	sorrel, chopped	2 oz
1	bouquet chervil, chopped	1
3	sage leaves, finely chopped	3
$\frac{1}{2}$ tsp	finely chopped savory	$\frac{1}{2}$ tsp
1 tbsp	flour	1 tbsp
2	egg yolks, lightly beaten	2
2 tbsp	lemon juice	2 tbsp

Melt 15 g ($\frac{1}{2}$ oz) of the butter in a large pan and lightly sauté the onion, 15 g ($\frac{1}{2}$ oz) of the parsley, and the celery. Add the mussels and season with salt and pepper. Pour in the white wine and cook over a high heat, covered, until all the mussels have opened. Remove the mussels from the pan, shell them, and put them in a shallow dish. Moisten with a little of the cooking liquid. Cover and keep them warm.

Put another 15 g ($\frac{1}{2}$ oz) of the butter in a saucepan with the sorrel, the remaining parsley, the chervil, sage, and savory. Cook over a low heat for about 5 minutes. Strain the mussel cooking juices into the saucepan. Blend the remaining butter with the flour and whisk this *beurre manié* into the herb sauce. Cook gently for 2 minutes. Off the heat blend in the egg yolks and lemon juice. Pour over the mussels and serve.

EMMANUELLE JANVIER
LES MEILLEURES RECETTES AUX FRUITS DE MER

Combined Seafood Dishes

━━━━━━━━━━━━ ◆ ━━━━━━━━━━━━

Mixed Fried Seafood Italian-Style

Fritto Misto di Pesce

(Options: any fresh fish or shellfish suitable for frying)

This recipe is for the classical Neapolitan version of the dish. Even in Naples, other fish might be added. Elsewhere in Italy the choice could be quite different, but will usually include squid, cut into rings, which is deliciously scrunchy when correctly fried. The technique of cleaning squid is demonstrated on page 24. The seafood can be deep fried in a batter coating (recipe, page 175), if you prefer.

To serve 6		
Six 15 g	red mullet, cleaned	Six 5 oz
750 g	small squid	1½ lb
	oil for deep frying	
	flour	
	salt	
4 to 6	sprigs parsley	4 to 6
1	lemon, cut into 6 segments	1

Clean the squid: remove the cartilage from the hood, and discard the ink sac. Cut the squid bodies into rings, and cut off the tentacles, keeping them whole for frying.

Heat the oil and, as it is approaching the correct temperature, roll the fish and squid in flour to which a little salt has been added. Shake them free of any excess flour, and fry them in the hot oil until they are of a golden colour and crisp. Then lift out the seafood, drain, and serve it on a heated platter with a garnish of parsley and lemon wedges.

JEANNE CARÓLA FRANCESCONI
LA CUCINA NAPOLETANA

Provençal Fish Stew

(Options: firm and tender-fleshed fish; see page 48)

To serve 8 to 10		
2 kg	mixed whole fish of medium size, 150 to 300 g (5 to 10 oz) each, cleaned: red snappers, grey sole, lemon sole, mullet, whiting	4 lb
500 g	mixed fish, trimmed and thickly sliced: sea bass, fresh cod, halibut	1 lb
500 g	conger eel, cut into slices about 4 cm (1½ inches) thick	1 lb
500 g	live soft-shelled crabs	1 lb
¼ litre	olive oil	8 fl oz
1 tsp	mixed herbs (thyme, savory, oregano, marjoram)	1 tsp
About ½ tsp	powdered saffron	About ½ tsp
10 cl	pastis	4 fl oz
500 g	leeks, white parts only, finely chopped (discard tough green parts and keep greenish parts for the fumet)	1 lb
2	medium-sized onions, finely chopped	2
750 g	firm, well-ripened tomatoes, skinned, seeded and chopped	1½ lb
1 tsp	whole saffron threads	1 tsp
1	strip dried orange peel	1
	sea salt and freshly ground pepper	
About 20	slices French bread, dried out in a very slow oven, but not toasted	About 20
6 or 7	garlic cloves, peeled	6 or 7
Fumet		
2.75 litres	water	4¾ pints
500 g	fish heads, carcasses and trimmings (ask your fishmonger for carcasses from fish that have been filleted)	1 lb
	reserved green parts of leeks, chopped	
1	onion, coarsely chopped	1
4 or 5	garlic cloves, crushed	4 or 5
1	branch fennel or 1 tsp fennel seeds	1
1	strip dried orange peel	1
1	sprig thyme	1
1	bay leaf	1
	salt (preferably coarse sea salt)	

Sponge all the fish and crabs, dry them with paper towels, spread them out on a large platter and sprinkle them evenly with about 4 to 5 tablespoons of the olive oil, then with the herbs, a pinch of powdered saffron, and finally with half the pastis. Gently rub the fish in your hands, inside and out, until they are all equally yellowed by the saffron. Then leave the fish to marinate, turning them from time to time, while you prepare the fish fumet.

Heat the water in a saucepan and add the heads, carcasses and trimmings of fish, the leek greens, onion, garlic, fennel, dried orange peel, thyme, bay leaf and salt. Bring to the boil and cook, covered, over a medium heat, for about 30 minutes. After 15 to 20 minutes, crush all the solid material with a wooden pestle or spoon. Pour the contents of the pan into a fine sieve set over a bowl, and press the debris well with the pestle or spoon in order to extract all the flavour possible.

Pour the remaining oil into a very large saucepan. Put the leeks and onion to cook gently in the oil, stirring them regularly with a wooden spoon. Ten minutes later, add the tomatoes, the remaining powdered saffron, the whole saffron and the dried orange peel. Continue to cook for another 5 minutes or so, salt lightly (bearing in mind that the fish stock has already been salted to taste) and add a generous amount of freshly ground pepper.

Place the pan over the highest possible heat and add the fish fumet and the remaining pastis. From this moment count about 15 minutes' cooking time. The liquid should be kept at a rapid boil and the pan uncovered. The fish should be added at three different intervals; those of firm and somewhat gelatinous flesh should be added first along with any crustaceans; 5 to 6 minutes later, the larger specimens of the more tender-fleshed fish varieties; and 5 minutes after that, the smallest of the soft-fleshed fish. This timing is inevitably arbitrary, everything depending on the variety, the size, and the kind of fish used. Sometimes only two intervals rather than three are needed, and it may be that 10 to 12 minutes' total cooking time will be sufficient.

During the time in which the fish is cooking, rub the dried-out bread slices with the garlic cloves; count 1 medium-sized clove for 3 slices of bread.

Lift out the fish carefully with a large wire skimming spoon and arrange them on a heated serving platter. Moisten them with 2 to 3 ladlefuls of broth and pour the remainder of the broth into a soup tureen. Send the fish and the broth to the table at the same time, accompanied by the garlic-flavoured crusts. Serve, first, a ladleful of broth poured over a garlic crust, and, after, the fish, moistened with an additional ladleful of broth for each guest.

Should there be leftovers, the whole thing may be thrown together, boiled up, strained, and served, with a handful of boiled pasta thrown in, as a fish soup.

RICHARD OLNEY
THE FRENCH MENU COOKBOOK

Mixed Fish Stew with Herbs and Wine

Une Bonne Chaudrée

(Options: haddock, hake, dab, John Dory, squid)

If using squid for this recipe, cook it in the same way as the cuttlefish; slices of haddock, hake, dab or John Dory will require about 10 minutes' cooking time.

To serve 6 to 8

1½ to 2 kg	cuttlefish, small skate, small eels, small sole and small cod in equal quantities, all cleaned, washed, and thickly sliced	3 to 4 lb
50 g	sprigs parsley	2 oz
1	garlic head, cloves separated, lightly crushed but not peeled	1
¾ litre	dry white wine	1¼ pints
¼ litre	water	8 fl oz
	salt and pepper	
1	bouquet garni	1
2 tbsp	lemon juice	2 tbsp
50 g	butter	2 oz
2	lemons, quartered	2

Put the parsley and garlic at the bottom of a large pan. Put in the cuttlefish, pour on the wine and water, and season with salt and pepper. Add the bouquet garni. Bring rapidly to the boil, and cook, uncovered, over a high heat for 10 minutes. Add the skate and eels and boil 10 minutes more. Add the sole, cod, lemon juice and half of the butter. Cook for 10 minutes more, or until all the fish are cooked.

Put the remaining butter, cut in small pats, into a warmed deep serving dish. Transfer the stew to the dish and serve accompanied by lemon quarters.

MAURICE BÉGUIN
LA CUISINE EN POITOU

Braised Mixed Seafood

Zarzuela de Pescado

In its original title, this famous Spanish dish is called a musical comedy of seafood because so many kinds of fish and shellfish are combined. The fish, molluscs and crustaceans suggested by the author can be replaced with substitutes according to what is available; for example, halibut instead of angler-fish and cockles instead of the small clams. But a mixture is essential, and all of the fish must have firm flesh which will not disintegrate in the cooking. The zarzuela *is best served in an earthenware casserole, which should be preheated unless you have used it for the cooking.*

To serve 4

12	plump mussels, scrubbed	12
24	small clams, scrubbed	24
400 g	angler-fish, thinly sliced	14 oz
300 g	squid, sliced into rings	10 oz
200 g	Dublin Bay prawns	7 oz
200 g	prawns	7 oz
15 to 20 cl	olive oil	6 fl oz
1	onion, chopped	1
1	garlic clove, finely chopped	1
1	sprig parsley, finely chopped	1
250 g	tomatoes, finely chopped (and then passed through a sieve, if preferred)	8 oz
	salt	
2 tsp	lemon juice	2 tsp
2	peppercorns	2
6 tbsp	sherry	6 tbsp
1 tbsp	cognac	1 tbsp
3 tbsp	stoned black olives (optional)	3 tbsp

Put the mussels and clams in a pan over a gentle heat, so that their shells open. Remove and discard the empty half-shells.

Put about 15 cl ($\frac{1}{4}$ pint) of oil in a frying pan. Add the onion, garlic, parsley and tomatoes, and cook over a low heat for about 15 minutes. The frying should be gentle and light.

Sprinkle the fish slices and the squid rings lightly with salt. Fry them, covered, in a large fireproof earthenware casserole over a low heat, using a little olive oil, and adding a little lemon juice.

After about 10 minutes, when the fish and squid are cooked, add the mussels, clams and prawns and the fried tomato mixture. Season with salt and leave to cook, covered, over a gentle heat for 15 to 20 minutes. Add the peppercorns, sherry and cognac, and remove from the heat without delay. A typical finishing touch is to add stoned black olives.

LEONORA RAMIREZ
EL PESCADO EN MI COCINA

Fish Stew Fisherman-Style

Caldeirada à Fragateira

(Options: hake, whiting, conger, sea bream)

Caldeirada is the Portuguese national fish stew, which has many variations. The following is a simple version. The author recommends the addition of 2 small lobsters but they are not necessary. The important thing is to have a good mixture of fish and shellfish.

To serve 10 to 12

4 to 5 kg	mixed fish, cleaned, heads and skins reserved	10 lb
1 kg	prawns, plunged into boiling water for 1 to 2 minutes, peeled and shells reserved	2 to 2$\frac{1}{2}$ lb
1 kg	mixed live mussels, clams and cockles, scrubbed	2 to 2$\frac{1}{2}$ lb
2	large onions, chopped	2
5	sprigs parsley	5
1	bay leaf	1
2 tbsp	lemon juice	2 tbsp
20 cl	white wine	7 fl oz
	salt and pepper	
10	peppercorns	10
20 cl	olive oil	7 fl oz
4	large onions, finely sliced	4
4	garlic cloves, crushed	4
500 g	tomatoes, skinned, seeded and chopped	1 lb
3	sprigs coriander	3
300 g	bread, sliced and oven-dried	10 oz

Put the mussels, clams and cockles in a pan, cover and place over a high heat until the shells have opened. Strain the cooking juices, and remove the shells.

Take a cooking pot with a capacity of 5 to 6 litres (9 to 11 pints). Line the bottom of it with the fish heads and skins, the prawn shells, the chopped onions, 2 parsley sprigs, the bay leaf, lemon juice, wine, 1 teaspoon salt and peppercorns. Add about 2 litres (4 pints) water, bring to the boil, and continue boiling over a high heat for 30 minutes, stirring frequently. Then strain and reserve the broth.

Heat the olive oil in a large fireproof casserole—preferably earthenware—and add the sliced onions and garlic. Cook over a brisk heat until the onions are golden, then add the tomatoes. Reduce and add a parsley sprig, the coriander and the strained fish broth and shellfish broth. Bring to the boil, lower the heat and simmer for 10 minutes. Add the fish, prawns and mussels, clams and cockles. Bring back to the boil and simmer for a further 10 minutes. Chop the remaining parsley sprigs. Season the stew with salt and pepper, add the chopped parsley, and serve with the bread slices.

Another way of serving this dish is to line the bottom of a warmed serving dish or tureen with the bread and pour the fish stew on top of the bread.

ANTÓNIO MARIA DE OLIVEIRA BELLO OLLEBOMA
CULINÁRIA PORTUGUESA

Brazilian Fish Stew

Vatapá

(Options: cod, angler-fish, turbot, halibut)

Vatapá is an Afro-Brazilian dish, a speciality of Bahia.

To serve 6		
500 g	fresh firm fish, sliced	1 lb
250 g	dried shrimps	8 oz
500 g	fresh prawns, peeled	1 lb
1	coconut, drained, shelled and grated	1
1	onion, sliced	1
1	garlic clove, sliced	1
1	bay leaf	1
1 to 4	fresh chili peppers stemmed, halved, seeded and crushed	1 to 4
5 tbsp	olive oil	5 tbsp
	salt	
125 g	roasted peanuts, finely ground or 60 g (2 oz) almonds, blanched and finely ground	4 oz
150 g	yellow cornmeal	5 oz

Spread the grated coconut over the bottom of a roasting tin. Sprinkle it with a little hot water and set the tin in a very low oven, 130°C (250°F or Mark ½), to warm slightly for about 20 minutes. Transfer the coconut to a cloth. Squeeze out all the coconut milk, reserving both the milk and the coconut gratings. Spread the dried shrimps on a sheet of foil, and toast them under a grill until thoroughly dried out, about 3 to 4 minutes. Grind them very finely.

Cook the onion, garlic, bay leaf, chili peppers and 3 table-spoons of the olive oil for a few minutes in about 40 cl (¾ pint) of water in a large, heavy saucepan. Season with salt and add

the fish and the fresh prawns. Cover and simmer until the fish is done, about 15 minutes. Lift out the fish and prawns.

Remove the skin and bones from the fish; strain the broth and set all aside. In a small pan, add 1.25 litres (2 pints) water to the grated coconut. Bring to the boil. Simmer for a few minutes. Strain, pressing out and reserving all the liquid, but throwing the coconut away.

Put the coconut broth into a heavy saucepan and add the nuts and the dried shrimps. Bring to boiling point and simmer, uncovered, for about 20 minutes, or until the nut and shrimp flavours have been extracted. Add the strained broth from the fish. Heat together and then strain. Return the strained liquid to the saucepan and bring to the boil. Season with salt and gradually stir in the cornmeal. Cook over a low heat for 30 minutes, stirring frequently to prevent scorching, to make a smooth, thick mush. Add the fish, prawns, coconut milk and the remaining oil.

Serve the stew in soup plates. The consistency of the dish should be that of thick cream, with prawns and bits of fish scattered throughout.

CORA, ROSE AND BOB BROWN
THE SOUTH AMERICAN COOK BOOK

Fish Pudding

Le Poupeton

This Provençal recipe provides a good way of using up fish left over from a fish stew. If desired, the mould can be decorated, as demonstrated on page 88.

To serve 3 or 4		
300 to 400 g	leftover cooked fish	10 to 14 oz
100 g	bread, crusts removed, soaked in milk and squeezed	3½ oz
3	eggs, yolks separated from whites	3
50 g	Parmesan cheese, grated	2 oz
	salt and pepper	
15 g	butter	½ oz

Carefully remove all skin and bone from the fish. In a large mortar, pound the fish flesh with the bread. Beat in the egg yolks, one at a time, then the Parmesan cheese. Beat the egg whites until they stand in soft peaks and fold them into the mixture; lightly season with salt and pepper.

Butter a 1 litre (2 pint) soufflé dish or charlotte mould and pour in the mixture. Place the dish in a bain-marie, and bake in a warm oven, preheated to 170°C (325°F or Mark 3), for about 40 minutes, or until the pudding is firm to the touch. Turn the pudding out on to a warmed serving dish and surround it with sautéed tomatoes.

IRÈNE BORELLI
LA CUISINE PROVENÇALE

Sauces and Standard Preparations

A Basic White Sauce

This recipe can be used whenever béchamel sauce is required.

To make about 40 cl (¾ pint) sauce

30 g	butter	1 oz
2 tbsp	flour	2 tbsp
60 cl	milk	1 pint
	salt	
	white pepper	
	freshly grated nutmeg (optional)	
	double cream (optional)	

Melt the butter in a heavy saucepan. Stir in the flour and cook, stirring, over a low heat for 2 to 5 minutes. Pour in all of the milk, whisking constantly to blend the mixture smoothly. Raise the heat and continue whisking while the sauce comes to the boil. Season with a very little salt. Reduce the heat to very low, and simmer for about 40 minutes, stirring every so often to prevent the sauce from sticking to the bottom of the pan. Add white pepper and a pinch of nutmeg if desired; taste for seasoning. Whisk again until the sauce is perfectly smooth, and add cream if you prefer a richer and whiter sauce.

Beurre Blanc

To make about 30 to 40 cl (½ to ¾ pint) sauce

6 tbsp	dry white wine	6 tbsp
6 tbsp	white wine vinegar	6 tbsp
3	shallots, very finely chopped	3
	salt	
	pepper	
250 to 400 g	cold unsalted butter, diced	8 to 14 oz

In a heavy stainless steel or enamelled saucepan, boil the wine and vinegar with the shallots and a pinch of salt until only enough liquid remains to moisten the shallots. Remove the pan from the heat and allow it to cool for a few minutes. Season the mixture with pepper. Place the pan on a fireproof mat over a very low heat and whisk in the butter, a handful at a time, until the mixture has a creamy consistency. Remove from the heat as soon as all the butter has been incorporated.

Hollandaise Sauce

This sauce can be turned into a mousseline sauce by the addition of cream. Whip 10 to 15 cl (6 fl oz) single or whipping cream until foamy but not stiff and stir it into the prepared hollandaise sauce, off the heat.

To make about 30 cl (½ pint) sauce

3	egg yolks	3
1 tbsp	cold water	1 tbsp
250 g	cold unsalted butter, finely diced	8 oz
	white pepper, cayenne pepper, and salt	
1 tsp	strained lemon juice	1 tsp

In a large pan, heat some water until it simmers, then reduce the heat to low. Place a saucepan on a trivet in the water bath, put the egg yolks and the cold water in the saucepan and beat them until the yolks are smooth. Whisk a handful of the butter into the yolks and, when the butter has been absorbed, continue adding the diced butter in this way until all of it has been used. Beat until the sauce becomes thick and creamy. Season the sauce with white pepper, cayenne pepper and salt to taste, and add the lemon juice.

Montpellier Butter

To make about 40 cl (¾ pint) sauce

2 tbsp each	parsley and chervil leaves	2 tbsp each
2 tbsp	chopped chives	2 tbsp
1 tbsp	tarragon leaves	1 tbsp
4 or 5	spinach leaves, stems removed	4 or 5
60 g	watercress, main stems removed	2 oz
3	sour gherkins, chopped	3
2	shallots, chopped, parboiled and squeezed dry	2
4	salted anchovy fillets, soaked and drained	4
2 tbsp	capers	2 tbsp
1	garlic clove, peeled	1
	salt, pepper and cayenne pepper	
3	hard-boiled egg yolks	3
250 g	butter, softened	8 oz
10 cl	olive oil	4 fl oz
1 tsp	wine vinegar	1 tsp

Blanch the herbs, spinach and watercress by plunging them into boiling water for 1 minute. Drain the herbs and leaves, refresh them briefly in cold water and squeeze them dry in a towel. Put them into a mortar with the gherkins, shallots, anchovy fillets, capers, and garlic. Season with a little salt, pepper and cayenne pepper. Pound the mixture to a paste with a pestle. Add the hard-boiled egg yolks and the butter, and pound until they are thoroughly incorporated into the mixture. Using a plastic pastry scraper, rub the mixture through a drum sieve placed over a plate. Wipe out the mortar and return the puréed mixture to it. Slowly add the olive oil, beating constantly, until all the oil is incorporated and the sauce looks glossy, smooth and creamy. Taste for seasoning and beat in the vinegar.

Sabayon Sauce

To make about 30 cl (½ pint) sauce

30 cl	fish fumet (*page 174*)	½ pint
3	egg yolks	3
250 g	cold unsalted butter, diced	8 oz

In a small saucepan, boil the fish fumet until it has been reduced to about 5 to 6 tablespoons. Meanwhile, partly fill a larger pan with water and bring to a light simmer. Put the small saucepan on a trivet in the simmering water, and whisk the egg yolks into the reduced fumet. Add the butter, a handful at a time, whisking between each addition. Continue adding butter and whisking until all the butter is incorporated and the sauce has the consistency of a light, foamy custard. Remove the saucepan from the water bath, and whisk the sauce for a further 30 seconds.

Mayonnaise

To prevent curdling, the egg yolks and oil should be at room temperature and the oil should be added very gradually at first. Mayonnaise will keep for several days in a covered container in a larder. Stir it well before use.

To make about ½ litre (18 fl oz) mayonnaise

3 or 4	egg yolks	3 or 4
	salt and white pepper	
1 tbsp	wine vinegar or lemon juice	1 tbsp
1 to 2 tsp	Dijon mustard (optional)	1 to 2 tsp
½ litre	olive oil	18 fl oz

Put the egg yolks in a bowl. Season with salt and pepper and add 1 teaspoon of the vinegar or lemon juice, and the mustard if used. Mix thoroughly with a small whisk. Add the oil, drop by drop to begin with, whisking constantly. When the sauce

starts to thicken, pour the remaining oil in a thin, steady stream, whisking rythmically. Whisk in the remaining vinegar or lemon juice and taste for seasoning.

Aïoli

Aïoli, a garlic-flavoured mayonnaise, is traditionally served with salt cod. The ratio of olive oil to egg yolk can be varied according to taste: 1 yolk will take between 15 to 20 cl (6 fl oz) to ½ litre (18 fl oz) of oil. The amount of garlic used is also a matter of individual preference. You can include as much as 1 clove per person. To prevent curdling, both oil and egg yolks should be at room temperature before use.

To make about ¾ litre (1¼ pints) aïoli

3	large garlic cloves, peeled	3
1 tsp	sea salt	1 tsp
2	egg yolks	2
60 cl	olive oil	1 pint
1 to 2 tsp	lemon juice	1 to 2 tsp
1 to 2 tsp	warm water	1 to 2 tsp

In a marble mortar, pound the garlic and salt to a purée with a wooden pestle. Add the egg yolks and stir with the pestle until they turn pale in colour. Add the olive oil, drop by drop, to the side of the mortar, stirring constantly and always in the same direction. When the sauce starts to thicken, pour in the oil in a thin, steady stream, still stirring constantly. When the sauce is quite stiff, add the lemon juice and the water. Stir in the remaining oil until the sauce reaches a thickish consistency.

Tartare Sauce

Make a mayonnaise (*left*), and add finely chopped sour gherkins, capers and *fines herbes* according to taste.

Velouté Sauce

To make about 30 cl (½ pint) sauce

60 cl	fish fumet (*page 174*)	1 pint
30 g	butter	1 oz
2 tbsp	flour	2 tbsp

Melt the butter in a heavy saucepan over a low heat. Stir in the flour to make a roux and cook, stirring, for 2 to 3 minutes. Pour the fumet into the pan, whisking constantly. Raise the heat and continue to whisk until the sauce comes to the boil. Reduce the heat to low, and move the saucepan half off the heat so the liquid on only one side of the pan simmers. A skin of impurities will form on the still side. Remove the skin periodically with a spoon. Cook the sauce for about 40 minutes to reduce it and to eliminate the taste of flour.

Fish Fumet

To make about 2 litres (3½ pints) fumet

1 kg	fish heads, bones and trimmings, rinsed and broken into convenient sizes	2 to 2½ lb
1 each	onion, carrot and leek, sliced	1 each
1	stick celery, diced	1
1	bouquet garni	1
2 litres	water	3½ pints
	salt	
½ litre	white wine	18 fl oz

Place the fish, vegetables and herbs in a large pan. Add the water and season lightly with salt. Bring to the boil over a low heat. With a large, shallow spoon, skim off the scum that rises to the surface as the liquid reaches a simmer. Keep skimming until no more scum rises, then cover and simmer for 15 minutes. Add the wine and simmer, covered, for a further 15 minutes. Strain the fumet through a colander placed over a deep bowl. The fumet is now ready for use as a poaching medium. If the fumet is to be used for a sauce or for aspic, do not press the solids when straining lest they cloud the liquid.

Aspic

The technique of coating fish with aspic is shown on page 41.

To make about ½ litre (18 fl oz) aspic

½ litre	fish fumet (*above*)	18 fl oz
15 g	gelatine	½ oz
1	egg white and crushed eggshell	1
1 to 2 tbsp	Madeira or other fortified wine	1 to 2 tbsp

Strain the fumet into a bowl through a fine sieve lined with muslin. Place the bowl in the refrigerator for several hours to allow the fine solids in the fumet to form a sediment. Decant the clear liquid into a saucepan and warm it over a low heat. In a small bowl, soften the gelatine with 2 to 3 tablespoons of cold water. Add a little of the warmed fumet, then stir the softened gelatine into the fumet in the saucepan. Refrigerate a spoonful of the fumet. If it does not set within 10 minutes, soften a little more gelatine and add it to the saucepan.

To clarify the fumet completely, beat the egg white until it forms soft peaks and add it to the saucepan with the crushed eggshell. Place the pan over a high heat and whisk the fumet continuously until it reaches the boil. Remove the pan from the heat for 10 minutes. Bring the fumet to the boil twice more, letting it stand for 10 minutes between each boil.

Strain the fumet into a bowl through a fine sieve lined with 3 or 4 layers of dampened muslin or cheesecloth. When all the fumet has dripped through the cloth, leave it in the bowl to cool. Taste the cooled aspic for salt and add the Madeira. The aspic is now ready for use.

A Wine Court-Bouillon

This court-bouillon is a general-purpose poaching liquid for most fish and shellfish. The amount of wine can be increased or decreased according to taste. A couple of fennel stalks and a clove of garlic may also be included if desired.

To make about 2 litres (3½ pints) court-bouillon

1 each	large onion, carrot and leek, sliced	1 each
1	stick celery, diced	1
60 g	parsley	2 oz
2	sprigs thyme	2
2	sprigs dill (optional)	2
1	bay leaf	1
1½ litres	water	2½ pints
	salt	
½ litre	white or red wine	18 fl oz
5 or 6	peppercorns	5 or 6

Put the vegetables, herbs and water into a large pan, and season with a pinch of salt. Bring to the boil, then lower the heat, cover, and simmer for about 15 minutes. Pour in the wine and simmer for a further 15 minutes, adding the peppercorns for the last few minutes of cooking.

A Vinegar Court-Bouillon

Use the same ingredients as for a wine court-bouillon, but substitute 15 to 20 cl (6 fl oz) red or white wine vinegar for the wine. Add the vinegar to the pan with the vegetables, herbs and water, bring to the boil, cover and simmer for 30 minutes, adding the peppercorns for the last few minutes of cooking.

A Milk and Lemon Court-Bouillon

To make about 1½ litres (2½ pints) court-bouillon

30 cl	milk	½ pint
1.25 litres	salted water	2 pints
1	lemon, skin and pith removed, thinly sliced and seeds removed	1

Combine the milk and salted water in the pan that will be used for poaching the fish, and add as many lemon slices as you like. The court-bouillon requires no cooking before being used as a poaching medium.

Mousseline

This recipe is for a rich mousseline, suitable for use as a stuffing or in a moulded fish dish. For a more delicate mousseline, increase quantity of cream to 35 cl (12 fl oz).

For a firmer mousseline that can be used as a casing for a prepared fish filling, or formed into dumplings or quenelles and poached, use 2 small egg whites and 15 cl ($\frac{1}{4}$ pint) cream, and do not whip any of the cream.

If desired, a pinch of cayenne pepper, or $\frac{1}{4}$ teaspoon of powdered saffron dissolved in 1 teaspoon of boiling water, can be added while pounding the fish. For texture and flavour, any of the following can be mixed into the purée after the cream has been incorporated: chopped pistachios; cooked, chopped prawns, shrimps or mussels; a mushroom and onion *duxelles*; sautéed chopped mushrooms; chopped truffles.

To make about 60 cl (1 pint) mousseline		
250 g	skinned fillets of whiting, pike, sole, salmon, hake or John Dory, chopped	8 oz
	pepper	
1	large egg white	1
$\frac{1}{4}$ litre	double cream	8 fl oz
	salt	

In a mortar, pound the fish to a smooth purée with a pestle. Season with pepper and add the egg white, pounding until it is completely incorporated. A little at a time, rub the purée through a fine meshed sieve, using a plastic pastry scraper for a drum sieve or a wooden pestle for any other sieve. Pack the purée into a glass or metal bowl and press plastic film against the surface. Place the bowl in a larger bowl containing crushed ice and refrigerate for at least 1 hour.

Remove the bowls from the refrigerator. Using a wooden spoon, work a little double cream into the mixture. Return the bowls to the refrigerator for 15 minutes. Continue beating in small quantities of cream, refrigerating for 15 minutes between each addition. Beat the mixture vigorously as soon as it becomes soft enough. When about half the cream has been incorporated, season the mixture with salt and refrigerate for a few minutes. Lightly whip the remaining cream and incorporate it into the purée. Refrigerate until ready for use.

Shortcrust and Rough-Puff Pastry

One simple formula produces dough for both plain shortcrust and rough-puff pastry. The difference is in how you roll it out.

To make about 250 g (8 oz) pastry—enough to cover a 20 cm (7 to 8 inch) pie dish		
125 g	flour	4 oz
$\frac{1}{4}$ tsp	salt	$\frac{1}{4}$ tsp
125 g	cold unsalted butter, cut into small pieces	4 oz
3 to 4 tbsp	cold water	3 to 4 tbsp

Mix the flour and salt in a mixing bowl. Add the butter and cut it into the flour rapidly, using 2 table knives, until the butter is in tiny pieces. Do not work for more than a few minutes. Add half the water and, with a fork, quickly blend it into the flour and butter mixture. Add just enough of the rest of the water to

allow you to gather the dough together with your hands into a firm ball. Wrap the dough in plastic film or waxed paper and refrigerate it for 2 to 3 hours, or put it in the freezer for 20 minutes until the outside surface is slightly frozen.

To roll out shortcrust pastry. Remove the ball of pastry dough from the refrigerator or freezer and put it on a cool floured surface (a marble slab is ideal). Press the dough out partially with your hand, then give it a few gentle smacks with the rolling pin to flatten it and render it more supple. Roll out the dough from the centre, until the pastry forms a circle about 1 cm ($\frac{1}{2}$ inch) thick. Turn the pastry over so that both sides are floured and continue rolling until the circle is about 3 mm ($\frac{1}{8}$ inch) thick. Roll the pastry on to the pin, lift up the pin and unroll the pastry over the pie dish. Trim the pastry to within 1 cm ($\frac{1}{2}$ inch) of the rim of the dish, turn the edges under, press the double thickness of pastry to the rim firmly with thumb and forefingers and crimp the edges.

To roll out rough-puff pastry. Place the dough on a cool floured surface and smack it flat with the rolling pin. Turn the dough over to make sure that both sides are well floured, and roll out the pastry rapidly into a rectangle about 30 cm (1 foot) long and 12 to 15 cm (5 to 6 inches) wide. Fold the two short ends to meet each other in the centre, then fold again to align the folded edges with each other. Following the direction of the fold lines, roll the pastry into a rectangle again, fold again in the same way and refrigerate for at least 30 minutes. Repeat this process two or three more times before using the pastry to cover a pie. Always let the pastry dough rest in the refrigerator in between the times it is rolled out.

Batter for Deep Frying

The consistency may be varied by increasing or decreasing the proportion of liquid to flour. A thin batter will cook crisper and lighter, but some of it will be lost in the oil during frying; a thicker batter clings better, but tends to be more stodgy.

To coat about 12 to 15 pieces		
125 g	flour	4 oz
	salt and pepper	
1 tbsp	olive oil	1 tbsp
20 cl	beer or water	7 fl oz
2	egg whites	2

Sift the flour into a bowl and season with salt and pepper. Make a well in the centre of the flour. Add the oil, and gradually whisk in the beer or water, working from the centre outwards. Whisk for only as long as it takes to produce a smooth batter: do not overwork the mixture. Leave the batter to rest for about 1 hour at room temperature, otherwise it will shrink away from the fish pieces and provide an uneven coating. Beat the egg whites until they form soft peaks, and fold them gently into the batter mixture just before using.

Recipe Index

English recipe titles are listed by fish and shellfish categories; within each category, the recipes appear alphabetically. At the end of each category are the page numbers of recipes for which that particular fish or shellfish—though not mentioned in the recipe title—is an appropriate option. Recipe titles in foreign languages are listed alphabetically without regard to category.

General Index/Glossary

Included in this index are definitions of many of the culinary terms used in this book; definitions are in italics. The recipes in the Anthology are listed in the Recipe Index on page 176.

Recipe Credits

The sources for the recipes in this volume are shown below. Page references in brackets indicate where the recipes appear in the Anthology.

Académie Culinaire de France, *Cuisine Française*. © Éditions Universitaires aux droits des Éditions Le Bélier-Prisma, 1971. Published by Éditions Le Bélier-Jean-Pierre Delarge, Éditeur, Paris. Translated by permission of Éditions Le Bélier-Jean-Pierre Delarge, Éditeur (*pages 100, 166*).

Acton, Eliza, *Modern Cookery*. Published by Longman, Green, Longman and Roberts, London, 1860 edition (*page 120*).

Adam, Hans Karl, *German Cookery*. © The Wine and Food Society Publishing Company, 1967. First published by David and Charles (Holdings) Limited, Newton Abbott. By permission of Pitman Publishing Ltd. (*page 121*).

Ainé, Offray, *Le Cuisinier Méridional*. Imprimeur-Libraire, 1855 (*page 95*).

Audot, L. E., *La Cuisinière de la Campagne et de la Ville ou la Nouvelle Cuisine Économique*. Published by Librairie Audot, 1881 (59th edition) (*Pages 114, 126*).

Ayrton, Elisabeth, *The Cookery of England*. Copyright © Elisabeth Ayrton, 1974. Published by Penguin Books Ltd., London. By permission of Penguin Books Ltd. (*page 115*).

Aznar, Marina Pereyra de and Froud, Nina, *The Home Book of Spanish Cookery*. First published in 1956 by Faber and Faber Ltd., London. New material © Marina Pereyra de Aznar and Nina Froud 1967, 1974. By permission of Nina Froud (*page 158*).

Barberousse, Michel, *Cuisine Provençale*. Privately published by Michel Barberousse, Seguret. Translated by permission of Michel Barberousse (*pages 110, 117*).

Beard, James, *James Beard's Fish Cookery*. Copyright 1954 by James A. Beard. Published by Little, Brown and Co., Boston. By permission of Little, Brown and Co. (*page 156*).

Beard, James, *James Beard's New Fish Cookery*. Copyright 1954, © 1976 by James A. Beard. Published by Little, Brown and Co., Boston. By permission of Little, Brown and Co. (*page 165*).

Becker, Fritz. *Das Kochbuch aus Mecklenburg, Pommern und Ostpreussen*. Copyright © 1976 by Verlagsteam Wolfgang Hölker. Published by Verlag Wolfgang Hölker, Munster. Translated by permission of Verlag Wolfgang Hölker (*page 154*).

Beeton, Mrs. Isabella, *The Book of Household Management* (1861). Reproduced in facsimile by Jonathan Cape Ltd., London (*page 119*).

Béguin, Maurice, *La Cuisine en Poitou*. Published by La Librairie Saint-Denis, c. 1933 (*page 169*).

Bergese, Nino, *Mangiare da Re*. © Giangiacomo Feltrinelli Editore, 1969. Published by Giangiacomo Feltrinelli Editore, Milano. Translated by permission of Giangiacomo Feltrinelli Editore S.p.A. (*page 106*).

Besson, Joséphine, *La Mère Besson "Ma Cuisine Provençale"*. © Éditions Albin Michel, 1977. Published by Éditions Albin Michel, Paris. Translated by permission of Éditions Albin Michel (*page 112*).

Blancard, Eugène, *Souvenirs de Villégiature—Mets et Produits de Provence*. Published by Imprimerie Bordato, Toulon, 1926 (*page 151*).

Blanchard, Marjorie Page, *Treasured Recipes from Early New England Kitchens*. Copyright 1975 by Harrington's In Vermont, Inc. Published by Garden Way Publishing Company in association with Harrington's of Richmond, Vermont, Inc. By permission of Writers House, Inc., author's agents (*page 113*).

Bocuse, Paul, *The New Cuisine*. © 1976 Flammarion. English translation, Copyright © 1977 by Random House, Inc. Published by Hart-Davis, MacGibbon Ltd./Granada Publishing Ltd. By permission of Hart-Davis, MacGibbon Ltd./Granada Publishing Ltd. (*pages 116, 164*).

Boni, Ada, *Italian Regional Cooking*. Copyright © 1969 s.c. by Arnoldo Mondadori. English translation, copyright © 1969 s.c. by Thomas Nelson & Sons Ltd. and E. P. Dutton and Co., Inc. Published by Bonanza Books, a division of Crown Publishers, Inc. By permission of Arnoldo Mondadori (*pages 112, 136*).

Bontou, Aloïde, *Traité de Cuisine Bourgeoise Bordelaise*. Published by Feret et Fils Éditeurs, Bordeaux. Translated by permission of Feret et Fils Éditeurs (*pages 108, 146*).

Borelli, Irène, *La Cuisine Provençale*. © Solar. Published by Solar, Paris 1975. Translated by permission of Solar (*pages 106, 117, 155 and 171*).

Borgström and Danfors, *Scandinavian Cookbook*. Published by Wezäta Förlag, Stockholm. By permission of Wezäta Förlag (*page 108*).

Born, Wina, *Het Groot Visboek*. © 1972 by J. H. Gottmer—Haarlem. Published by J. H. Gottmer—Haarlem. Translated by permission of J. H. Gottmer—Haarlem (*page 138*).

Boyd, Lizzie (Editor), *British Cookery*. Copyright © British Farm Produce Council and British Tourist Authority. Published by Croom Helm, London. By permission of British Farm Produce Council and British Tourist Authority (*pages 105, 111, 119 and 145*).

Bouzy, Michel, *Les Poissons-Crustacés-Coquillages*. Published by Blondel la Rougery, Paris. Translated by permission of Blondel la Rougery (*page 113*).

Brissenden, Rosemary, *South East Asian Food*. Copyright © R. F. and R. L. Brissenden, 1970. Published by Penguin Books Ltd., London. By permission of Penguin Books Ltd. (*page 128*).

Brown, Cora, Rose and Bob, *The South American Cook Book*. First published by Doubleday, Doran & Company Inc., 1939. Republished in 1971 by Dover Publications Inc., New York (*pages 145, 146 and 171*).

Caillat, A., *150 Manières d'Accommoder les Sardines*. Privately published, Marseilles, 1898 (*page 111*).

Calera, Ana Maria, *La Cocina Vasca*. © Editorial "La Gran Enciclopedia Vasca", 1971. Published by La Gran Enciclopedia Vasca, Bilbao. (*pages 106, 121 and 133*).

Carnacina, Luigi, and Veronelli, Luigi, *La Buona Vera Cucina Italiana*. © 1966 by Rizzoli Editore. Published by Rizzoli Editore, Milan. Translated by permission of Rizzoli Editore (*pages 138, 153*).

Carrier, Robert, *The Robert Carrier Cookery Course*. © Robert Carrier, 1974. Published by W. H. Allen and Co. Ltd. By permission of W. H. Allen and Co. Ltd. (*page 108*).

Cass, Elizabeth, *Spanish Cooking*. Copyright © Elizabeth Cass, 1957. First published by André Deutsch Ltd., 1957. Also published by Mayflower Books Ltd., 1970. By permission of André Deutsch Ltd. (*page 140*).

Cavanna, Guelfo, *Doni di Nettuno*. Privately published, Florence, 1913 (*page 159*).

Chanot-Bullier, C., *Vieilles Recettes de Cuisine Provençale*. Published by Tacussel, Marseilles. Translated by permission of Tacussel, Éditeur (*pages 134, 160 and 167*).

Chantiles, Vilma Liacouras, *The Food of Greece*. Copyright © 1975 by Vilma Liacouras Chantiles. Published by Atheneum, New York. By permission of Vilma Liacouras Chantiles (*pages 141, 161*).

Chao, Buwei Yang, *How to Cook and Eat in Chinese*. Published by Faber and Faber Ltd., London. By permission of Faber and Faber Ltd. (*page 96*).

Chapelle, Vincent de la, *Le Cuisinier Moderne*. Paris 1735 (*page 132*).

Cholcheva, Penka, *Kniga za Vseki den i Vseki Dom*. Published by Technika Publishing House, Sofia, 1978. Translated by permission of Jusautor Copyright Agency, Sofia (*page 146*).

Claudian, *À Table*. Published by Publications Périodiques, Paris, 1963. Translated by permission of Publications Périodiques (*page 105*).

Colutta, Flavio, *Cucina e Vini della Toscana*. © Copyright 1974 Ugo Mursia Editore, Milan. Published by Ugo Mursia Editore. Translated by permission of Ugo Mursia Editore (*page 148*).

Correnti, Pino, *Il Libro d'Oro della Cucina e dei Vini di Sicilia*. Copyright © 1976 Ugo Mursia Editore, Milan. Published by Ugo Mursia Editore. Translated by permission of Ugo Mursia Editore (*pages 110, 137*).

Costantini, Simone, *Gastronomie Corse et ses Recettes*. Published by U Muntese, Corsica. Translated by permission of U Muntese (*page 142*).

Courtine, Robert J., *Mon Bouquet de Recettes*. © Les Nouvelles Éditions Marabout, Verviers, 1977. Published by Les Nouvelles Éditions Marabout, Verviers. Translated by permission of Les Nouvelles Éditions Marabout (*pages 107, 132*).

Curnonsky, *Bons Plats, Bons Vins*. Published by Ponsot, Paris, c. 1950 (*page 127*).

Curnonsky, *Cuisine et Vins de France*. Copyright © 1953 by Augé, Gillon, Hollier-Larousse, Moreau et Cie (Librairie Larousse), Paris. Published by Librairie Larousse, Paris. Translated by permission of Société Encyclopédique Universelle (*pages 148, 163*).

Dauzvardis, Josephine J., *Popular Lithuanian Recipes*. Published by the Lithuanian Catholic Press, Chicago, 1967. By permission of the Lithuanian Catholic Press (*page 95*).

David, Elizabeth, *French Country Cooking*. Copyright © Elizabeth David, 1951, 1958, 1966. Published by Penguin Books Ltd., London. By permission of Penguin Books Ltd. (*page 166*).

David, Elizabeth, *French Provincial Cooking*. Copyright © Elizabeth David, 1960, 1962, 1967, 1970. First published by Michael Joseph Ltd., London 1960. Also published by Penguin Books Ltd., London. By permission of David Higham Associates Ltd., for the author (*page 126*).

David, Elizabeth, *Summer Cooking*. Copyright © Elizabeth David, 1955. Published by Penguin Books Ltd., London. By permission of Penguin Books Ltd. (*page 124*).

Davidson, Alan, *Mediterranean Seafood*. Copyright © Alan Davidson, 1972. Published by Penguin Books Ltd., London. By permission of Penguin Books Ltd. (*page 123*).

Davidson, Alan, *North Atlantic Seafood*. Copyright © Alan Davidson, 1979. Published by Macmillan London Ltd., 1979. By permission of Penguin Books Ltd. (*pages 139, 160*).

Davidson, Alan, *Seafood of South-East Asia*. Copyright © Alan Davidson, 1977. Published by Federal Publications, Singapore. By permission of Federal Publications (*page 137*).

Davidson, Alan and Jane, *Dumas on Food*. Selec

tions from *Le Grand Dictionnaire de Cuisine* by Alexandre Dumas translated by Alan and Jane Davidson. © Alan and Jane Davidson, 1978. Published by the Folio Society, London. By permission of the Folio Society (*page 127*).

Dege, Hroar, *Fra Neptuns Gaffel*. Published by H. Aschehoug and Co., Oslo, 1966. Translated by permission of H. Aschehoug and Co. (*page 114*).

Derys, Gaston, *L'Art d'Être Gourmand*. Copyright by Albin Michel, 1929. Published by Éditions Albin Michel, Paris. Translated by permission of Éditions Albin Michel (*page 142*).

Diat, Louis, *French Cooking for Americans*. Copyright 1941 by Louis Diat. Copyright © renewed 1969, by Mrs. Louis D. Diat. Published by J. B. Lippincott Company, New York. Reprinted by permission of J. B. Lippincott Company (*pages 128, 138*).

Dougall, Anton B., *Kċina Maltija: Maltese Cuisine*. Copyright Anton B. Dougall M.C.F.A. (C.G.) 1974. Published by A. B. Dougall Co. Ltd., Malta. By permission of Anton B. Dougall Co. Ltd. (*page 148*).

Dubois, Urbain, *École des Cuisinières*. Published by Dentu, Paris, 1876 (*page 97*).

Durand, Charles, *Le Cuisinier Durand*. Privately published by the author, Nîmes, 1843 (*pages 115, 124*).

Eren, Neset, *The Art of Turkish Cooking*. Copyright © 1969 by Neset Eren. Published by Doubleday & Company Inc., New York. By permission of Neset Eren (*pages 135, 144 and 154*).

Es, Ton van, *Het Volkomen Visboek*. © 1975 by Meijer Pers b.v., Amsterdam, Holland. Published by Meijer Pers b.v. Translated by permission of Meijer Pers (*pages 119, 125*).

Escoffier, Auguste, *Le Carnet d'Épicure*. (Magazine.) 1912, no. 10. Translated by permission of Pierre Escoffier (*page 101*).

Escudier, Jean-Nöel, *La Véritable Cuisine Provençale et Niçoise*. Published by U.N.I.D.E., Paris. Translated by Permission of U.N.I.D.E. (*page 107*).

Feng, Doreen Yen Hung, *The Joy of Chinese Cooking*. First published by Faber and Faber Limited, London in 1952. By permission of Faber and Faber Ltd. (*page 130*).

Flower, Barbara and Rosenbaum, Elisabeth, *The Roman Cookery Book, A critical translation of "The Art of Cooking by Apicius"*. © E. Rosenbaum, 1958. Published by George G. Harrap and Co. Ltd., London. By permission of George G. Harrap and Co. Ltd. (*page 144*).

Francesconi, Jeanne Caróla, *La Cucina Napoletana*. Published by Casa Editrice Fausto Fiorentino, Naples, 1965. Translated by permission of Jeanne Caróla Francesconi (*page 168*).

Frederick, J. George and Joyce, Jean, *Long Island Seafood Cook Book*. Copyright 1939 by Business Bourse, New York. Republished in 1971 by Dover Publications Inc., New York (*page 163*).

Gosetti della Salda, A. (editor in chief), *La Cucina Italiana*. (Magazine.) Published by Casa Editrice "La Cucina Italiana". Translated by permission of A. Gosetti della Salda (*page 136*).

La Gastronomie (Magazine) 1953, no.7(*page 130*).

Giniés, Louis, *Cuisine Provençale*. Published by U.N.I.D.E., Paris. Translated by permission of U.N.I.D.E. (*page 110*).

Gouffé, Jules, *Le Livre de Cuisine*. Published by Librairie Hachette, Paris, 1867 (*pages 120, 156*).

Government of Canada, Fisheries and Oceans, *The Canadian Fish Cookbook*. By permission of Government of Canada, Fisheries and Oceans (*page 94*).

Government of Canada, Fisheries and Oceans, *Canadian Fish and Shellfish Cookbook Series*. By permission of Government of Canada, Fisheries and Oceans (*page 118*).

Grigson, Jane, *Fish Cookery*. Copyright © Jane Grigson, 1973. Published by Penguin Books Ltd, London. By permission of Pitman Publishing Limited (*pages 121, 148 and 162*).

Guérard, Michel, *Michel Guérard's Cuisine Minceur*. © Macmillan London Ltd., 1977. Published by Macmillan London Ltd. Originally published in French as "La Grande Cuisine Minceur". © Éditions Robert Laffont S. A., Paris, 1976. By permission of Macmillan London Ltd. (*page 99*).

Guinandeau, Z., *Fez Vu par Sa Cuisine*. Published by J. E. Laurent. Translated by permission of Madame Guinandeau (*page 112*).

Hartley, Dorothy, *Food in England*. Published by Macdonald & Jane's, London 1975. By permission of Macdonald & Jane's (*page 109*).

Hastings, Macdonald and Walsh, Carole, *Wheeler's Fish Cookery Book*. © 1974 by Macdonald Hastings and Carole Emmanuel. Published by Michael Joseph Ltd., London 1974. By permission of Michael Joseph Ltd. (*page 150*).

Heath, Ambrose, *Herrings, Bloaters and Kippers*. Published by Herbert Jenkins Ltd., London. By permission of the publisher, Herbert Jenkins Ltd. (*page 109*).

Heyraud, H., *La Cuisine à Nice*. Privately published, Nice, 1922 (*page 161*).

Jakobsson, Oskar, *Good Food in Sweden*. © 1968 G. L. A. and Oskar Jakobsson. Published by Generalstabens Litografiska Anstalt, Stockholm. By permission of G. L. A. and Oskar Jakobsson (*pages 96, 129*).

Jans, Hugh, *Bistro Koken*. Copyright © 1973 Unieboek b.v. C. A. J. van Dishoeck, Bussum. Published by Unieboek/C. A. J. van Dishoeck Bussum. Translated by permission of Unieboek/C. A. J. van Dishoeck (*page 106*).

Janvier, Emmanuelle, *Les Meilleures Recettes aux Fruits de Mer*. Copyright Elsevier Séquoia, Bruxelles, 1977. Published by Elsevier Séquoia, Bruxelles. Translated by permission of Elsevier Séquoia (*page 167*).

Jouveau, René, *La Cuisine Provençale*. Copyright © Bouquet & Baumgartner, Flamatt, Switzerland. Published by Éditions du Message, 1962, Berne. Translated by permission of Bouquet & Baumgartner (*page 157*).

Junior League of Charleston, The, *Charleston Receipts*. © 1950 by The Junior League of Charleston, Inc. Published by the Junior League of Charleston, Inc. South Carolina. By permission of the Junior League of Charleston (*pages 150, 155*).

Kahn, Odette, *La Petite et la Grande Cuisine*. © Calmann-Lévy, 1977. Published by Éditions Calmann-Lévy, Paris. Translated by permission of Éditions Calmann-Lévy (*pages 98, 151 and 166*).

Käkönen, Ulla, *Natural Cooking the Finnish Way*. Copyright © 1974 by Ulla Käkönen. Published by Times Books, a Division of Quadrangle/The New York Times Book Co. Reprinted by permission of Times Books, a Division of Quadrangle/The New York Times Book Co. (*page 94*).

Karaoglan, Aida, *A Gourmet's Delight, Selected Recipes from the "Haute Cuisine" of the Arab World*. Copyright © 1969 Dar An-Nahar. Published by Dar An-Nahar, Beirut. By permission of Caravan Books (*pages 143, 145*).

Katz, Heinz, *Maritime Leckereien, Das Fischkochbuch von der Waterkant*. © Ditzen Druck und Verlags—GmbH, Bremerhaven. Published by Ditzen Druck und Verlags—GmbH, 1976. Translated by permission of Ditzen Druck und Verlags—GmbH (*page 128*).

Kouki, Mohamed, *Poissons Méditerranéens*. Published with the collaboration of the Office National des Pêches, Tunis (*page 135*).

Labarre, Irène, *La Cuisine des Trois B*. © Solar 1976. Published by Solar, Paris. Translated by permission of Solar (*page 116*).

Lagunov, L. L. *et al*, *Rȳbnȳe Blyuda*. Published by Pishchevaya Promyshlennostj, Moscow, 1973. Translated by permission of USSR Copyright Agency for Pishchevaya Promyshlennostj (*page 113*).

Lal, Premila, *Sea-Food Dishes*. © Premila Lal 1971. Published by India Book House Pvt. Ltd., 29, Nathalal Parekh Marg, Bombay 400 039. By permission of Premila Lal and India Book House Pvt. Ltd. (*pages 132, 154*).

Lane, Lilian, *Malayan Cookery Recipes*. © Lilian Lane, 1964. Published by Eastern Universities Press Sdn. Bhd., Singapore, in association with Hodder & Stoughton Educational, London. By permission of Eastern Universities Press Sdn. Bhd. (*page 153*).

Lassalle, George, *The Adventurous Fish Cook*. Published by Pan Books Ltd., London, and Macmillan London Ltd. By permission of Pan Books Ltd. (*pages 115, 130*).

Lazarque, E. Auricoste de, *Cuisine Messine*. Published by Sidot Frères, Libraires-Éditeurs, Nancy, 1927 (*page 102*).

Macilquham, Frances, *Fish Cookery of North America*. Copyright © 1974 by Frances MacIlquham. Published by Winchester Press, New York. Reprinted by permission of Winchester Press (*page 165*).

MacMiadhacháin, Anna, *Spanish Regional Cookery*. Copyright © Anna MacMiadhacháin, 1976. Published by Penguin Books Ltd., London. By permission of Penguin Books Ltd. (*pages 122, 157*).

Magyar, Elek, *Kochbuch für Feinschmecker*. Printed in Hungary, 1967. Published by Corvina Verlag, Budapest. Translated by permission of Dr. Bálint Magyar and Dr. Pál Magyar (*pages 94, 102*).

A Maine Cookbook. Copyright 1969 by Twin City Printery. Published by Twin City Printery, Lewiston, Maine, 1969. By permission of Twin City Printery (*page 165*).

Mallos, Tess, *Greek Cookbook*. © Copyright Tess Mallos, 1976. Published by The Hamlyn Publishing Group Ltd. By permission of The Hamlyn Publishing Group Ltd. (*page 140*).

Martini, Dario G. and Ferrer, Manuelli, *Pesto e Buridda*. Copyright © Marco Sabatelli Editore, Savona. Published by Marco Sabatelli Editore, Savona. Translated by permission of Marco Sabatelli Editore (*page 111*).

Martin, Peter and Joan, *Japanese Cooking*. Copyright © 1970 Peter and Joan Martin. First published 1970 by André Deutsch Limited. By permission of André Deutsch Limited (*page 135*).

McNeill, F. Marian, *The Scots Kitchen*. Published by Blackie and Son Limited, London. Reproduced by permission of Blackie and Son Limited (*page 120*).

Medécin, Jacques, *La Cuisine du Comté de Nice*. © Juillard, 1972. Published by Penguin Books Ltd., London, 1979. Translated by permission of Penguin Books Ltd. (*page 142*).

Meer, Janny van der and Mansur, Beatrice R., *Tanzanian Food with Traditional and New Recipes*. Published by the Food and Agriculture Organization of the United Nations. By permission of the Food and Agriculture Organization of the United Nations (*page 146*).

Menon, *La Cuisinière Bourgeoise*, Paris 1745 (*page 103*).

Minchelli, Jean et Paul, *Crustacés, Poissons et Coquillages*. Published by Éditions Jean-Claude Lattès. Translated by permission of Éditions Jean-Claude Lattès (*page 167*).

Molchanova, O. P. *et al*, *Kniga o Vkusnoĭ i Zdorovoĭ Pishche*. Published by Pishchepromizdat Publishing House, Moscow, 1952 (*pages 97, 103*).

Molokhovets, Elena, *Podarok Molodým Khozyaĭkam*. Published in St. Petersburg, 1892 (*page 104*).

Monselet, Charles, *Lettres Gourmandes*. Published by Jacques Grancher, Éditeur, Paris. Translated by permission of Jacques Grancher, Éditeur (*page 139*).

Montagné, Prosper, *Larousse Gastronomique*. © The Hamlyn Publishing Group Limited, 1961. Published by The Hamlyn Publishing Group Limited, London. By permission of The Hamlyn Publishing Group (*pages 123, 126*).

Montagné, Prosper and Gottschalk, A., *Mon Menu—Guide d'Hygiène Alimentaire*. Published by Société d'Applications Scientifiques, Paris (*page 133*).

Murray, Janet, *With a Fine Feeling for Food*. Copyright © Janet Murray, 1972. By permission of Janet Murray (*page 108*).

Nightingale, Marie, *Out of Old Nova Scotia Kitchens*. Copyright, 1971 by Marie Nightingale. Published by Pagurian Press Ltd. By permission of Pagurian Press and Mrs. L. A. Nightingale (*page 116*).

Olleboma, António Maria de Oliveira Bello, *Culinária Portuguesa*. Privately published by the author, Lisbon, c. 1936 (*pages 122, 170*).

Olney, Richard, *The French Menu Cookbook*. Copyright © 1970 by Richard Olney. Published by Simon and Schuster, New York. By permission of John Schaffner, Literary Agent (*pages 99, 124 and 168*).

Olney, Richard, *Simple French Food*. Copyright © 1974 by Richard Olney. Published by Atheneum, New York. Reprinted by permission of Atheneum and A. M. Heath & Company Ltd., Author's Agents (*pages 118, 143*).

Orga, Irfan, *Cooking with Yogurt*. First published 1956 by André Deutsch Limited, London. By permission of André Deutsch Limited (*page 131*).

Ortiz, Elisabeth Lambert, *Caribbean Cooking*. Copyright © Elisabeth Lambert Ortiz, 1973, 1975. Published by Penguin Books Ltd., London. By permission of Penguin Books Ltd. (*page 140*).

Pakhuridze, N, (editor), *Blyuda Gruzinskoĭ Kukhni*. Published by Planeka Publishing House, 1972 (*page 114*).

Paradissis, Chrissa, *The Best of Greek Cookery*.

Copyright © 1976 P. Efstathiadis & Sons. Published by P. Efstathiadis & Sons, Athens. By permission of P. Efstathiadis & Sons (*page 158*).

Peck, Paula, *Paula Peck's Art of Good Cooking*. © 1966 by Paula Peck. Published by Simon & Schuster, New York. By permission of John Schaffner, Literary Agent (*page 101*).

Peter, Madeleine, *Grandes Dames de la Cuisine*. © 1977 by Éditions Robert Laffont S. A. Published by Éditions Robert Laffont S. A. (*page 141*).

Petits Propos Culinaires, © 1979, Prospect Books. Published by Prospect Books, Washington D.C. By permission of the publisher (*page 149*).

Petroni, Paolo, *Il Libro della Vera Cucina Marinara*. © Copyright 1976 by Casa Editrice Bonechi—Via Cairoli 18b-Firenze. Published by Casa Editrice Bonechi. Translated by permission of Casa Editrice Bonechi (*page 134*).

Piruzyan, A. S., *Armyanskaya Kulinariya*. Published by Ekonomika Publishing House, Moscow, 1971 (*page 100*).

Point, Fernand, *Ma Gastronomie*. © Flammarion. Translated and adapted by Frank Kulla and Patricia Shannon Kulla. English language edition © 1974, Lyceum Books, Inc. Published by Lyceum Books, Inc. Wilton, Ct., U.S.A. By permission of Lyceum Books, Inc. (*page 152*).

Pomiane, Édouard de, *Cuisine Juive: Ghettos Modernes*. Copyright 1929 by Albin Michel. Published by Éditions Albin Michel, Paris. Translated by permission of Éditions Albin Michel (*page 104*).

Les Princes de la Gastronomie, © 1.2.1975—Les Éditions Mondiales. Published by Modes de Paris. Translated by permission of Les Éditions Mondiales (*pages 98, 147, 150 and 164*).

Ray, Elizabeth (Editor), *The Best of Eliza Acton*. © Longmans, Green & Co. Ltd., 1968. Introduction Copyright © Elizabeth David 1968. Published by Penguin Books Ltd., London. By permission of Penguin Books Ltd. (*page 125*).

Ramirez, Leonora, *El Pescado en mi Cocina*. Published by Editorial Molino. Translated by permission of Editorial Molino (*pages 160, 170*).

Reboul, J. B., *La Cuisinière Provençale*. Published by Tacussel, Marseilles. Translated by permission of Tacussel, Éditeur (*pages 134, 159*).

Reynière, La, *200 Recettes des Meilleures Cuisinières de France*. © Éditions Albin Michel, 1977. Published by Éditions Albin Michel, Paris. Translated by permission of Éditions Albin Michel (*page 131*).

Sarvis, Shirley, *Crab and Abalone, West Coast Ways with Fish and Shellfish*. Copyright © 1968 by Shirley Sarvis and Tony Calvello. Published by Bobbs-Merrill

Company Inc. By permission of Shirley Sarvis (*pages 101, 129*).

Sigurdardóttir, Helga, *Matur Og Drykkur*. Published by Isafoldarprentsmidja H. F. Reykjavik. Translated by permission of Isafoldarprentsmidja (*page 129*).

Steinmetz, Emma W. K., *Onze Rijsttafel*. © Unieboek b.v./C. A. J. Van Dishoeck, Bussum. Published by C. A. J. van Dishoeck, Bussum. Translated by permission of Unieboek b.v./C. A. J. van Dishoeck (*page 152*).

Straub, Maria Elisabeth, *Grönen Aal und Rode Grütt*. © LN-Verlag Lübecker Nachrichten GmbH, Lübeck, 1971, 6th Edition 1977. Published by LN-Verlag Lübecker Nachrichten. Translated by permission of LN-Verlags, Lübeck (*page 96*).

Tada, Tatsuji, *Japanese Recipes*. Published by Charles E. Tuttle Company Inc., of Tokyo, Japan. By permission of Charles E. Tuttle Company, Inc. (*page 152*).

Tibbott, S. Minwel, *Welsh Fare*. © National Museum of Wales (Welsh Folk Museum). Published by the National Museum of Wales (Welsh Folk Museum). 1976. By permission of the National Museum of Wales (Welsh Folk Museum) (*page 163*).

Troisgros, Jean and Pierre, *Cuisiniers à Roanne*. Éditions Robert Laffont, S. A., 1977. Published by Éditions Robert Laffont, Paris. Translated by permission of Éditions Robert Laffont (*pages 98, 102*).

Valente, Maria Odette Cortes, *Cozinha Regional Portuguesa*. Published by Livraria Almedina, Coimbra, 1973. Translated by permission of Livraria Almedina (*pages 118, 146 and 158*).

Varenne, La, *Le Cuisinier François*, 1651 (*page 162*).

Vermeersch, Fons, *Op Zoek Naar Spijs en Drank*. © Uitgeverij Lannoo, Tielten Utrecht. Published by Lannoo, Belgium. Translated by permission of Lannoo (*pages 104, 149*).

Wretman, Tore, *Svensk Husmanskost*. © Tore Wretman, 1967. Published by Forum Publishers, Stockholm. Translated by permission of Tore Wretman (*page 109*).

Wright, Carol, *The West Country*. Copyright © Carol Wright 1975. Published by Cassel & Company Ltd., an imprint of Cassel & Collier Macmillan Publishers Ltd. By permission of Cassell & Company Ltd. (*page 110*).

Zeitoun, Edmond, *250 Recettes Classiques de Cuisine Tunisienne*. Published by Jacques Grancher, Éditeur, Paris. Translated by permission of Jacques Grancher, Éditeur (*page 131*).

Zerańska, Alina, *The Art of Polish Cooking*. Copyright © 1968 by Alina Zerańska. Published by Doubleday & Company, Inc., New York. By permission of Doubleday & Company, Inc. (*page 128*).

Acknowledgements and Picture Credits

The Editors of this book are particularly indebted to Jeremiah Tower, San Francisco; and Pat Alburey, Royston, Hertfordshire.

They also wish to thank the following: John Bridge, Estuary Products, Leigh-on-Sea, Essex; Pamela Davidson, London; Jennifer Davidson, London; Cécile Dogniez, Paris; J. Audrey Ellison, London; Dorothy Frame, London; Diana Grant, London; Maggie Heinz, London; Marion Hunter, Sutton, Surrey; Agneta Munktell, London; C. J. Newnes, Fish

Merchant, Billingsgate, London; E. B. Smith, Wells Next-to-Sea, Norfolk; J. M. Turnell & Co., Vegetable Merchants, New Covent Garden, London; Eileen Turner, Brighton, Sussex.

Photographs by Alan Duns: Cover, 4, 18, 19—top right and bottom, 20 to 23, 26 to 29, 30—top, 31—top, 32, 34—bottom centre and right, 35 to 37, 40 to 46, 50 to 52, 54, 55, 56—top, 58, 60 to 65, 66—top, 67—top, 68, 69, 72, 73—top, 74, 76 to 82, 84 to 87, 92.

Photographs by Tom Belshaw: 19—top left and centre, 24, 25, 30—bottom, 31—bottom, 34—bottom left, 38, 39, 49, 53, 56—bottom, 57, 66—bottom, 67—bottom, 70, 73—bottom, 75, 88 to 91. Photograph by Louis Klein: 2.

Illustrations: 8 to 17, research and artwork by Annabel Milne and Peter Stebbing; all line cuts from Mary Evans Picture Library and private sources.

Colour separations by Gilchrist Ltd.—Leeds, England
Typesetting by Camden Typesetters—London, England
Printed and bound by Brepols S.A.—Turnhout, Belgium.

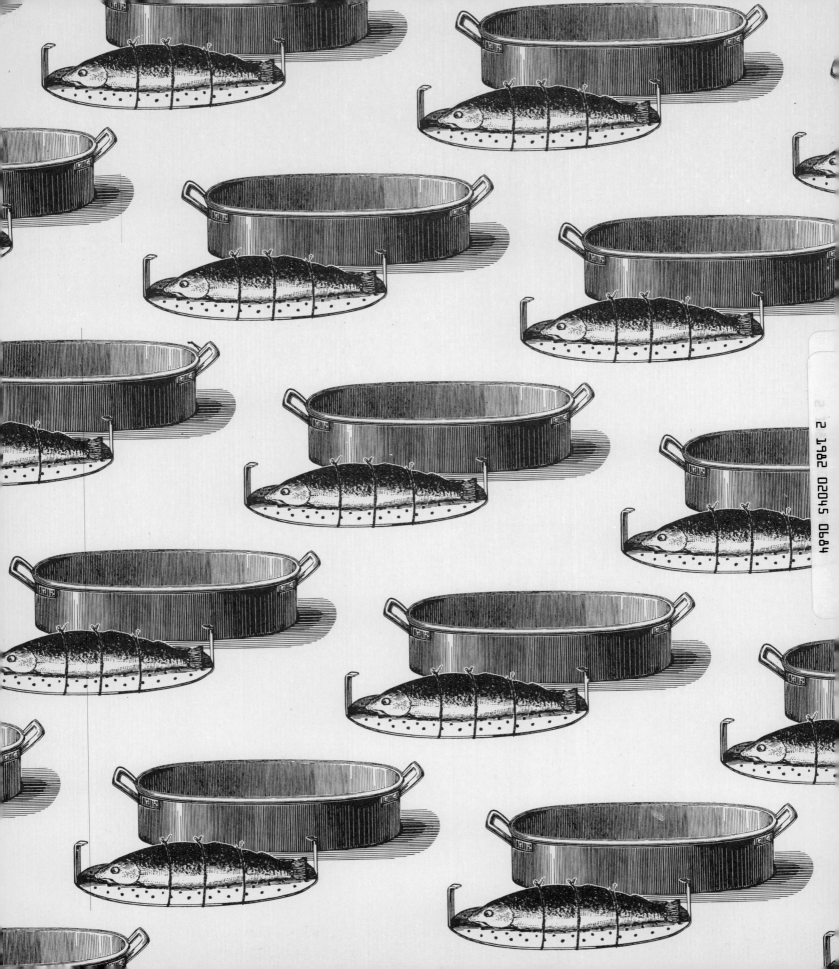